TORN APART
United by Love, Divided by Law

TORN APART

United by Love, Divided by Law

JUDY RICKARD

FINDHORN PRESS

Published in 2011 by Findhorn Press, Scotland

ISBN 978-1-84409-548-3

Edited by Nicky Leach
Cover design by Richard Crookes
Cover photograph of Judy Rickard, left, and Karin Bogliolo, right,
© 2010 Venture, UK. Used by permission.
Interior design by Damian Keenan
Printed and bound in the USA

1 2 3 4 5 6 7 8 9 17 16 15 14 13 12 11

Published by
Findhorn Press
117-121 High Street,
Forres IV36 1AB,
Scotland, UK

t +44 (0)1309 690582
f +44 (0)131 777 2711
e info@findhornpress.com
www.findhornpress.com

CONTENTS

CONTENTS

CONTENTS

MEA CULPA IN ADVANCE

Of course, someone or something may have been left out that should have been included, try as hard as I did to think of everyone and everything. Something might not have been written as well as it could have been. Chalk that up to age, stress and human error of a tired old lesbian trying to do the best she can. This book is my effort to educate, advocate, and fundraise. Hope it works!

NOTE: The phrase "United by Love, Divided by Law" was coined by Out4Immigration, an all-volunteer, grassroots organization working to end the discrimination same-sex binational couples face when Americans cannot sponsor their permanent partners for immigration. The phrase is used here by permission from Out4Immigration, San Francisco, California.

DEDICATIONS

For Karin Grace Darling, who committed.

For John, who lost his battle with pancreatic cancer
before he could hold this book in his hands.

For Joan and Kate, who lost John
before they could hold this book in their hands.

For Dad Everest, my birth father, who started all this
and was thrilled to meet me when I was 56.

For my birth mother, who did the hardest thing for her
and the best thing for me.

For Mom and Dad, who adopted me and loved me and raised me well.

For Mom Everest, my bonus Mom!

For my newer family in Europe and Florida,
thanks for welcoming me!

Our family knows what the words Torn Apart really mean…

This book is dedicated to anyone who has not been able to be who they are and with whom they want, for reasons they cannot control. That means a lot of folks!

But it is especially dedicated to gay men and lesbians born in America who struggle to be with their permanent partners who were not born in America. That's not because I think America is the best place in the world. It's because noncitizenship is the accidental issue that separates these men and women.

To the children of these couples, I can only say that I am ashamed for the reality you and your parents face. Bless you all!

WHITE HOUSE STATEMENT ON
UNITING AMERICAN FAMILIES ACT (UAFA)

This week, the White House issued a statement about the Uniting American Families Act, saying "President Obama thinks Americans with partners from other countries should not be faced with a painful choice between staying with their partner or staying in their country."

— *IMMIGRATION EQUALITY BLOG,*

MARCH 27, 2009

WHITE HOUSE STATEMENT ON
SAME-SEX MARRIAGE

A White House statement regarding Wednesday's ruling overturning Proposition 8 said President Barack Obama had spoken out against the measure because it was "divisive and discriminatory." A White House spokesperson sent the following statement to *The Advocate* regarding Wednesday's ruling declaring Proposition 8 unconstitutional: "The President has spoken out in opposition to Proposition 8 because it is divisive and discriminatory. He will continue to promote equality for LGBT Americans."

— *THE ADVOCATE,*

AUGUST 4, 2010 BY KERRY ELEVELD

PRESIDENT OBAMA ON
CIVIL UNIONS

President Obama supports civil unions over full marriage equality for same-sex couples, but he has increasingly walked a fine line on the issue now that six states have legalized same-sex marriage. The President has also said that he believes states should have the right to determine the question of marriage, and as such he supports full repeal of the Defense of Marriage Act, which prohibits the federal government from recognizing legal same-sex marriages. His administration, however, continues to defend the law in the courts.

— *THE ADVOCATE, KERRY ELEVELD,*

OCTOBER 16, 2009

PRESIDENT OBAMA ON
SAME-SEX MARRIAGE

President Barack Obama told progressive bloggers his attitude about marriage equality may be evolving. "I think that it is an issue that I wrestle with and think about because I have a whole host of friends who are in gay partnerships. I have staff members who are in committed, monogamous relationships, who are raising children, who are wonderful parents. And I care about them deeply," Obama said. Obama also rejected the idea that the LGBT community should be disappointed in his administration, listing accomplishments that he said make his presidency the most LGBT-supportive in history.

— *AMERICABLOG.COM/GAY BLOG,*

OCTOBER 27, 2010

WHITE HOUSE PRESS STATEMENT ON
CIVIL UNIONS

The President has long opposed divisive and discriminatory efforts to deny rights and benefits to same-sex couples, and as he said at the Human Rights Campaign dinner, he believes "strongly in stopping laws designed to take rights away." Also at the dinner, he said he supports, "ensuring that committed gay couples have the same rights and responsibilities afforded to any married couple in this country."

— *WHITE HOUSE PRESS RELEASE ON THE SUBJECT OF CIVIL UNIONS,*

OCTOBER 29, 2010

BY ELIZABETH GILBERT

After reading these stories I am almost ashamed to share my story, although at the time it happened it was the biggest crisis in my life. It pales in comparison to what lesbian and gay binational families go through, and what many people I have met while working with the Immigration Equality Action Fund are going through.

Those of you who have read *Eat, Pray, Love* know that it has a very romantic ending. I meet this lovely Brazilian guy, who's being played in the movie version by Javier Bardem, who looks about as much like my husband as I look like Julia Roberts.

My husband, who in the book goes by the name Felipe, is really named José. He and I were coming into the country together when we had our problem. We were sort of beginning to build a life in the United States, and like all binational couples we were doing an enormous amount of expensive and complicated commuting to work around the United States visa restrictions.

We came in through the Dallas–Ft. Worth Airport and I went through customs first. I waited for him on the other side, which is something we had become used to over the years that we had been together. I immediately knew that something was wrong when he went through the foreign citizens' line.

Normally, there's this librarian-like thunk of the welcoming visa entry stamp that people who are in binational relationships live and die by. It didn't come. The guy just sat there looking through José's passport, looking again and again.

I remembered my husband, who is a world traveler, had told me once that on any given day, any given border guard in any given part of the world can define your life for you. We learned this that day.

This guy decided that he just didn't want to let José in. I need to say that José hadn't broken any laws. He hadn't overextended his visa time. It's just that, as the Immigration and Customs Enforcement gentleman explained later, he felt that my now-husband had been coming to the country too much. That's it—just a random, arbitrary decision.

He was taken away from me and put in custody for six hours. I was unable to find out what was going on. In the end days of the Bush administration this was not a comfortable position to be in, to have your foreign-born sweetheart taken away by a guy in a Homeland Security uniform.

I waited for six hours and was finally brought in after he had been interrogated. I was told that he would not be allowed into the country again. Obviously this was a huge blow. We were frightened and terrified. But we were offered this wonderful piece of news by Officer Tom of the Department of Homeland Security. He very nicely informed us that there was a loophole.

Because I was an American citizen, I could bring my partner in. He could "jump the line" in the phrase that we were given. José could be allowed to apply for permanent citizenship. We would have to marry to do that.

What I remember most about that moment was the phrasing that Officer Tom used. He said: "We, the United States government (he was at that moment the face of the United States government), Elizabeth, offer this to you as a courtesy for your citizenship."

He was a nice guy. He was certainly a courteous guy. He had impeccable manners. He couldn't have been kinder to us in a very horrible situation. But there was something about that phrasing that gnawed at me from the moment it came out of his mouth. It has continuously bothered me since. It was the use of the word "courtesy."

My citizenship is not a courtesy that is offered to me by my government. It is my birthright. It is my right as an American citizen. My rights are not something that are offered to me out of politeness or friendliness by the United States government. They don't do this to me because they like me. My rights are a hard-fought-for and hard-defended series and maze of entitlements and obligations that are part of the contract that I share with my government.

And it, too, has its side of the contract. We negotiate our contract based on obligations, responsibilities, and entitlements that have been fought for and challenged in the courts for as long as we've been a country—and before. Central to those rights is the idea that I will obey the law and pay taxes and be a good citizen. The government will do its part, which is to first and foremost insure the safety and the well-being and the privacy of my family, however I should choose to create that family.

The fact that I'm entitled to this, that a Homeland Security officer after five minutes of conversation was able to toss me this loophole (what my friends call the hetero card), that I was able to play that card, when LGBT families who have been together 30 years are unable to play that card… well, it is quite simply unconscionable.

It makes these civil rights I enjoy as an American seem like a country club, with very limited and exclusive membership. There are certain people in the neighborhood who are allowed to be part of that country club, and there are certain people who are not. That's just not tenable.

After what I've now learned from seeing other people's immigration stories, ours ends with what was a relatively easy year in exile—both of us fighting very hard for the right to come back. We came back. José's now on the track to citizenship.

What I want to express is the ending of the story, which is not our union or even the paperwork we went through. The ending of the story is that we now live in New Jersey. We live in a small community. We are homeowners. My husband has started a very successful business in the town where we live. He employs out-of-work Americans. We pay an enormous amount in taxes because we live in New Jersey. We are involved in the business of the town. We are contributors to everything that happens in the town. We march in the Memorial Day parade. We are part of the fabric of this society. I hate to say it, because it kind of messes with my street cred as an alleged Bohemian, but we're sort of pillars of our society. We sort of accidentally have ended up as that.

All of that energy and all of that money and all of that goodwill that we put into this town—all that work and all those jobs and all of that—we would have taken out of this country had they not let José in.

That's what's happening right now. There's this drain. So in addition to being unjust and cruel and unconscionable, these laws are stupid. They are taking away some of the best and brightest minds and prospects out of the country. These laws force gay and lesbian families to do nothing but fight for their lives, rather than putting their shoulder to the wheel and working for the betterment of the society.

And they are in a fight for their lives. I am proud to be part of that fight. I'm humbled and honored to be part of that fight. I'm happy not only to have been honored by Immigration Equality, June 8, 2010, but to say also that I am a donor to Immigration Equality. On September 30, 2010, I also became a lobbyist for Immigration Equality Action Fund and this work to get immigration reform for lesbian and gay binational couples.

I hope you will all join me in that. It's worthy. Until there's fairness on this for everybody there is fairness for no one.

PREFACE

Author Elizabeth Gilbert, whose best-selling memoir *Eat, Pray, Love* was filmed as a Hollywood movie starring Julia Roberts and Javier Bardem, joined Immigration Equality's efforts in 2010 and began lobbying Congress to push for passage of the Uniting American Families Act.

In her memoir, Gilbert related how she met her husband—but the story that resonated for my lesbian and gay binational families community was her subsequent book *Committed: A Skeptic Makes Peace with Marriage*. That book dealt with her experience as the American half of a binational couple and how she and her partner overcame many obstacles.

The pair (both committed to not marrying after divorces that left them scarred) dealt with visa restrictions, being separated, being out of America alone and together, and all the same hoops binational couples like mine have had to jump through to keep their families together.

While they were traveling out of the United States, things were fine in the immigration challenges realm; it was only after José began traveling back and forth to the United States to be with Gilbert there that problems arose. That's when they learned the struggles that the couples you will meet in these pages deal with all the time.

As Gilbert relates in her foreword, José was barred from entering the United States, immediately incarcerated, and required to submit to voluntary deportation. Although Gilbert and her partner did not want to marry, they started the process that would bring them together safely. They obtained a fiancé visa and got married in the United States, where they live happily together today.

That's not unusual. Many Americans have spouses who were born in other countries. As long as you are a man and a woman, there is a clear-cut process that involves fees for a fiancé/fiancée visa and steps to follow. For information on how heterosexual binational couples go through the system that same-sex binational couples are denied, see Pertinent Definitions and Information, Chapter 37.

The only way a U.S. citizen's partner can apply for permanent residency is if they are legally married. In 1996, in the Defense of Marriage Act (DOMA), the federal government legally defined marriage as only between a man and a woman. Despite the fact that same-sex marriage is legal in several states and the District of Columbia, for immigration purposes, federal law takes precedence over laws in the few states or the nation's capital where same-sex marriage is legal.

At the last count, some 36,000 gay and lesbian binational couples like mine have been affected by unfair immigration laws. Elizabeth Gilbert talked about our issue in her book *Committed* and on her book tour. Then she went farther: She partnered with Immigration Equality to advocate for lesbian and gay immigration rights.

In *Committed*, Gilbert shared: "In the spirit of full disclosure, I should make clear here that I'm a supporter of same-sex marriage. Of course I would be, I'm precisely that sort of person. The reason I bring up this topic at all is that it irritates me immensely to know that I have access, through the act of marriage, to certain critical social privileges that a large number of my friends and fellow taxpayers do not have. It irritates me even more to know that if Felipe and I had happened to be a same-sex couple, we would have been in *really* big trouble after that incident at the Dallas/Ft. Worth Airport. The Homeland Security Department would have taken one look at our relationship and thrown my partner out of the country forever, with no hope of future parole through marriage. Strictly on account of my heterosexual credentials, then, I am allowed to secure Felipe an American passport."

She continued the discussion with her country club analogy, which admits some and excludes others, and remarked that the topic of gay marriage as a social debate is too hot a topic to write about "that it's almost too early to be publishing books about it yet" since things keep changing and evolving. She does insist that legalized gay marriage is coming to America, she knows, "because non-legalized same-sex marriage is already here. Same-sex couples already live together openly these days, whether their relationships have been officially sanctioned by their states or not. Same-sex couples are raising children together, paying taxes together, building homes together, running businesses together, creating wealth together, and even getting divorced from each other. All these already existing relationships and social responsibilities must be managed and organized through rule of law in order to keep civil society running smoothly. (This is why the 2010 U.S. Census will be documenting same-sex couples as 'married' for the first time in order to chart clearly the actual demographics of the nation.)"

Her opinion about this situation is that the federal courts will get fed up, "just as they did with interracial marriage, and decide that it's far easier to let all consenting adults have access to matrimony than it is to sort out the issue state by state, amendment by amendment, sheriff by sheriff, personal prejudice by personal prejudice." She has more to say, so Karin and I recommend you get her book *Committed* and read it.

My opinion? She is spot on! My reaction? Wow! My hope? She can help people listen who might not listen to me or to others who are in same-sex binational couples. Thank you so much, Elizabeth!

Karin and I met her in New York City on June 8, 2010, at the Immigration Equality's Safe Haven Awards celebration where she was being recognized for her work on behalf of gay and lesbian immigration rights. We told her how important her book *Committed* was to us—that it was hard to keep reading and made us cry it touched so close to home. I had shared with Gilbert earlier that I had hoped she could write a book about LGBT binational families, which she agreed was a worthy topic, but she told me she was too busy on new projects. She encouraged me to do it myself! I didn't think that would happen at the time, but two months later I took the plunge. This book needed to happen.

At the awards ceremony, Gilbert didn't pull any punches in offering her opinion of current immigration laws: "In addition to being unjust and cruel and unconscionable, these laws are stupid because they are taking away some of the best and brightest minds and prospects out of the country," she said. Gilbert acknowledged the fight LGBT families are in because of American marriage and immigration laws and said she was "proud to be part of that fight."

On September 30, 2010, Gilbert went to Washington, D.C. to lobby for us with legislators leading the fight for Uniting American Families Act (UAFA). She joined the Immigration Equality Action Fund to lobby Congress for passage of UAFA and to meet with key Congressional lawmakers and call on elected leaders to pass UAFA. At that time, Uniting American Families Act had 130 co-sponsors in the House and 25 in the Senate.

The lobbying effort's afternoon press event included Congressman Jerrold Nadler (D-NY-8), lead House sponsor of Uniting American Families Act, (UAFA) in the 111th Congress; UAFA co-sponsor Congressman Michael Honda (D-CA-15), Chair of the Congressional Asian Pacific American Caucus and lead sponsor of the LGBT-inclusive Reuniting Families Act (RFA); and Rachel B. Tiven, executive director of the Immigration Equality Action Fund.

Gilbert was in great company. Gordon Stewart, Immigration Equality board member and the American half of a gay binational couple living in England with his Brazilian husband, was also there, as well as Julie Kruse, policy director for Immigration Equality. Most of the Immigration Equality staff was there too. These are legislators and activists who have been working a long time to help same-sex binational couples with the immigration reform that will allow them to sponsor their non-American partners.

To coincide with Gilbert's visit to Capitol Hill, the Immigration Equality Action Fund launched an online campaign entitled "Engage, Lobby, Love," to encourage allies to join Gilbert in a virtual campaign to call on Congress to pass the Uniting American Families Act.

Whatever the 111th Congress did or didn't accomplish about comprehensive immigration reform, this book is designed to throw open the windows and let the light in on the shattered lives of many same-sex binational couples struggling for equality under immigration law in the United States.

The book can be read on many levels. It is a cautionary tale about discrimination and its outcomes. It is a testament to families who love each other and manage to stay together in spite of what the government throws at them. It is a love story on many levels—mine and Karin's and the convoluted life that we must lead in order to stay together, an echo of the Byzantine arrangements other same-sex binational couples, including those profiled in this book, must make in order that love can triumph. It is the chilling story of those of us who are struggling to be together when America won't allow it—a cautionary tale detailing what happens to people who just want to be able to be with their families. At its worst, it is the story of parents who face separation from their children.

A NOTE ABOUT THE TIMING OF TORN APART:
UNITED BY LOVE, DIVIDED BY LAW

This book was completed in November 2010. At that time, those working on our issue were all hoping Congress would pass Uniting American Families Act as a stand-alone bill or one of the two newer bills that included UAFA to create immigration reform for LGBT families as part of comprehensive immigration reform—a contentious battle for years.

For a quick look at the history of the first two bills designed to solve this problem and their progress, go to: *http://en.wikipedia.org/wiki/Uniting_American_Families_ Act#Legislative_History_and_Recent_Action*

For updates on Uniting American Families Act (UAFA) go to: *www.thomas.loc.gov/* and search for updates to it under the current Congressional term.

Karin and I were thrilled to be at the Senate Judiciary Committee hearing for UAFA on June 3, 2009 in Washington, D.C. We met people who were helping us and we met people who shared their stories in this book. The bill had a hearing finally and had more co-sponsors than ever before in the 111th Congress.

For updates on Reuniting Families Act (RFA) which includes UAFA go to: *www. thomas.loc.gov/* and search for updates to it under the current Congressional term.

This bill is dear to our hearts because it was introduced by my Congressman, Michael Honda (D-CA-15), who I have known for years. Karin and I were at the press conference June 4, 2009, in Washington, D.C. when he announced the bill he introduced that day in the House of Representatives.

For updates on the newest effort to help us as it helps all who need immigration assistance, Comprehensive Immigration Act of 2010 (CIR 2010) go to: *www.thomas. loc.gov/* and search for updates to it under the current Congressional term.

This bill, S.B. 3932, which also includes UAFA, was introduced late in the 111th Congress (September 29, 2010) by Senator Robert Menendez (D-NJ) and Senator Patrick Leahy (D-VT). It was the last effort at CIR that included UAFA before this book went to press. At the time this bill was introduced, both the House of Representatives and Senate had bills dealing with comprehensive immigration reform that included us: same-sex binational couples. In America today, thousands of people need immigration reform to keep their families together. The issue is not easy. It is a divisive, hot topic. We are not even included in much of the rhetoric. Most of it is centered on the code words "illegal aliens," which to me means racial and economic bias, as it always seems to apply to Central or South American country citizens illegally crossing the California, Arizona, New Mexico, and Texas borders, rather than to citizens of other countries who are in the United States without proper papers.

Added to the mix when we point it out—but generally ignored or hidden—is our group: same-sex binational couples. LGBT Americans with partners from other countries get left out of discussions or worse, picked off in bargaining and compromises. We need to be included in the solution!

I am tired of how easy it is for people in charge to leave us behind, (even throw us under the bus as they say) in dealings to create Comprehensive Immigration Reform. Gay and lesbian permanent partners need Comprehensive Immigration Reform (CIR), just like UAFA defines, but achieving it has been hard because we face a challenge from U.S. marriage and immigration laws.[*]

At the time I finished this manuscript, the CIR process was nowhere near settled. The struggles you will read about here go on. The challenges go on. The separations go on. The expenses go on. The disappointments go on. The sadness goes on. The hurt goes on. And on.

Stories here have been presented so that they were timely when written. Circumstances about legislation are presented with an historic overview approach. My biggest fear—but at the same time greatest joy—is that the book would turn out to be out of date by the time it was published because the law had passed. If that happens, it would mean that this long challenge Karin and I and so many others have faced would all be past history by 2011. If I am right, I can live with it. If not, I'm still helping to get it changed.

This book is a plea for help. Won't you help us get a fair immigration bill passed in the United States? It's the right thing to do.

---

[*] See Pertinent Definitions and Information, Chapter 37

"First they came for the Socialists, and I did not speak out because I was not a Socialist. Then they came for the trade unionists, and I did not speak out because I was not a trade unionist. Then they came for the Jews, and I did not speak out because I was not a Jew. Then, they came for me, and there was no one left to speak for me."

—*PASTOR MARTIN NIEMOLLER, GERMAN PROTESTANT MINISTER*
AND LEADER OF THE CHURCH'S OPPOSITION TO HITLER,
WHO WAS INTERNED IN NAZI CONCENTRATION CAMPS, 1938-1945

"I believe all Americans, no matter their race, no matter their sex, no matter their sexual orientation, should have that same freedom to marry… I support the freedom to marry for all. That's what Loving, and loving, are all about."

—*MRS. MILDRED LOVING, WHO WITH HER HUSBAND, RICHARD LOVING*
(BOTH DECEASED), WAS A PLAINTIFF IN THE HISTORIC SUPREME COURT CASE,
LOVING V. VIRGINIA, WHICH STRUCK DOWN RACE RESTRICTIONS ON
THE FREEDOM TO MARRY JUNE 12, 1967.

"I swore never to be silent whenever and wherever human beings endure suffering and humiliation. We must always take sides. Neutrality helps the oppressor, never the victim. Silence encourages the tormentor, never the tormented."

—*ELIE WIESEL, NOBEL LAUREATE AND HOLOCAUST SURVIVOR*

"Cowardice asks the question: Is it safe? Vanity asks the question: Is it popular? Expediency asks the question: Is it political? But conscience asks the question: Is it right? There comes a time when one must take a position that is neither safe, popular or political, but because it is right."

—*DR. MARTIN LUTHER KING, JR., MINISTER,*
CIVIL RIGHTS LEADER AND NOBEL PEACE PRIZE WINNER

"No government has the right to tell its citizens whom to love. The only queer people are those who don't love anybody."

—*RITA MAE BROWN, LESBIAN AUTHOR*

"If you can, help others; if you cannot do that, at least do not harm them."

—*HIS HOLINESS THE 14TH DALAI LAMA OF TIBET*

"Promise me you'll always remember: You're braver than you believe, and stronger than you seem, and smarter than you think… says Christopher Robin to Pooh."

—*A.A. MILNE, ENGLISH AUTHOR*

"If you believe you are equal, then act like you are."

—CLEVE JONES, AIDS AND LGBT RIGHTS ACTIVIST
WHO CONCEIVED THE NAMES PROJECT AIDS MEMORIAL QUILT
AND CO-FOUNDED THE SAN FRANCISCO AIDS FOUNDATION

"All, too, will bear in mind this sacred principle, that though the will of the majority is in all cases to prevail, that will to be rightful must be reasonable; that the minority possess their equal rights, which equal law must protect, and to violate would be oppression."

—THOMAS JEFFERSON, FIRST INAUGURAL ADDRESS, MARCH 4, 1801

"I believe all Americans who believe in freedom, tolerance and human rights have a responsibility to oppose bigotry and prejudice based on sexual orientation."

—CORETTA SCOTT KING, CIVIL RIGHTS ACTIVIST AND
WIDOW OF DR. MARTIN LUTHER KING, JR.

"Never doubt that a small group of thoughtful people could change the world. Indeed, it's the only thing that ever has."

—MARGARET MEAD, CULTURAL ANTHROPOLOGIST (1901–1978)

"When I was in the military, they gave me a medal for killing two men and a discharge for loving one."

—TOMBSTONE OF LEONARD MATLOVICH,
THE FIRST GAY SERVICE MEMBER TO FIGHT THE BAN ON GAYS IN THE MILITARY (1943–1988)

"Because no one has the right to deny another their life even though they disagree with it, because everyone has the right to live the life they so desire if it doesn't harm another and because discrimination has no place in America."

—BRAD PITT, ACTOR AND ACTIVIST ON PROPOSITION 8
AFTER DONATING $100,000 TO FIGHT THE BALLOT MEASURE

"I want you to know that nothing has changed between us."

—ERMA RICKARD, MY MOM, WHEN I CAME OUT TO HER IN 1973.

"But all we know about homosexuals is that they hang out at public restrooms looking for sex."

—EMMETT RICKARD, MY DAD, WHEN I CAME OUT TO HIM IN 1973.

"That's okay, honey."

—*DAD EVEREST, MY BIRTH FATHER, WHEN I CAME OUT TO HIM IN 2004,*
THE DAY WE MET FOR THE FIRST TIME.

"That's okay, honey. Everyone deserves to be happy."

—*MOM EVEREST, MY BONUS MOM, WHEN I CAME OUT TO HER IN 2004,*
THE DAY WE MET FOR THE FIRST TIME.

PART I

JUDY AND KARIN

CHAPTER ONE

NEARLY NAKED ON THE TRAIN TO PARIS

There I was, wearing nothing but my underpants—sitting in the corridor of the TGV, the "bullet train," hurtling toward Paris. It was my birthday trip in January 2010, and it was starting out badly. I hadn't planned to turn 62 that way, but there you go: just another day in the life of a love exile.

In order to be with my British partner, Karin, who had been forced by U.S. immigration law to leave the United States, I had taken early retirement from my university job of 30 years and left California. Now, we were both seminomadic, living out of her car and my two suitcases in order to comply with temporary visa requirements that require Karin to leave the United States and not return for six months.

Karin is already retired. Like me, though, she would rather stay in one place, not travel in four countries in six months. But because we don't want to jeopardize any chance of being together in the United States in the future, she left the country as required. The difference this time is that she had taken me with her, introducing me—a California girl who had barely left America—to places throughout Europe where she had lived and to her family and friends.

Suffering from food poisoning anywhere is not fun. This particular incident started for me with a cheese tart in Montblanc, in the south of France, where we had rented a flat for two months; it ended with me losing my lunch, then having to take the walk of shame the length of the train car while all the other passengers held their nose or ran for the exit. My favorite sweatshirt took a beating on this occasion, but I was lucky that it was in my lap at the time. Not so fortunate was that it, and the rest of my clothes, ended up in a garbage bag abandoned on the TGV.

We had taken Karin's red Renault hatchback Twingo, optimistically named Hope, to the station in Agde, to catch the regional train to Montpellier. There, we would catch Le Train à Grande Vitesse (TGV), which would take us to Paris. Karin had arranged and paid for everything. It was my birthday celebration. It was a big deal! First time to Paris. First time on the TGV. So much to look forward to. But it started off miserably, and what with my stomach and the terrible winter weather, never got much better.

We had taken the train through the Channel Tunnel ("Chunnel") from England and then traveled to Montblanc after spending 10 days driving west and south across France. The idea was to find the place in Europe with the warmest winter weather possible for December 2009 and January 2010. What we ended up with was the coldest French winter in decades.

Located less than half an hour from the Mediterranean, Montblanc is usually mild, even warm. Or so said Karin, who had once lived in the area for five years. But as luck would have it, global warming idiosyncrasies caught up to us. The swimming pool froze, the vineyards were covered with snow, and everyone we talked to said "*Jamais! jamais!*" ("Never! never!") as they apologized for their weather.

How did this TGV fiasco happen? A better question would be to ask what we were doing there in Montblanc living out of suitcases like two old broads on the run? We are not globetrotters. We are not rich people. We don't sit and plan travel around the world for months at a time because we have so much money and time we can't think of anything else to do. We do it now because we have to—and we both pay the price. But it means Karin and I are together. And that is where we want to be.

We are a lesbian family, a binational couple, and like thousands of other couples in our situation, we can't live legally as a couple in America. Our delight is that we found each other and are making a life together. Because Karin is not a U.S. citizen, it's no white-picket-fence-and-happily-ever-after situation for us in California. Instead, we spend our time figuring out how to keep spending time with each other between Karin's visa deadlines and hatching plans to be together elsewhere when we cannot be in California, a place I have lived my entire life. No matter what happens, we try to remember not to live in fear of our future. Much of the time we succeed.

CHAPTER TWO

AMERICA VS. SAME-SEX
BINATIONAL COUPLES

B y definition, an LGBT (Lesbian, Gay, Bisexual, or Transgendered) binational
couple is one with two men or two women where one partner is from one country
and the other partner is from another country. Specifically, we are talking about those
couples where one man or one woman is American and the other is not. That makes
life anything but simple for them, or us.

Unlike Elizabeth Gilbert and her husband, LGBT binational couples do not have
the option of a federally recognized marriage in America, thereby allowing the American citizen to sponsor the non-American partner for immigration purposes. According
to Immigration Equality's website, *www.immigrationequality.org/*

*Binational couples are couples in which the partners come from different
countries. Nineteen nations (at the time I wrote this book) allow their citizens
to sponsor their same-sex partners for immigration. Unfortunately, the United
States does not. Because of the Defense of Marriage Act, which defined marriage as between a man and a woman, even same-sex couples who had been
legally married in U.S. states or in foreign countries are not able to immigrate
based on their marriage.*

That leaves couples/families like mine with two terrible choices: to choose between family and country or to choose between family and career. What kind of choice is that?

That is the reality that thousands of other same-sex binational couple men and
women live with daily. In my case, Karin and I want her to be able to immigrate to the
United States; under the current immigration law, she can't. If I were to move to the
United Kingdom, Karin and I could enter into a civil partnership, with benefits and
full legal recognition of our status. But here's the thing: We prefer to live in California
and see family and friends in the United Kingdom and other parts of the world when
we want to and for however long we want to visit.

One important reason why we do not want to move to the United Kingdom is
my health. I am 62 years of age, a lifelong Californian, and every time I have been in

England or elsewhere in the United Kingdom I get sick with colds, earaches, sinus infections, and the like. According to Karin's doctor in England, this is not uncommon among expatriate Americans who are dealing with such a different climate. The other reason is family. It's hard for me to anticipate leaving everyone behind in another country, even though Karin has done that for years.

Karin and I have been interviewed long distance several times now by major media about our story. Our first interview by phone was with Seth Hemmelgarn from the *Bay Area Reporter*, a San Francisco gay paper, and later with Mary Gottschalk from *Silicon Valley Community Newspapers* in San José. Then things got kind of surreal as we were interviewed via Skype by CNN.com's Mallory Simon while we were in Canada. One time, we were even interviewed by Associated Press reporter Kevin Freking via cell phone in my car, Intrepid, on the side of the road in Oregon as we returned from Canada. And then there was the time we were interviewed by Matthew Bajko, another *Bay Area Reporter* staffer, as we waited in the Denver airport on our way out of the country together.

Karin and I just want what other couples have: the opportunity to marry and be together in the United States. That is not unreasonable. We aren't asking for anything special. We just want the same rights other Americans have. I should be able to marry my partner and sponsor her for immigration to America. Period. Just like Karin can do for me in the United Kingdom.

I'll say it again: We only want the same rights as other U.S. citizens. We are not asking for special rights. When people say we are asking for special rights they are clouding the issue and turning the discussion to their advantage, their perspective. It's a tactic used for years to vilify the LGBT community, and really, is it any wonder I find myself getting sick as we are forced to constantly move around the world instead of enjoy our retirement at home, in California, where we want to be?

CHAPTER THREE

AMERICAN LAWS IGNORE US

A question I often get asked (besides why Karin and I don't get married) is this: Why can't I, a U.S. citizen, sponsor Karin for immigration? There are two aspects to this question: federal marriage law and federal immigration and naturalization law.* Both laws need to change in order for Americans in same-sex binational couples like me to sponsor our partners for immigration to America.

For Karin to live with me in America, then, we have to deal on the federal level both with same-sex marriage and immigration and naturalization law. Imagine what a doubly scary proposition that is!

The online encyclopedia Wikipedia defines same-sex marriage* (also called "gay marriage") as "a legally or socially recognized marriage between two persons of the same biological sex or social gender." That sounds simple and straightforward, but not so fast: Same-sex marriage is barely recognized in American states and, as mentioned before, it is not recognized at all by the U.S. government.

It follows then that our relationship status as permanent same-sex partners is also not recognized by the U.S. Customs and Immigration Service (USCIS) and its Immigration and Customs Enforcement (ICE). Under American Immigration and Naturalization law, ICE does not allow non-spouses (we can't be our partners' parents or siblings) to sponsor non-spouses for immigration.

The Immigration and Naturalization Act of 1952 explains and defines how people can immigrate and get green cards to become Permanent Resident Aliens, which can later, after a waiting period, be converted into U.S. Citizenship.

Basically, there are three ways to immigrate to the United States, or receive what is euphemistically called a green card (it is no longer green): be sponsored by a family member, be sponsored through an employer, or become eligible for a green card as a refugee seeking asylum. As regards sponsorship through a family member, the United States Customs and Immigration Service (USCIS) website, *www.uscis.gov/* states the following:*

> Many people become permanent residents (get a green card) through family members. The United States promotes family unity and allows U.S. citizens

---

* See Pertinent Definitions and Information, Chapter 37.

and permanent residents to petition for certain relatives to come and live permanently in the United States. You may be eligible to get a green card through a family member who is a U.S. citizen or permanent resident, or through the special categories described.

Because Karin and I can't get married and have that union legally recognized, I cannot sponsor Karin as my spouse for immigration to the United States to live with me permanently. To America, we are not family. We are not recognized. We are, in legalese, "legal strangers." It's both that simple and that complicated.

The winds of change in America on both same-sex marriage and comprehensive immigration reform blow hot and angry these days. Mentioning either of these issues is the quickest way to make some folks go ballistic; put them together in the same discussion about solving the problem Karin and I and so many others face and you have a recipe for explosion for many Americans—even in Congress where the solution lies.

As it happens, I tried to sponsor Karin through my local Congressman Michael Honda's office. The application was rejected in Washington, D.C. It came back down to that old man-and-a-woman argument about legally defined marriage: I need to be a man, or Karin does, to be recognized as a spouse by the American government. And because of the government's law, we can't get married. Catch 22 anyone?

So we live our lives the best we can with these two problems hanging over our heads. But we are not going to roll over. We are trying to get those who can help fix this problem to do just that.

CHAPTER FOUR

FAMILIES UNVALUED

My country, America, proclaims it is a symbol of freedom. I have always believed that. But now I know it is not the symbol of freedom that I need or that welcomes my partner and those of so many others. That makes me heartsick! It's particularly ironic because my country is a nation of immigrants; it has been this way since the first outsiders met the indigenous residents. But immigrants had a better time coming into this country a long time ago than some of them do in the 21st century.

Immigration is a process that needs to be fair and inclusive. While family reunification is affirmed as a central concept of American immigration policy, gay and lesbian couples are not family to the federal government; in fact, we are "legal strangers." Strangers! Can you believe that?

Worse than that, should an Immigration and Customs Enforcement (ICE) officer at any entry point get wind of the idea that a couple like Karin and I are "more than friends," it is likely to arouse suspicions and lead to problems. If an ICE officer thinks Karin has a reason to overstay her visa (i.e., she is involved with me romantically), she can be denied entry to the United States. But Karin has never overstayed, nor will she. We have never broken the law. And we won't!

This issue with ICE is not an idle threat, either. We do know men and women who have been prevented from being with their permanent partners for this very reason. And until things change, it can keep happening. In fact, by writing this book and exposing ourselves to further scrutiny, we may be forced to leave the country to stay together. We know that and accept that.

As of the 2000 U.S. Census (the latest available data), more than 36,000 couples like mine are known to be dealing with this issue. That doesn't count the couples who don't let others know of their situation. It doesn't count the thousands more who have fled the United States to live together in another country. It doesn't count those who have terminated their relationships because of odds they couldn't overcome.

And it doesn't count those who wanted to be together but couldn't successfully begin a relationship because of the realities they faced and couldn't surmount. It also doesn't count the ones in the shadows—the couples where one partner is not only from another country but here illegally or has become undocumented by overstaying his or her visa.

No one really knows how many gay and lesbian families are impacted by American immigration law; and no one will ever know the real cost of what that law has done to individuals and families. If we could ever find out the real numbers, I would be even more sad and mad.

A report published in 2006 blew the lid off this underexposed problem. Human Rights Watch and Immigration Equality produced a report called *Family Unvalued*. In it, lesbian and gay binational couples told stories of abuse by immigration officials. Some even shared horror stories of deportation.

They described the devastating impact American immigration law had on their families, as well as their careers, homes and incomes. Most of all, *Family Unvalued* presented "the sometimes horrifying, always enlightening testimony of lesbian and gay families: people who simply sought to build a better future together."

Just as the 2000 census numbers showed how many couples were impacted at that time, they also showed that nearly half of those same-sex binational couples were raising children. The thought that a child's parents could be forced to separate by law is unimaginable, yet I have met kids whose parents face this challenge. It is not a pretty picture. The average age of the couples counted in the 2000 census was 38, meaning that many were younger and many older. That means all sorts of health, education, and other issues are included in the mix.

When they are available, the 2010 U.S. Census data will provide more information on lesbian and gay households, and perhaps a better picture of lesbian and gay binational couples in the United States today. Numbers tell the story. With better data comes the opportunity for better strategy and increased information to focus on solving the issues these binational couples face. I await the information and the changes I hope it brings.

CHAPTER FIVE

So Who Are
Judy and Karin?

Karin and I can serve as Exhibit A for what gay and lesbian binational couples face today in terms of not being able to live in America together. Our story is not as harsh as others you will read later in this book, but it is also not the typical story of two people who meet and fall in love and live happily ever after. We wish it was, but it can't be—at least the way things are as I wrote this. So here's a quick summary of my life, followed by Karin's.

Judy

I am Judy, the author. I turned 62 in 2010. I am an American citizen. I was born in Portland, Oregon, January 6, 1948, to an unwed teenage mother. That alone makes my life story different from many others, and it has only become more interesting as the months and years have gone by.

My adoption was unusual for its day: it was prearranged. In 1947, my birth mother was booted out of the small Bible college she attended when it became obvious she was pregnant. She spent the last couple of months of my gestation in a home for unwed mothers. She delivered me and gave me up in a hospital there. My earliest photo is an 8-by-10-inch, black-and-white exhibit photograph for my file. I am on my back in an incubator. It looks like an aquarium with an oxygen bottle on the floor and a tube going into the box. I am clenching my fists and kicking my feet and crying. Wouldn't you?

As it happens, my adoptive mother's brother and his wife in Yakima, Washington, were part of a network of people associated with that Bible college. They found out that my birth mother was pregnant with me and were the ones who made a connection with my future adoptive parents, who had been trying to get pregnant without success. So the deal was cut, and I waited to be born in Portland. Then in one of those twists in the tale that you couldn't make up if you wanted to, my future mother finally got pregnant. Now, they had to decide if they would go through with adopting me. I lucked out, because they decided to go ahead. That meant that they would have two babies close in age, but that was alright with them.

Photo of Judy Rickard, left, and Karin Bogliolo, right, by Gail Torr, from their private collection. Used by permission.

No sooner had they made that momentous decision then there came another, hard on its heels: My adoptive father got a teaching job in California that required he and his wife leave immediately. So before I was even born, my new adoptive family had moved to California. To complicate things still further (if that's possible), after I was born and ready to go to my new parents in California, my new adoptive mother was in the early stages of a very difficult pregnancy and Dad couldn't leave his new job. So that's how it ended up that my aunt Ruth and five-year-old cousin Ed from Yakima went to Portland on the train, picked me up, and took me to California to meet my new adoptive family. As a result, I have joked for years that I was delivered by the Southern Pacific Railroad.

My sister was born seven months after me, and we were basically raised as twins. I wasn't an only child for long, so I never experienced what it was like to grow up with my parents' undivided attention, as Karin, an only child, did.

Growing up in pre–Silicon Valley San José, California, in those post–World War II years was great. The population was only 50,000, but there were lots of houses and schools and businesses that made the town and the area hum, even though it was still an agricultural hub for America and the world. I went to local schools, played the typical games in the neighborhood, and tried to catch frogs in Guadalupe Creek right across the road from today's Mineta International Airport (in those days a Quonset hut). I had a very happy life.

I wasn't like all the other little girls. I had friends who were girls, but I didn't always want to do what they did. I got dolls for Christmas, like my sister, but I was known to mutilate them and render them useless. I took my bike apart and made it a hot rod without fenders. I built model cars and sold greeting cards door to door to finance my aquarium and buy things I wanted that were beyond my 25 cents a week allowance. I played games with the boys or did things by myself more often.

I didn't question why I was different from other girls, nor did others seem to think it was a problem. I was just me—a bit different, but luckily not so different I was teased a lot or excluded from everything. Even so, without support and information, I never knew until I was 26 years old that what I was had a name: lesbian.

In high school, I wrote for the student newspaper and worked on the yearbook. One year I had a lot of fun being the school mascot during basketball season. Later, I realized that I only took on the role of mascot so that I could hang out with the cheerleaders and pom pom girls. But while I was hanging out with the cheerleaders, they were hanging out with the guys on the team. I was more than a late bloomer; I was oblivious to the fact that I could be something known as a lesbian and be "more than friends" with other women.

I studied journalism and political science at San José State University, then later did my graduate studies there in mass communications. I worked part time while earning my B.A. and commuted from home on the bus for three of my four undergraduate years. At 20 years old, I moved out of my parents' house and lived with three other women in a house near campus. I graduated in 1970 and then worked full time and took night classes for several years to put myself through graduate school.

My social life (in high school and college) barely included men, although I had male friends in my classes. I went on a few dates with the same man in college, but physically we were miles apart in our desires and, although I really liked him, it was never going to work the way he would have wanted. And of course I didn't have it together enough to say that in a good way.

So, there you have it. My life in a nutshell: My family is all in America. I live in California. I have one sister I grew up with and a whole new family in Oregon I am getting to know. My sister lives in the same town as me and my niece is in graduate school not far away. My adoptive parents have both died. My mother passed in 1992, after a second bout with cancer, and my father passed in 2003 after years of diabetes-related problems. And now we have lost Joan's husband and Kate's father and Karin's and my brother-in-law, John.

After I lost Mom, but before I lost Dad, I decided to look into finding my birth parents. I started with my birth mother. I found her, but unfortunately there was never a reunion as she didn't want to meet me. Then after Dad died, when I was aged 56, I found and met up with my birth father. He was ecstatic to learn of my existence and meet me, because it turns out that he had never even known his then-fiancée was pregnant. He lost track of her when her family moved while he was in another part of Oregon working as a logger. When he went home after being on the job for weeks, he found the love of his young life was gone. No one would tell him where the family had moved. So he moved on with his life without her and didn't know I existed until I showed up at his home in 2004.

My sister and niece are in California. My genetic family is in Oregon and Washington. And my lifelong cousins and other family I keep in touch with are in California, Oregon, Washington, Tennessee, Hawaii, Arizona, Florida, New York, and Virginia. So, as you can see, family and my home have great meaning for me, especially now, when I have lost so much already.

Karin

When I was 57 years old, I met Karin, the love of my life. I knew what life was by then, and I knew what love was, too. I have both in full measure now, and it is wonderful. But we face serious challenges to be together and keep our love and life the way we want it. So that takes a lot of our focus, both together and individually.

Karin is as much my opposite as she is like me, and we are a terrific fit. We so mirror each other that we make each other better people. Karin loves to chatter; I usually prefer to listen. We both like movies, but not always the same kinds. It's the same with music. Karin tries to rein me in, and I try to make her more loose. Of course, I think I know her—but she sometimes surprises me. Bet she would say the same about me!

We are both funny, and we have lots of fun. We love to be together at home. We love to visit family and friends. We love to travel. We love to explore new places. We love to take photographs. We love to cuddle. We love to share. We love to see how our adventure will unfold next. We chat about that and lots of things over cups of tea that Karin loves to make and drink. I love to drink tea now, too—the British way with lots of milk.

It seems almost impossible that we would have met, let alone be together. But it happened. I am a butch lesbian, easily identified by most people in the know. Karin is far from that and has lived a much different life prior to meeting me. I love how Karin takes care of me and nurtures me and complements me. She doesn't always understand all of my quirks, but on the whole she gets who I am, and that is very important.

Karin was 65 when we met. She turned 70 in 2010. She was visiting America in 2005, and we met online before we met in person. Karin was born in Germany on August 6, 1940. Her German mother and Austrian father experienced a terrible time during World War II. Karin's father was killed in Stalingrad two years after she was born. He briefly met his daughter at her birth, but had to return to war and never lived to return to Germany. That makes Karin's story not so different from many Germans or other Europeans or Americans of her age group, but her story goes on to be very different.

After being relocated because of the war and living in a refugee camp, then finally returning to her bombed hometown, Karin and her family put their life back together as best they could. Karin was raised mostly by her grandparents while her mother worked as a translator for the Church of Scotland.

Karin's childhood included playing with her friends in bombed-out buildings in her hometown of Muelheim Ruhr and floating little boats made of twigs in the puddles left by the rain.

She remembers riding on a special seat her grandfather (Opa) made for his bicycle, and she remembers helping her grandmother (Oma) in the kitchen and drinking malz bier at the local watering hole when she would accompany Opa.

Things changed as Germany rebuilt and the occupying army left. Karin moved to England at age 12 with her mother and new stepfather, an officer in the British army who got a job as a biscuit (cookie) salesman after the war. As a result, her accent is British and she has British citizenship and passport. By birth, though, she is German.

Karin has lived in Germany, England, Spain, Scotland, and France, and you might say she is traditionally European. But she has also lived in the United States before—in Florida for a few years—and now has visited me in California several times. I think these visits to the West Coast may be helping her to be slightly more informal, more American than European. We'll see how that goes…

Karin's path to recognizing that she is a lesbian has been different from mine, more gradual. Like me, she received little information and support about her sexuality in the 1940s and 1950s. But she had her crushes. She was exhibiting the behavior we call lesbian, even though she could not identify it as such. She fell in love with German actress Greta Garbo and had her photos on her bedroom wall, and she rode her bike for miles just to look at her favorite female teacher's house.

After completing high school, she decided that she wanted to be a journalist but didn't have the money to go to university. Living at home and studying was not an option because of Karin's difficult relationship with her stepfather. She applied to be a stewardess for Pan American Airlines, potentially based in Los Angeles, but didn't follow through on that job in the end because she had the opportunity to work in a hotel on Jersey, an island off the coast of England, where she had full room and board and began her long career as a hotel manager. At the hotel, Karin met the first of her three husbands. During two of the marriages, she bore a child. She also helped raise five stepchildren.

The whole time she was married to, or involved with, men, she didn't really like being sexual with them. After she had her second child, she fell in love with a woman and had a loving and sensual, not sexual, relationship for years. Then, while she was married to her third husband, a gay man, she fell for a whiskey-drinking, cigar-smoking Haitian woman in Paris, but, as Karin explained, there was only one chaste kiss between them.

Karin's road to being a lesbian brought her a new awareness late in life and radically changed her future because, as she sums up her current immigration challenge, "I fell in love with a U.S. citizen!" She added, "I still am in love with this woman," but we both know our relationship makes life challenging, to say the least.

Though our beginnings had some similarities, the exact parts of our younger lives were different enough that by the time we met in 2005 I had been in three long-term lesbian relationships, as well as a couple of shorter ones. Karin's experiences were with men, although she had always been attracted to, and had tried to have relationships with, women.

"I came out, in a way, when I was 39 years old, at Findhorn in Scotland, where I lived for more than two decades," Karin told me. It's hard for her to say exactly when it happened. "Not until I was around 60 years old did I truly get it," she said.

So, that's Karin in a nutshell. She is an only child who was married or partnered with men, although she acknowledges she was always attracted to women. She has a son in Scotland, a daughter in England and seven grandchildren. She also keeps up with some of her stepchildren and their children. One stepson in England has already passed on.

With her few short and rocky lesbian relationships behind her, Karin was still looking for a real, successful one by her mid-60s. That's when she found me on an online dating site she explored one Sunday evening. That's when our story began. Now my family in America and her family in England and Scotland and France and Florida are our family.

■

CHAPTER SIX

FROM CYBERSPACE TO OREGON

I met Karin online when she was visiting friends in Oregon. She was poking around a lesbian dating site I had joined. I don't know why I was even there, really. I had quit the whole dating scene, discouraged and disgusted at how some things had turned out, and I figured I would be alone for the rest of my life. I was pushing 60, and it just seemed that my fate was sealed. But a friend had convinced me to try the site, so I did. I put up several pictures. I wrote the profile of my life. And Karin found me.

She didn't know that clicking on my profile meant I would know that she had seen it. She was surprised a few days later to receive a brief e-mail from me asking why she had clicked on my profile. She told me later that at first she thought she would just ignore it. Then she said she felt guilty and decided to be polite and respond. So she answered me. And then I answered her. And then we chatted a lot online.

One day we talked on the phone and things progressed from there. She invited me to Oregon to a PFLAG (Parents, Friends and Family of Lesbians and Gays) dance. I told her I didn't dance. She said she didn't, either. But I went to visit her. My friends in California and her friends in Oregon thought we were out of our minds for doing it. Two groups of friends in two states thought an axe murderer was going to be in the mix!

We had a fun three-day weekend in southern Oregon. To me, the dance was the biggest fishbowl in the world. All Karin's friends were there checking me out, and I was there all on my own. Even Karin was mostly a stranger at that point. We talked. We watched other people. We danced a bit. We spent time together. We shared stories. We laughed over meals. We goofed around taking pictures in the park.

We separated after that first weekend visit knowing that we liked each other and wanted to meet again. I thought we might have a long-distance relationship. Karin had more reservations about it than I did. Neither of us knew then what would really happen—and we couldn't have predicted or anticipated exactly how our binational relationship was going to play out with ICE down the road. At that time we had the bliss of ignorance on that score.

As I got to know Karin, she explained that she had a B1/B2 visa that would allow her to visit America for six months at a time. Though she had lived and worked in America in the past, she had not been here long enough to apply for and receive a green card. She didn't feel the need to do so at the time. She had been in Florida and found it too conservative and closed-minded, she said. She had returned to the more progressive and open-minded culture in Europe and was living in France.

I'll be honest: During those first heady days, when Karin explained her visa situation to me it seemed like an annoyance, a blip. But as we fell in love and moved down that road of togetherness, it became an ugly intruder—a bad dream that would not go away. It began to take over our lives like a ticking clock with an alarm no one ever wanted to hear.

Karin's visa situation was not foremost in our minds in late 2005 and early 2006. We were still getting to know each other and figuring out how we felt about each other. Karin visited me in California, then returned to stay with her friends in Oregon. During that time, things were relatively normal for a new relationship. We would probably see each other every month or so. Lots of people do that. And I was feeling that that was the limit of what we could do at the time. After all, Karin would be returning to Europe before long, anyway.

Things changed when Karin called me one day, upset. She was getting ready to go and stay with a different friend who lived in a different location and was having a panic attack about it. She realized that even though she had said that's what she wanted to do, she couldn't go through with it. She cried on the phone, saying she wanted to be with me. She was upset that I had not invited her to visit me longer in California.

Shocked, I told her that she was welcome to come and visit me in California. We worked out logistics, then she drove south two days in snow and rain to my home. Our agreement was that she would visit for a month, regardless of what happened, and see how things turned out.

Karin's first extended stay with me was both difficult and interesting. We are from very different cultures, and though we both speak English, it's really Californian and British. Karin likes neat, tidy places with lots of white and light. I am not fastidious, and my house is colorful and full of eclectic treasures from travel and shopping in ethnic shops in America.

Believe me, the habits, idiosyncrasies, dislikes, likes, and just plain stubbornness of a younger person are greatly magnified when one of you is 57 years old and the other is 65. Now add to the mix that one of you is American and has never visited Europe and the other is European, and you'll get the picture. Food is different. How you see the world is different. Even when and how you eat dinner is different. What you think about things is different.

I am a lifelong lesbian, and Karin was finally beginning a serious lesbian relationship after taking a long time to come out. It's a wonder we didn't run away or kill each other just getting through each day as virtual strangers staying in the same house. And the visa issue was becoming all too clear now: Even if we were to make a go of it, Karin would not be able to stay in America with me. If we were going to be together, we would have to figure out where we would live and how we would work that out.

After our first small, incremental commitment to be together for a month and see how that went, we did it again—this time, for three months. After that we were clear: We were destined to be together!

Even as our comfort and familiarity with each other grew, so too did the apprehension and uncertainty of what the future held. We were becoming a couple, and that was a very good thing, but because we were becoming a lesbian binational couple the future posed uncertainties.

CHAPTER SEVEN

COMMITTING TO EACH OTHER

Karin and I had just a few months of getting to know each other before she had to leave the country in order to meet her temporary visa requirement. She went back to England and her family, and I kept going to work and hoping all would be well.

When she returned for a visit, we decided we needed a good vacation together. An Olivia (lesbian) cruise in December 2006 sounded like a terrific idea. I used some of my inheritance money and took unpaid time off work. We flew to Honolulu and spent a week there, then boarded the ship for a cruise among the Hawaiian Islands and an amazing open ocean voyage to Fanning Island, a coral atoll in the Republic of Kiribati. We couldn't get enough of paradise and spent some more time on the island of Oahu before flying to California—time and money well spent, we know now.

One special event during that cruise stood out. At night, with no one else around, with a view of lava eruptions from Kilauea on the Big Island of Hawaii in the background, Karin and I committed to each other and a future together. We knew enough of the promise and enough of the danger to make a true resolve, regardless.

We both had cheap adjustable rings that Karin had insisted on buying in a cool store in Silverton, Oregon, called Stone Buddha. Explorer rings, Karin called them. They certainly weren't comfortable, and Karin left hers off. I, however, kept mine on all the time, as a symbol of our relationship. It was all we had to show us and anyone else that we were committed to each other.

That night, as we promised to be together and be fearless about the future, we twisted the rings together and tossed them overboard, along with our purple vanda orchid leis. Drama! Commitment! We promised Hawaii we would return. Magic! We stepped into a new future together without fear.

When I look back on it, it seems like the honeymoon came before the wedding for us, since the Hawaii cruise was everything a honeymoon should be. But none of that could compensate for the fact that we couldn't marry legally. Even if we could get married in California, it would not be recognized by the federal government for purposes of immigration.

In a very sad twist of fate, marriage was our worst enemy at that time. If Karin and I married in the United States, it would cause Immigration and Customs Enforcement

(ICE) to see Karin as a risk to overstay her visa. It could mean that she might not leave when her visit period was up. And even though we can marry in the United Kingdom (it's called civil partnership), it wouldn't change our status in the United States and allow me to sponsor Karin for immigration.

Undaunted, when we returned from our vacation, we decided to celebrate our commitment to each other with a special afternoon tea, complete with little sandwiches and proper British black tea and special treats. We had the tea party reception in September 2007 in San José, the date determined by vacation schedules of European family members who wanted to attend. We made the food and drinks with the help of family and friends. We rented our local LGBT Center ballroom and splurged on a four-tier "wedding" cake. Everyone who attended got a special tea bag favor. The individually packaged bags had two tea cups pictured with our names and date and the title Perfect Blend. Usually I don't go for things like that, but this was special. It was so special I got teapots and tea cups at thrift stores and made an entry arbor covered with them and ferns and tulle to guide people into the hall.

Two hundred people helped us celebrate that day, and we loved every minute of it. We explained that we were not married and why we couldn't be, even though that was a downer for a "wedding" reception. For us, though, it was just another symptom of our status, and it opened lots of eyes when we shared our dilemma with our guests. Family came from all over—England, Scotland, France, Florida, Oregon—and joined the locals in what was a terrific celebration. But nagging on the heels of that wonderful event was the ticking visa clock: Karin had to be out of the country two weeks after our party. No excuses!

As it turned out, the journey out of the country and back was all quite straightforward. While our daughter and son-in-law from England, Tamsin and Terry, visited Las Vegas and New Mexico, Karin and I visited Canada with Michael, our son from Scotland. After some fun sightseeing in Seattle, Vancouver, and Victoria, Karin was easily welcomed back to America and got another six-month visitor's visa. In fact, the border guards spent more time questioning Michael about why he was there and what he was up to than they did Karin. We were glad to get back in the rental car and drive back to Seattle to fly to California.

After our Canadian trip, the visa cycle started all over again. Over the next six months, I kept going to work and Karin kept living her life. This was normal existence for us. At the end of the visa period, we decided to go to Mexico for a vacation in Puerto Vallarta with friends. Several years earlier, I had won a raffle for a stay in an oceanside condo for a week and never could get anyone to go with me. So Karin and I asked our good friends, who are really family, Cathy and Bill and one of their sons, Eric, to join us. Karin struggled with the idea of going. She was nervous about leaving, in general, then returning and having to go through being questioned at the border. But in the end, she agreed to go.

On our way south, we met some gay guys from Canada in LAX airport. They told us it was Bear Week in Puerto Vallarta, a time when gay men known as Bears from everywhere descend on the resort for fun. Karin and Bill and I shared what we had learned about Bears from the guys in the airport with Cathy and Eric, who arrived in Puerto Vallarta before we did. None of us knew there were so many types of Bears. I have to admit I thought it just meant big, hairy men. I was wrong!

Cathy wasn't worried about teenaged Eric being in Puerto Vallarta for Bear Week; she was worried he might be bored being on a week's vacation with four older folks. But after helping launch Ridley turtle hatchlings into the ocean and going dune buggy riding with his dad, among other fun things, Eric had as much fun as anyone, if not more.

In fact, everyone had a wonderful time. We went to the local market. We saw iguanas in the trees. We ate crêpes from a nighttime vendor and delicious pastries for breakfast from a man who walked along the ocean. I had my hair braided with beads. We took the bus to a wonderful botanical garden. I explored on my own and found an interesting vegetarian restaurant. Karin and I went on a day-long gay and lesbian catamaran cruise, where we turned out to be the only lesbians among a gang of Bears. They took us under their wings, and we had a good time (even if a wave did knock me down and sweep away my brand new glasses!).

After that warm and happy week staying beside the ocean and playing in a rooftop swimming pool, Karin was welcomed back into the United States without incident. We could breathe easier for a while. We even began to feel like things wouldn't be so bad after all.

Karin's next trip took her back to England, and this time I joined her. It was my first trip to England and Europe, and while we were there, we went searching for my genetic family roots. We discovered my birth father's ancestors had worked for Anne Boleyn's family at Hever Castle! Who knew? The story was still pretty fresh to me, and I had never imagined I would find that I was descended from English ancestors. When I learned about Hever Castle, in Kent in southeast England, I was anxious to go see the place where my genetic ancestors had worked and lived. Tamsin and Terry took us there and we saw all the grounds and inside the castle, which had been "modernized" by the Astor family, who bought it and lived in it for years. We also visited the church next to Hever Castle, St. Peter's, where my ancestors were christened, married, and buried.

We looked for the gravestones of my great, great, great, great-grandparents, Philadelphia Welfare Everest and Thomas Everest. Terry found the lichen-encrusted headstones, which were barely legible. More interesting than finding these Everests is the other amazing story of my ancestors. Thomas and Philadelphia's son William Richard Everest and his family went across the Atlantic to America in 1837. A decade later, they had crossed America on the Oregon Trail, got free land in Oregon Territory, and helped found the town of Newberg. Three of them even went to California and found gold in the Gold Rush of 1849.

Karin and I have now seen the headstones in England of William Richard's parents and seen his and his wife Jane Cole Everest's headstones in Oregon—a circle completed and my genetic history memorialized in stone on both sides of the Atlantic Ocean. We also followed their Oregon Trail journey in 2009, after I met Karin in Canada and she was allowed to reenter the United States on her visa again.

Of course, while in England we also had done our share of visiting tourist sights. We ate in pubs. We had Eton Mess for dessert. I tried several ales. In London, we rode the Underground, went to Trafalgar Square, saw Big Ben, and watched the water activity on the River Thames. We rode the London Eye, that enormous ferris wheel in central London, and saw the musical "Wicked" on the West End stage. After that small taste of England, I was anxious to return and spend more time with Karin's English family. In fact, I enjoyed England. It was a good thing because now I knew that I would be glad to visit Karin there when it came time for her to leave America once more.

And in one of the twists of my life, I now was connected to England through my birth father, Don Everest and my wife, Karin Bogliolo, who I had met less than a year apart and, get this—both in Oregon, where I was born, but never lived.

CHAPTER EIGHT

WHY YOU SHOULD CARE
ABOUT OUR STORY

If you don't know us, you might wonder why you should care about this problem, our issue. I understand that. I didn't know much about gay and lesbian binational couples until it became my day-to-day life. And now my everyday reality is in the spotlight. We face this threat to being together in America, as do thousands of others. We can't get married, and I can't sponsor Karin for immigration to live in America with me. That's why everyone should care.

You may know someone with a story like ours. If so, you can help them and advocate for them. Or if you are a lesbian or a gay man, at some time in your life you may find yourself part of a same-sex binational couple. If you do, you will want this situation fixed. Trust me!

If you are part of an LGBT binational family you should care a lot—and you should know that dedicated people are working to solve the problems you face. You can help, too. Check the Resource Groups and Websites, Chapter 35, and empower yourself to help fight this battle.

Even people who work with lesbian, gay, bisexual, and transgender (LGBT) civil rights issues are not all aware of the issue binational couples like us face. That's why it's good to know about us and our story. We need your help and advocacy so that we can keep our families together.

As I write these words in late 2010, the clock is again ticking for us. Karin has had to leave the United States again, and I am dealing with the post-writing portion of this project on my own. Although our story is not as dramatic as some you will read in this book, it is still sobering. Among the things that Karin and I have had to contend with since we became involved in 2005 are the following:

- Karin has to leave America every six months (or less) to be in compliance with her B1/B2 visa.*
- We cannot admit our relationship to the Immigration and Customs Enforce-

---

* See Pertinent Definitions and Information, Chapter 37.

ment (ICE) border officials of Homeland Security or Karin will be denied admittance because they will think she might want to overstay her visa.

- Karin has to keep paying for flights and living expenses out of the country. I pay for living expenses while we are together in America, while we are separated, and while we are out of the country together.

- We are both draining our savings accounts, which are not bottomless! Karin has taken on the task of turning things in the house into exile income. Our 2009 garage sale earned us nearly $3,000, which helped a lot. Our 2010 garage sale liberated much of my Mexican folk art collection, along with assorted other things from cupboards and closets, but didn't net as much. We didn't have as much to sell, and Karin scolds me for pricing things too low…

- My awesome stash of more than 100 lesbian pulp fiction books just went to one lucky online buyer in New York for enough money to keep Karin in food and shelter for a month or so in the United Kingdom. It's hard to see my treasures disappear, but there is no choice really. We have to live in two countries at this point in time and we have to pay for it.

- I took early retirement in 2009, at age 61, so we could be together. I have a reduced pension because I couldn't work to full pensionable age. I made the difficult decision to retire after Karin and I had been forced to live apart for nine months. In an event I will relate shortly, ICE told Karin she was visiting too often and forced her to leave the country for a longer period, so we had to take drastic action.

- We have to leave behind aging parents in Oregon when we are out of the country. Mom and Dad Everest don't like it when we are not in California.

- We have had to be separated from family in California while they dealt with a serious health issue.

- When Karin left the country on October 27, 2010, we were separated again. We had agreed I would stay in California to help John and Joan as he battled pancreatic cancer.

- Now, when Karin and I leave California, Joan will be more alone in San José, since John lost his battle with pancreatic cancer on October 28, 2010, the day after Karin left the country.

John, our brother-in-law, kept reminding me to remind our Congressman Mike Honda that when we have to leave, they lose us and we lose them. Karin and I agree. We know firsthand the pain of separation. We don't like it, but we do it to be together. We work as hard as we can to get the law changed so that we and the estimated 36,000 other couples and families like us can stay together. Our separations and the stress we share take a toll on us physically, mentally, emotionally, and spiritually. We fight depression, anxiety, fear, panic, and more. No one should have to live like this!

So, this is Judy and Karin's basic story. Today we are yo-yo people, living in two countries, trying to hold on until Uniting American Families Act (UAFA), or Reuniting Families Act (RFA), or Comprehensive Immigration Reform of 2010 (CIR 2010), or another truly comprehensive immigration reform bill that includes LGBT families[*] passes the U.S. Congress and is signed into law. We are hopeful that this will happen before long. We need it to happen. So do thousands of others.

We are sharing our story, and our hopes for change in the law, with no small risk involved. By telling our story openly, this book reveals who we really are. While we are "legal strangers" to the U.S. government, we are, in fact, a couple like any other married couple—except for the fact that we don't have the law on our side, and with it, the 1,138 federal rights that legal American marriage confers.

Sharing our story may make it impossible for Karin to return to the United States on her visa to visit me, as it will alert Immigration and Customs Enforcement to our situation. We are willing to take that risk to help the cause. We are willing to relocate if necessary to be together. We have information that makes us nervous about Karin's likelihood of reentry after she had to leave again in October 2010. We also have information that makes us more secure as elected officials and organizations promise to help us.

This book is an overview—a history if you will. It is the story of a harsh reality gay men and lesbians face trying to keep their families together. Many have dealt with this issue much longer than Karin and I have. As you read the stories that follow you will see what others have done and will do to stay together. You will meet brave lesbians and gay men who have faced tremendous challenges and have solved their issues in various ways. They are our heroes, and they should be to all Americans who believe in equal rights for all.

Karin and I were horrified when we heard the stories you will read here. We can barely imagine what some couples and families have to go through to live together. We are in awe of their perseverance and grit and determination and all they have done to stay together. They inspire us. I hope they inspire you as you read their stories.

Karin and I came to this story, the LGBT family binational immigration issue, late in life. I am embarrassed that I knew little about it all the years I was working on civil rights for the LGBT community. And, until Karin and I were together, it wasn't her issue—or mine.

Our story is presented here as one example of coping with an unfavorable reality.

---

[*] See Pertinent Definitions and Information, Chapter 37.

Stories of the various ways other people cope are included, so that you can see what sort of challenges the American immigration system presents for adults and children who are left out of the legal definition of family in America.

Since federal recognition of same-sex partnerships was nonexistent, gay men and lesbians (like me) could not sponsor their partners (like Karin) for immigration. That was the simple problem.

But the answers were not simple; they were problems, too. Here's what I thought as I wrote this book:

No American should have to choose between family and country!

No American should have to choose between family and career!

Yet, as it turned out, I would have to do both those things. That's because eventually what we were dreading did, in fact, happen: In April 2008, Karin was challenged and detained in a cell-like room by three uniformed members of Immigration and Customs Enforcement (ICE), in the San Francisco International Airport, as she came back from the United Kingdom to visit me in California. What happened during that nightmare scenario was a call to action that we could no longer ignore.

CHAPTER NINE

OUR AIRPORT SCARE
WITH ICE

Karin and I made a second visit to England in 2008. On April 21, Karin and I flew to California on the same flight from the United Kingdom. That day is impossible to forget. We had been in the air for 12 hours. We were tired. We were jet lagged. I hadn't been able to sleep because the guy in front of me kept his seat way back the whole time and someone behind me kicked my seat constantly.

While on the plane, I had asked Karin if she had anything she should take out of her purse. She said there was nothing in there that would be a problem. That oversight came back to bite her in a few hours.

Because our passports are from different countries, we don't go through the same line at U.S. Immigration and Customs. We had agreed to meet at the baggage claim. I walked through customs quickly and went to get the bags. I got a luggage cart and loaded things, glancing back to see how Karin was doing at the customs desk. I saw her in line. Then I saw her talking to an agent. The next time I glanced back she had disappeared. I felt my guts go to the floor; they had taken her away! I didn't know where she was or what had happened, but I knew it couldn't be good.

I was panicking, but I tried to look calm. I just stood there with the luggage cart feeling helpless and scared—no, terrified. The security guard kept eyeing me, and I knew I had to do something. I asked him if I could wait there for my friend, but he said I was loitering and to take my bags out into the lobby area. So I left through the double doors and called Joan and John, my sister and her husband who were meeting us, to tell them to park the car and meet me inside. Something was terribly wrong, and they didn't need to sit in the cell phone waiting area indefinitely, wondering what was going on.

Ordinarily, the routine is for Joan and John to come to the curb to pick us up after we claim our bags. But this was not an ordinary day. The three of us ended up sitting in the waiting area outside the international arrivals doors for three hours, never knowing what was going on with Karin—or if we would be allowed to see her.

When she finally came out of the arrival area, Karin was shaken. I was so relieved to see her I jumped up and grabbed her. She was nervous and wanted to rush to the car and get away, so we did. "What happened?" I asked. "I'll tell you in the car," she said. She was very upset, and it took her some time to calm down.

It was late at night by then. We had landed in the early evening, so being delayed for hours with customs and the luggage and the detention really left us exhausted. But we felt hungry. We found a place to get some food and rode home in a daze, worried about what would happen next. By the time we got the luggage upstairs and found and greeted the cat, we had been up nearly 24 hours straight.

When Karin had finally told us what had happened, we were shocked, and Joan and John got a really good look at what Karin and I have to deal with. Even for me, somewhat prepared for trouble at some point in our lives, it was hard to hear what happened. It made me realize that our future was now compromised big time.

Karin had renewed her B1/B2 visa at the U.S. Embassy while we were in London on that trip. In general, according to the *www.ImmigrationDirect.com* website, "the B-1/B-2 visa is used by foreign visitors who enter the U.S. for a temporary period for business or pleasure. A B-1/B-2 visa is generally valid for six months and can be extended once the visa holder is in the U.S."

The site continues with: "A B-1/B-2 visa is the most commonly used U.S. visa. It authorizes a fairly wide range of activities, and individuals who enter the U.S pursuant to this status are generally authorized to change to a status that authorizes work or study after entering the U.S." [*]

This B2 visa code is the same one that ICE issues Karin every time she visits the United States; however, on this particular day, the ICE folks at the airport in San Francisco challenged the visa and proceeded to question her. It was our very own Day of Infamy, the day when our future really took a turn. We knew we would have to make more long-term plans, and things were going to be very different—probably for the rest of our lives.

What happened to change things was very simple: The guards (a woman and two men) who detained and questioned Karin that day went through her purse. When they did so, they found a picture of Karin and me, and asked Karin to identify who the other woman was. Then they found Karin's Oregon driver's license and wanted to know why she had that.

She told them the second woman in the photo was her friend. She explained that she had been visiting in Oregon and didn't want to drive without a license. They asked a bunch of other questions, and Karin answered them all. They wanted to know why she had the kind of visa she did and why she was in the United States as often as she was. Karin and her former husband owned a small publishing company, Findhorn

---

[*] See Pertinent Definitions and Information, Chapter 37.

Press, based in the United Kingdom. So on that day, Karin explained that while in the United States, she met with authors and worked with book publishers and continued to do work as she had for years with Findhorn Press.

Unfortunately, the agents weren't buying it. Karin was told she had been visiting the United States too often, and that she hadn't been leaving enough time between visits to the United States. As a result, on that day in April 2008, ICE refused to give Karin a six-month entry visa. The guards told her she would have four months to get her affairs in order in the United States, and after she departed the country, she would have to stay away from the United States for an indefinite period of time. Three abbreviated notations were written in Karin's passport, which we believe refer to "no extension of stay" and "no adjustment of stay," with the third possibly referring to "no offer of stay."

So, to cut a long story short: Just four months later, Karin had to return to England and ended up staying there for nine months. Since I still had a full-time job at San José State University, I could not go with her, and we were separated for an excruciatingly long time. We kept our relationship going with Skype and e-mail and did our best with what we faced. It was our biggest Torn Apart experience to date and we didn't like it at all—so we now know more what other families deal with and are anxious to help fix our problem with immigration.

CHAPTER TEN

KARIN'S LONG GOODBYE

Before Karin had to leave America in the summer of 2008, we prepared ourselves for the separation in lots of ways. One thing we did was to get ready to leave California for good by clearing out our house and having a huge garage sale. At the garage sale, we made several thousand dollars. People kept asking why we were selling such good stuff. It was a wonderful teachable moment, as they say, and we took the opportunity to explain to people why we were selling things.

But my day was ruined in a heartbeat by one lady, who got a car full of stuff practically for free. She hugged me when I told her our story. She seemed sympathetic, but then she floored me by whispering in my ear, No, she couldn't vote No on Proposition 8 (California's initiative to allow same-sex marriage). I'll tell you: I felt like taking all my stuff back!

We had friends over for dinner to say goodbye to Karin. We visited Mom and Dad Everest in Oregon and our Cole cousins in Washington. Mom and Dad and the Everest/Verhelst/Soesbe/Handy clan had a party for us with a wedding cake. We brought two plastic brides to put on top.

Back in California we went to a few places for fun, just the two of us. We even spent several terrific days in Las Vegas at Green Valley Resort and found out how the rich and famous live on a special-price online deal I got for Karin's birthday. We sat by the pool in a cabana room—an enormous splurge for us. We walked the strip and saw the sights. We even won prizes at the arcade games.

And then the day came when I had to take Karin to San Francisco for the long flight to London and the "stay out of the country for a long time" separation we were dreading. Chatting on the drive to the airport was hard. Sitting at the airport was harder.

It got so weird sitting there in the food court area that Karin said: "Why don't you just go home, honey?" There wasn't anything we could really do but sit there being miserable, and she was trying to cut that experience short. I didn't want her to go, and I didn't want to leave her. It was a real lose-lose situation.

"I didn't buy anything for you," I said, feeling bad and embarrassed. "That's okay," she replied. "We have each other." I tore a corner off a paper in my wallet and wrote "I love you" on it and handed it to her. Silly thing to do maybe, but it felt good at the time.

I walked Karin to the security station to get the goodbye over with, so we wouldn't suffer any more at the airport together. She asked me if I would be okay, and I told her I would. I knew I would, but I didn't want her to leave. I kissed her goodbye and realized how awful this whole thing was. It was a big dose of discrimination. I felt we didn't deserve it one bit.

She waved once and then waited in line without watching me. I didn't want to just stand there, so I walked toward the parking garage. I hurt so much! It felt like the biggest hand in the universe had punched me in the gut and the heart. And there was nothing, nothing I could do about it. If you've ever lost someone you really love, you know the feeling—beyond sad, beyond loss, the worst—the feeling of being torn apart.

Through tears, I watched my beloved Karin leave without me. That was the day our nine-month separation began. That August day in 2008 was the day we were really Torn Apart.

For us, Torn Apart is not because of something I did or she did. It's not because of death or breakup. It's because the American government won't let me and my partner stay together. So many gay and lesbian families face this terrible set of challenges, there might have even been another couple like us saying goodbye to each other that very day. Hard to realize, hard to visualize, men and women and families with children face this all the time. So we faced it the best we could on this day in San Francisco, California, of all places, a gay and lesbian capital for the world!

Thankfully, our life returned to its routine (for us) in May 2009, when I drove to Canada and picked up Karin, who had flown there from England. From that day on, we planned to be together again always—in or out of America for the rest of our lives. That worked for 2009 and most of 2010, but John's illness changed that plan. We both agreed I needed to stay in California when Karin had to leave. On October 27, 2010, Karin left the United States again to comply with her visa.

CHAPTER ELEVEN

FAST FORWARD TO ANOTHER SAD AIRPORT GOODBYE FOR JUDY AND KARIN

Part One: Judy's Story

OCTOBER 29, 2010, SAN JOSE, CALIFORNIA. It's a terrible thing to think, let alone say, but the more practice you have kissing your partner goodbye for a long time, the easier it gets. It's sort of true—the scab is forming on emotions. But it isn't fun. I don't like doing it. No one should have to do it.

After a year where I took early retirement and joined Karin in Europe because she was unable to be with me in the United States, here we were back to the same old, same old. I had to see Karin off again on October 27, 2010. She was again forced to leave to meet her visa requirements, and I wasn't going with her this time. I was staying home to be with my family while we faced a serious health problem. We had not made arrangements to have someone take care of the house and cat, because we had planned for months that Karin would go and I would stay behind. We knew it was the right thing to do, and we each of us supported the other's position.

Aside from the fact that Karin and I want to be together, it's a real pity that she could not stay to help our family. My brother-in-law John was suffering from his second bout with cancer, this time pancreatic, and Karin is a trained hospice caregiver. She would have been a great help as she is experienced in the needed care and procedures.

To add more stress, the U. S. State Department had issued a travel alert for Americans to be vigilant about possible plots for terrorist attacks originating in Pakistan and North Africa aimed at Britain, France, and Germany. Furthermore, we were separating in Los Angeles, nowhere near home, because Karin had found a much cheaper fare from there. In our life now every penny counts double.

But the biggest problem with our goodbye was this: Much as I don't want to believe it, we have no assurance that I will see Karin again in America. No assurance at all! If she is not allowed back in, we will have to relocate, unless the law changes.

So after finding the least expensive airfare to London, we drove to Los Angeles to follow through on the schedule imposed on us by ICE. We had planned to take a leisurely drive down the California coast, but we abandoned that to stay with family an extra day before we left. Our mood in the car was colored by the sadness that enveloped us as we faced being torn apart from our life together and torn apart from John, who was losing his battle day by day.

Life was bittersweet for us. Happy was mixed with sad. Fun was mixed with work. We had feelings pulling us in many directions. On the happy side: We were excited about this book being completed and meeting the publisher, his publicist, and an LGBT book promoter in Los Angeles on the day that Karin had to fly out of the United States. Karin wanted to be at the meeting, so we didn't postpone it until the day after she left, as I had suggested. We were sad that we had to go all the way to Los Angeles for the flight, but we were excited to talk about the book project. We steeled ourselves to do what we had to do and hoped that doing something we wanted to do would make it somehow better. I can't really say that it worked, though.

After the meeting about the book was over and I had seen Karin off at LAX, I couldn't hold it in any longer: I puddled up. It wasn't so different from the time I had to see her off at San Francisco airport two years earlier.

But I knew what I had to do, so I kept on going. I met with the publisher and publicist once more the day after Karin left. Then I took the publisher to LAX for his flight to France. I checked in with my sister and said hi to John on speakerphone. By that day, October 28, it was nearly impossible for John to talk, but I told him I would see him the next day when I got home. Later that night, while I was in a motel on the way north, I got the call I dreaded. John had died before I could get back to San José. We now had one more tragedy to add to our story in *Torn Apart*; it hurt more than it would have because Karin was out of the country and I was grieving alone. Though I couldn't help with John, which is why I had stayed behind, I was glad to be in California to help Joan and my niece Kate and sped north to be at their sides.

So, I'm counting on you, and you, and you, and you. Help me bring Karin back home to live with me where we want to live. Help me be an American citizen who has the rights of American citizens who are not lesbians or gay men or bisexual or transgendered persons.

The time is now!

Part Two: Karin's Story

OCTOBER 30, 2010, GUILDFORD, ENGLAND. I have now been back in England for two days, still feeling rather jet-lagged. And yet so much more than jet-lagged. Two days ago, I left Judy alone at Los Angeles International Airport. I took a last picture of her as I looked down from the security area. She gave me a wan smile and a tired wave. I felt totally numb; I could not cry or feel anything. Sometimes survival means moving into a space of nothingness. I was not only leaving Judy again for an indefinite time, I was leaving our dear sister Joan and her dying husband John. I had seen him a couple of days earlier and kissed him goodbye. He had said, "See you when you come back." We both knew that would not happen. He died shortly after I flew back to Europe across the Atlantic.

I am feeling almost unbearable pain at being torn away from these loved ones as we all go through this transition from life to death. It is a time for family to be together, to hold each other, to support each other. I have been denied the opportunity to grieve with my dearest Judy, and with my family in California. For what reason? Nothing except some unfair, unjust law that keeps families apart.

I am beginning to feel my own mortality. This year I celebrated my 70th birthday. I am moving into those years when death begins to feel like a reality, something to consider. It is also a time when I want to be with the person I love most in the world. Yet much of that time is denied to us by a country unwilling to accept that families come in many different forms.

I know that what I am going through right now is also happening to thousands upon thousands of other couples and families, children, grandparents; it is not only a couple that makes a family. We are told that families are the basic unit of relationships of the human race. So what about MY family, my partner and her parents, her brothers and sister, nieces and nephews and cousins and their families? Am I not part of this family? Why am I thrown out, even at the point of death of a dearly loved one?

I am angry. I am in despair and pain. I want the physical presence of my beloved, not just a fuzzy picture on Skype, where I see her tears and sorrow. There is no reason for this, no justice in it.

So to whomsoever is reading this book, I ask that you care, that you are willing to act and bring this stupidity and injustice to an end. For Judy and me, for our family, and for all the other countless families affected by the same laws.

For now I must spend the winter alone. I will spend Christmas alone, and New Year, and all the other days in between. I have no idea when I will be allowed to see my darling Judy again. Please help us.

STORIES OF OTHER
SAME-SEX BINATIONAL
COUPLES

CHAPTER TWELVE

PHILIPPA AND INGER:
YO-YO GEOGRAPHY

*This is the ongoing situation Karin and I were dealing with in 2009/2010,
but it will change one way or the other soon, based on whether the law
changes. One day, we will be together in one country; it's just that, right now,
we don't know which one. It's stressful and disruptive and expensive, and we
don't want to keep doing it. We are older ladies, as they say, so we want to
settle down. We want to stop our yo-yo geography as soon as we can.*

*I'll admit, Karin and I don't really get lots of sympathy from friends who
think it's cool to be in Europe or somewhere else half the year. They tell us
they're jealous. But if they had to go through what we do, they would find the
gild off the lily after awhile, I'm sure.*

*Our inconvenience is not as bad as some gay and lesbian binational
couples, though. For example, we don't have a young child to figure into the
equation like the following couple does. We just have to figure out how to deal
with where my cat will live if we have to relocate—and sell everything we own
before I leave the country.*

In February 2008, when Philippa and Inger (no last names shared) began chatting
on an online site for tattoo enthusiasts called InkNation, they didn't know it would
mean that they would become a binational couple with a problem staying together.
After getting to know each other online, Philippa flew from her home in England, to
see Inger in the United States.

"That's when we fell in love," she smiled. "After that visit, I made four more trips to
the United States (which included one for three months), and Inger made two trips to
the United Kingdom."

Inger and her 10-year-old daughter live in Denver, Colorado. "She cannot come
here, to England," said Philippa, "because we do not want to take our 10-year-old
away from her father. And I cannot go to the United States to live because American
immigration laws will not allow Inger to sponsor me."

Photo of Philippa, left and Inger, right, from their private collection.
Used by permission.

"Right now we don't know when we will see each other again," said Inger. "Due to Philippa's frequent visits to the United States, she was detained by ICE on the last trip." "They questioned me about working," said Philippa, "which I have not been doing in America."

This couple wants to be together in the United States, but because one is American and female and the other is not American—and female—Inger cannot sponsor Philippa for immigration, which could lead to permanent residence with her in Colorado.

They are trying everything they can to get their story out and get help passing the law that will make things work for them and for so many other couples.

"We have tried to raise awareness in order to encourage change by doing two radio interviews," said Inger.

"We have made a video that has made an impact on various equality and immigration websites," added Philippa. "We have created a Facebook page, and my wife has volunteered for Out4Immigration at Denver Pride."

"Besides that, I have talked to politicians and lawyers," said Inger. "I have worked with the GLBT Commission in Denver to get unanimous support for Uniting American Families Act from the Denver City Council. I have approached media and magazines, and we have had our story published online by *She Wired*."

The situation is ridiculous and exceedingly expensive, Philippa and Inger agree. "It is extremely difficult to rationalize any of this to our 10-year-old daughter," Inger said, "as the situation really doesn't make any sense."

Philippa and Inger would enjoy living anywhere they could be together, they say, but with their 10-year-old daughter and her father to consider, they know the United States is the destination of choice, at least until she is older. That is not possible right now, though, because of "the United State's archaic and homophobic visa requirements," said Philippa. So these two have yo-yo geography, getting together when they can and hoping ICE cooperates.

Philippa, 33, came out in 1994 and has been out and active as a lesbian. Inger, 42, came out in 1985 but faced external pressure and tried to live a heterosexual life. "After years of trying, I realized this was not being true to myself or my daughter," she said. Her daughter has a good relationship with both her mother and father, and now has a new mom, Philippa, too.

But her moms live in two different countries, and it is hard on all of them, Philippa shared. They say it is hard to explain the situation to a young girl old enough to know something is not right, but not old enough to really understand the political situation. She just knows that one mom has to keep leaving after she visits a short time.

"We need to pass UAFA so that our family and many families can be reunited," said Inger.

"We need to pass UAFA so that people can have legal status and not live in fear of deportation or detainment," added Philippa. "People are made to feel like criminals in their own country the way things are," she stressed, "and have to live in exile away from their families, friends and communities."

Inger and Philippa's story is important because it involves a disrupted family.

"It is important because it represents a situation that affects so many more people than publicized," said Philippa. "If we don't make a stand, the situation will never change. There are many couples and families who for one reason or another cannot have their voices heard."

Inger added, "We represent a reality that people need to be aware of because this is a story of discrimination and basic human rights."

The situation remained grim for these women and their family in late October 2010, as I finished writing their story.

"We have no idea when we will see each other again," stressed Philippa.

"UAFA needs to pass. The jury is out, but we remain hopeful and continue to fight," added Inger.

They know they need to be in the United States to be together—until their daughter is old enough to decide where she will live and what she will do. They have not given up on living in America together.

"I will not give up on that," emphasized Philippa, "because Inger and our daughter are my life!"

While Philippa has moved in with her father because her trips to America cost so much, Inger continues to fight in Denver.

"I constantly call my legislators," she shared. "Staffers say 'Thank you' when I call, and 'I'll pass along this message.'" She has contacted the following elected officials in Colorado and elsewhere: Senator Michael Bennet (D-CO), Senator Charles Schumer (D-NY), Senator Dick Durbin (D-IL), Senator Mark Udall (D-CO), Senator Harry Reid (D-NV), Congresswoman Diana DeGette (D-CO-1), Congressman Ed Perlmutter (D-CO-7), and State Representative Daniel Kagan (D-HD3).

"Inger has also contacted: Christine Mastin, immigration lawyer and Republican candidate for Colorado's House District 3; Sarah Palin; and Speaker of the House Nancy Pelosi (D-CA-8). She has also made continuous calls to the White House," said Philippa.

She has contacted Immigration Equality and Out4Immigration and volunteered for them. She has e-mailed Love Exiles.

"Inger has been very active on our issue," said Philippa. "She met with National Center for Lesbian Rights (NCLR), phoned the Gay and Lesbian Task Force, and has contacted Get Equal, the American Civil Liberties Union (ACLU), Human Rights Watch, Human Rights Campaign (HRC), Stonewall, DREAM Act, Pride Nation, Standing on the Side of Love, The Center, 365gay.com, lezgetreal.com and others."

These women are determined to keep their family together and will continue to educate and advocate for Uniting American Families Act or legislation that includes it to solve the problem they share with so many other couples and families.

Philippa's family in England includes her father and three brothers. In the United States, Inger's family includes her parents and a sister and her daughter.

"They are all sympathetic and want the law to change," says Philippa.

"Our families sign petitions we send to them," said Inger, "and they have donated to Immigration Equality."

While they wait to be together one day, Philippa works in retail in her hometown. Inger is a part-time legal assistant in Denver.

"We were led to believe I could stay in the United States," says Philippa. "So I quit my career in the care industry, which has subsequently lead to a change in career."

While employers have not been able to help Philippa and Inger with their immigration situation, they provide sympathy and support, which is important and welcomed.

"When Inger thought I was going to be able to stay in Denver, she rescued a Pug for me to go with our Akita crossbreed, our Rottweiler crossbreed, and the three diva cats," smiled Philippa. "Not only do I leave my wife and child behind but all the animals, too."

Here's a transcript of a video the couple made on the last night they spent together in Denver in 2010:

Philippa and Inger Reality Check Video Transcript

(INGER SPEAKING). Hi everyone, this is Inger and Philippa here, and we said we'd make a video and so we are. It is the last full night we will spend together for God knows how long, and I for one am not coping. I don't want this. I need everybody out there to realize that this is wrong. You all need to vote, talk to your Congress people, your Senators. I'm not going to give you a sermon, but it is so hard to know, that... uh... the life we share together is on the whim of a government that doesn't even know we exist.

"Philippa had difficulty coming in through immigration and the U.S. border control. She was interviewed twice and got her documents taken off her, which means that, after waiting six and one-half months, the likelihood of her coming in the next year seems pretty slim, unless there are some changes made.

"We've had a good three weeks. It's been really wistful, but we've had some great times, a lot of smiles. But now we are down to the wire. She's going to leave tomorrow evening, and my heart's breaking. I don't want to keep doing this... but I will. I'll wait as long as I have to to be with my family. But... for those of you who are with the ones you love... treasure every minute you have. And for those of you in our same situation, contact me. We have to figure out a way to change things... this can't keep happening. If you are in a binational couple, it's worth it.

"It's hard. God, I know it's hard. Living on phone calls and living on webcam and living on letters and packages, planning the occasional trip. It's difficult, but it beats a half-life of living alone or settling for something other than true love. That's my sermon.

"Hi Jo! I was promised... I promised that, uh, I'd say that." (To Philippa): "Anything you wanna say? Talk to the nice people."

(Philippa shakes her head no and continues crying).

(INGER CONTINUED): "We love all of you and we are so grateful for your support, and uh, we'd be in much worse shape if we didn't have...

(TURNING TO PHILIPPA): "I love you so much" (facing forward), "and I don't ever want to be without her" (crying). "We need to change the world, and we can't do it alone, I can't do it alone, but I'm going to do everything I can. And if any of you know how to contact the people at Logo and get them interested, so we can get the word out, contact me on Facebook, on e-mail. I'll give you my phone number, I don't care. SOMEBODY has to make a big deal out of this... people have to know!

"I spent two days at Pride talking to hundreds and hundreds and hundreds of people and... I would say 75 percent of them had no idea, and there were a few binational couples who I met who were either they couldn't make it, they couldn't last because it's so hard... or... they've gone the other way and are just flying under the wire, and I don't want to do either of those things. I want to do it right. I want to have this woman by my side, show the world that I love her (dog whining in background).

"And our pug (turning away, laughs) wants you to know that he loves his mommy, and he wants her to stay with us (Oscar the pug barks in agreement), and it's just not right (Oscar continues to whine, and Philippa and Inger turn away and back again, and laugh).

(Inger sniffling): "We haven't been moping the whole time, but this is to be expected, and so we are doing this tonight because I will be moderately hysterical tomorrow (fake smile) and, uh,... (dog barking) not be able to explain what I'm feeling. It's this tight wad of anger and sadness that I'm feeling... (breathes big sigh). I don't know what to do...so... anyone out there who can figure it out and help me out... help us out... I'd truly appreciate it.

(TURNING TO PHILIPPA): "I get it all?" (Philippa nods. Inger turns back to the cam). "We love all of you... and we're glad to have you in our lives (crying). I don't know what to tell you but thank you for everything (shakes head). We're gonna ask for more, so you might as well help us, so we'll shut up (voice breaking). Take care, all of you. 'Night" (cries and can't continue).

To see the video, go to *http://www.youtube.com/watch?v=SjsS4Xpzab0*

CHAPTER THIRTEEN

CHAD AND TIM:
I'M IN ONE COUNTRY, HE'S IN
ANOTHER—FOR A YEAR

Many gay and lesbian binational couples have to live in separate countries most of the time—visiting only when time, money, and career obligations allow. That's the story, though just for a year, of separation for Chad Tilley (not his real name), the American half of a gay binational couple and his partner, Tim Owen, from New Brunswick, Canada.

Unfortunately, this is also the story of many separated couples we will never hear about—terrified of consequences and afraid to ask for help because they see no way to right this wrong. To them, I say if you are reading this: Go to the Resource Groups and Websites, Chapter 35, and find the groups that are there to help you. Don't be afraid. Don't give up hope.

Talk to your federal elected officials: your two senators and your member of Congress. Talk to them about your story. Share it. Show them pictures of you and your partner and your family. Urge them to co-sponsor the legislation we need to fix this. On their websites, Out4Immigration (www.out4immigration.org/) and Immigration Equality (www.immigrationequality.org/) have guides to help you prepare to meet your elected officials and share your story.

Find out online from the Library of Congress THOMAS site (www.thomas.loc.gov/) if your senators have co-sponsored Uniting American Families Act (UAFA) or Reuniting Families Act (RFA) or the Comprehensive Immigration Reform (CIR) Act of 2010. Thank them for their support. Do the same for your member of Congress.

If your federal representatives have not co-sponsored these bills, urge them to do so NOW! We are all counting on their help, so that our families can stay together. Help me and Karin. Help Chad and Tim. Help the people in the other stories. Help people you will never meet but who will be thrilled by your support.

Chad Tilley, left, and Tim Owen, right. Photo by Tim Owen, from Chad and Tim's
private collection. Reproduced with his permission.

Chad Tilley (a pseudonym he is comfortable with, "just in case") and Tim Owen
met in December 1999 and fell in love almost right away, they shared.

"We met at Flex, a small Bear/Leather/Levi bar in Raleigh, North Carolina," said
Tim.

"I lived in Chapel Hill, North Carolina, " said Chad, "and Tim was in Raleigh, a
neighboring town, working for a company that placed IT professionals in contract
positions both locally and in Washington, D.C."

Tim said: "Our first year found us sometimes in a local relationship and sometimes
in a long-distance relationship. I was placed in Washington, D.C. for some assignments and then locally for some other assignments." They managed to see a lot of D.C.
while Tim was working there and made friends in both places.

But work changed for Tim, and he was placed in Raleigh in late 2000. "He moved
into my apartment," said Chad, "and it was less than 300 square feet, so we began the
search for a new home." The couple found a townhouse a few miles away in Durham.
"We celebrated our first anniversary packing for our move," Tim laughed.

"We always managed to keep Tim, who is Canadian, in the United States legally,"

Chad said, "until 2010." At that time, Tim was on a three-year visa teaching math and science at a local Quaker school. The three-year visa was renewable for an additional three years.

"We had planned to have the process started for a green card before the six years were up," said Chad, "but Tim's lawyer failed to inform him that the process had to be started before the end of the fifth year."

That meant Tim had to leave the United States for one full year in order to reset his visa eligibility. He left in August 2010. Planning on being separated for a year was hard, they shared, but Tim's job search was harder. He finally found a job in Cairo, Egypt. "He had searched for jobs in Canada and Mexico to no avail," said Chad.

"I was actually offered a job in an extremely remote and isolated village in northern Manitoba," Tim said, "but to be honest, it would be harder for Chad to visit me there than in Cairo."

Before this period of separation, Chad and Tim had continued to be together in America because of Tim's work visas most of the time. When he was without work, "he was here on a tourist visa," said Chad, "and we lived off my income and credit cards while he was unemployed."

They follow the law and play by the rules, even when it means they must be separated. "That's why Tim's in Cairo now," said Chad. "We've always played by the rules." These men know the penalties for not playing by the rules. "We know people who married opposite sex partners to get to stay in America," said Chad. "But we know the penalties are stiff," said Tim. "And we never wanted to risk permanent damage to our efforts to be together."

Like other couples who you will meet later, Chad and Tim were dealing with their situation when the law of hope was called the Permanent Partners Immigration Act. "For more than 10 years now, I've prayed for that law, now the Uniting American Families Act," said Chad.

Though hopeful as we might all be for change to happen with legislation, it's still not here. "It's hell being apart," fumed Chad. "We stay in touch, usually two or more times a day," he said. "We e-mail. We Skype. We call on calling cards."

"It's not the same, though," said Tim, sadly. "It's such a challenge. So much of the time we have together is spent discussing personal business issues or the nature of the problems of the communication methods themselves."

At the time I interviewed Chad and Tim they were only into the separation seven weeks. "I would have thought all the wrinkles would be ironed out by now," shared Tim, "but they aren't."

Chad agreed, saying "sometimes Skype is miraculous. The other night, we were able to watch a DVD together, using Skype. It was a hopeful evening," he shared. "But then our good feeling was shattered by the trials of using Skype the next day," lamented Tim. "Sometimes it's just not usable," he complained.

Just like LGBT binational families depend on politics to get the solution they need, sometimes politics in a couple's life is part of the mix. Chad and Tim had such a situation.

Tim explained, "I found out that I was going to need to leave for a year right before Thanksgiving 2009," he said. "I wanted to make sure we had an awesome holiday season, so I didn't tell Chad until January 2," he shared.

"It still makes me very emotional to think about that morning, said Chad. "I was in a good mood when I woke up, and I was happy to be next to Tim. When he woke up, he said he had some bad news."

"What is it?" I asked. "He said, 'What's the worst thing that could happen?' It wasn't the worst. The worst would have been that he was dying. But it wasn't good news. We had until his visa was up in August before he had to leave," said Chad.

Those seven and a half months were like being on death row, they shared—knowing the date is coming and not being able to do anything about it.

"It would have been very easy to withdraw and wallow in the depression the whole time," shared Tim, "but we fought against that."

"We became more cognizant of our every moment," revealed Chad. "I have to say that I've always tried to be fully aware of our time. I've been really stingy with it. Life is too short to waste it away, and when you're in a binational relationship, you really never know when something is going to separate your family," he continued.

So Chad continues to live in Durham, doing technical writing, while Tim is in Cairo for a year. The couple would be fine continuing to live in Durham, they say, but they would like to think about Santa Fe, New Mexico, maybe, "or anywhere we can be together," said Chad.

He came out at age 36, Chad revealed, "after running from who I am for about 18 years." He acknowledged that coming out is an ongoing process. "It's always a continuing process," he shared. "When I was 36, I said 'Enough!' and blew the door off my closet."

"My story is different," said Tim. "I've always known I was gay. But I didn't come out to my family until I was with Chad." He said it was almost like his siblings knew it, but just needed him to tell them.

Chad, 49, and Tim, 44, have been dealing with their immigration issue for more than a decade. They have strong feelings about how they have to live and how all gay and lesbian binational couples have to live. Why?

"Because the United States lags behind the civilized world in its recognition of gay families," stressed Chad, "and I'm in a binational relationship with a Canadian citizen."

"Our story is important," said Tim. "Everyone's story is important. Until there is justice, those of us who are cheated by society have to stand up and tell our stories. Ours is just another story of injustice," he said.

"Uniting American Families Act has to pass," said Chad. "It's a matter of fairness," he stressed. "I've paid my taxes ever since I started to work back in the 1970s. My partner has paid taxes the entire time he's been in the United States."

He skewered the system with this question: "Are my taxes worth less than people who marry someone of the opposite sex?" His answer? "Hell no! I should be allowed to sponsor my partner for immigration," he shouted.

"I SHOULD be allowed to marry," Chad continued. "In fact, Tim and I had never considered marriage. We felt we didn't need to mimic heterosexual habits, but as we've grown to realize the gross injustice we've experienced, we've changed our minds."

"Hell yeah, we're getting married... as soon as the federal government recognizes same-sex marriage, we're there," Chad continued. "We're registering at charities and department stores," agreed Tim. "SOCIETY OWES IT TO US. I've attended countless straight weddings and bought untold dollars worth of wedding gifts, and yet, I can't get married," he said.

These men are not really hiding, but using his real name might hurt them in their process, Chad felt. And though he shares the work he does, he does not want his employer identified.

"I have concerns that somehow it would work against us, and we've worked hard to be above board the entire time we've been together," Chad said. "We're not going to screw it up now."

Chad profiles them as a binational couple, working hard to do everything within the law. Part of it is their separation for a year, which he said "satisfies antiquated U.S. immigration laws."

Tim believes they will overcome their obstacles, though they haven't yet. "If we have to, we'll move to Canada and leave the United States to decay amidst the neocon fundamentalists," he said. "But what a shame that would be... for all the sane people to leave the country," smiled Chad. "Who will save it then?"

Grousing aside, Chad and Tim are very clear on what needs to happen to solve their problem and the problem faced by thousands of others. They list solutions as:

- Gay Marriage: Ideal solution
- Uniting American Families Act (UAFA): Second-best solution
- A Private Bill: Least likely solution
- Another Visa: Currently what we're working toward

They want to live in the United States and haven't given up on that yet. That desire keeps them focused on what they can do to help solve their problem. Chad has written many letters to the editor of the newspaper. They haven't been published, "but I will continue to try until they get tired of me and publish my letter," he said.

He has also spoken to legislators for his area, with mixed results, he said. "Congressman David Price (D-NC-4) has signed on to support Uniting American Families Act but will not be able to introduce a private bill on our behalf," Chad shared. "His office did discuss our situation and confirmed our actions are probably the best path," he added.

Senator Kay Hagan (D-NC) was somewhat sympathetic, according to Chad, "but flatly refused to even entertain the idea of a private bill. Her staff is sympathetic to our plight; however, it's unclear whether she will support the Uniting American Families Act," he added.

Chad has not had a good experience with Senator Richard Burr (R-NC), adding that he's willing to change his opinion of him if he gets some help from him.

Chad and Tim have turned to Immigration Equality for help. Equality North Carolina (ENC) has written stories on Chad and Tim and distributed flyers about their situation at North Carolina Pride in 2010. ENC has also written stories on the couple to help educate others about their challenge and advocate for their solution.

Chad has contacted Human Rights Campaign (HRC) and has created a Facebook page, "hoping to get more folks aware of the issues we face," he added. That's where I found their story and was able to contact them.

"I've also contacted my city council person and asked that she introduce a resolution of support for the Uniting American Families Act," said Chad, "but I still have heard nothing from her." He made the contact because he knows other cities have passed such resolutions. "I would like my city to be a progressive voice," he said.

Chad says his family is his partner Tim. "I have two brothers in the immediate metro area," Chad added. "One is heterosexual, married with two kids. The other is gay, partnered and living in a home they built on my parents' farm. My parents also live in the metro area," he added. He also has aunts, uncles, and cousins, mostly in the greater Durham-Raleigh area.

Tim shared that he has two brothers and one sister, two sisters-in-law, and numerous nieces and nephews. "Most live in Saint John, New Brunswick, near my dad," he said. The rest live farther north in New Brunswick. "I also have extended family in New Brunswick and in the United States in Maine," he added.

Both families "for the most part, try to support both of us in this hellish time," said Chad, adding they call, Skype, and send e-mails and cards." Chad says his family tells him they have contacted their legislators, but Tim's family can't expect American legislators to help them since they are Canadian.

Since both men are still working, their employment situation is critical to the whole picture. Chad's career has not been negatively impacted because of their status, but he prefers not to identify where he works and exactly what he does. "My employer has been supportive of my special needs for visiting," Chad shared. "My employers have sponsored visas," said Tim. But neither man's employer(s) have been able to solve their immigration situation.

"Tim's former U.S. employer said they would be willing to hire him back if they have an opening next year," Chad said, "but they refused to hold his position open or give him a leave of absence."

So in August 2011, Tim and Chad should be back together. If UAFA or another bill becomes law, they can start the process along with the rest of us to be together with our families in America.

[A sad update about Chad and Tim – Chad shared on Facebook that he was laid off from his job in November, 2010, adding to their stress and financial concerns. Karin and I hope he finds employment quickly.]

CHAPTER FOURTEEN

KATHY AND VIKI: HER WORK VISA KEEPS US TOGETHER IN AMERICA

Kathy Drasky and Viki Forrest met in San Francisco and have been together since 2001. Viki was working for an Australian tech startup during the dotcom era, but after September 11 and the dotcom crash, Viki's company went out of business and she lost her E2 visa.

At that point, Kathy and Viki knew they had a potential crisis. They found out the dangers of being a lesbian binational couple in terms of what it posed for Viki being able to stay with Kathy in the United States. Kathy said "that's when our odyssey through the U.S. immigration system began."

"But Viki was lucky," Kathy shared. "She is a highly skilled technology executive from a country—Australia—that has very good relations with the United States. There is even a special visa, the E3 visa, for Australians, as well as people from Chile and Singapore."

"I was able to get another job in the tech sector that would sponsor me for an H1B visa," said Viki. We thought our problems were solved when I went back to Australia to wait out the visa process."

"But she was denied!" said Kathy.

At that point, Kathy had never been to Australia. She had worked hard to build her own business, a reputable editorial services agency with clients on both the East and West coasts of the United States.

"I had never thought about living outside of America," said Kathy. "The idea of it hit me like a ton of bricks. I had moved from New York to California in my 20s, but now I was 40. Picking up and leaving everything you've worked for behind at pretty much a moment's notice isn't a simple decision."

"And," she shared, "Viki is a fighter! She did not take being denied a visa and the opportunity to work and further her career in the U.S. as a 'no'."

"Again, we were lucky," Kathy said. "Viki's prospective new employer connected her to one of the leading U.S. immigration attorneys, a man whose cases had set precedence for work experience qualifying as a bachelor's degree."

Kathy Drasky, left, and Viki Forrest, right.
Photo from their private collection. Used by permission.

"I don't have a college degree," said Viki. "I broke into the high-tech world as a computer programmer in the 1970s. "In short, we resolved this case by refiling the visa application with the new attorney," Viki said. One immigration attorney's strategy can be different from the next. You get recommendations for attorneys, and they may be very well respected; yet each visa application, no matter how expertly prepared, is at the discretion of the federal government. Nothing is ever certain," she added.

After being separated for three months, with Viki in Australia and Kathy in California, they traveled to Vancouver, Canada, where they waited out the six-week immigration refiling process together. This time the visa came through.

As CEO of ANZA Technology Network, which connects Australian and New Zealand companies to Silicon Valley, Viki ultimately met the criteria for a green card. She filed in 2008 and has qualified for each segment of the process to date.

"We are now waiting for the United States to clear up the backlog of people waiting for their green cards," said Viki. "We have been told this could take another three to seven years."

"I need to hold onto my job throughout this period in order to collect my green card," Viki stressed. She added, "I am very fortunate that I am a highly skilled worker and that Kathy and I were a bit older when this happened to us." Kathy echoed the thought, and said, "We were able to draw on some assets to keep us going and finance the periods of diminished income and costs that an employer doesn't traditionally cover."

Even though they consider themselves extremely fortunate compared to so many other gay and lesbian binational couples, life has still been stressful. They have been dealing with the tenuous combination of immigration linked to employment for almost 10 years. "We often wonder what our life and options would be like if we didn't have Viki's employment restrictions," said Kathy.

Kathy has been an out lesbian since her college days in the early 1980s. She has been involved with LGBT civil rights and helped launch Out4Immigration (*www.out4immigration.org/*), an all-volunteer grassroots group dedicated to ending the immigration discrimination she faces as an American citizen: the inability to sponsor her life partner for a green card.

Karin and I met Kathy with a group of volunteers from Out4Immigration at a meeting on September 17, 2009, with Senator Dianne Feinstein's staffers. We went to educate them about the issues facing gay and lesbian binational families and to tell them about Uniting American Families Act (UAFA) and Reuniting Families Act (RFA), which we hoped the senator would co-sponsor.

Kathy's work with Out4Immigration has taught her a lot about the challenges we face.

"American citizens are being denied basic civil rights," she explained. "Everyone needs to know that America's immigration system is more than broken—it blatantly discriminates against LGBT people with foreign partners and denies us the right to live in this country with the person we love. If the person you love can navigate the U.S. immigration system and its limited options, maybe they can get a green card through their work, but it's not something everyone can do."

Viki and Kathy know that Uniting Families Act or Reuniting Families Act or Comprehensive Immigration Reform of 2010 or another comprehensive immigration reform bill that includes LGBT binational families needs to pass.

"We need this so that no American will have to go through what so many of us have experienced: having to choose between the person you love and your country," Kathy stated. "My story is a classic case of an American being denied an equal right." In this case it directly denies me my right as a citizen to 'life, liberty and the pursuit of happiness.'"

Kathy, 49, knew a day when being gay in America was not as open or easy as people may find it today. Viki, 57, has had a similar life experience. She says that the Australian gay rights movement was about 10 years behind Stonewall but has since caught up and, in some cases, surpassed America. For instance, Australia recognizes same-sex relationships for immigration purposes. It does not have gay marriage, but it has many laws providing lesbians and gays with equal rights.

"I grew up and came out never expecting to be able to 'marry' my partner, or live an open and productive life as part of mainstream society," Kathy shared. "Wow! What changes have happened! For the longest time it was enough to be able to live this way. Marriage equality, state by state, was great and domestic partnerships gave you all the same protections, didn't they?" she said.

Kathy thought things were okay as far as being a lesbian in San Francisco was concerned until she became part of a same-sex binational couple and realized that none of the state and local laws provided the federal protections she would need to sponsor Viki under U.S. immigration laws.

"I never gave much thought to being a lesbian and American—but this has changed me," she remarked. "I have been forced to consider choosing between my partner and my country. I never knew how strongly I felt about America until that question was raised," she said.

"It brings tears to my eyes just to think about having to leave America. But it's a no-brainer: I would go anywhere not to be separated from Viki," Kathy said.

"I know we can live together in Australia," said Viki. "But do I really want that to be a deciding factor here? I came to the U.S. to work. While I was here I fell in love with an American. I'm still here working in this country, and I will continue to find a way to further and end my career here. But it is wrong that my partner is shut out from her government's system to have her relationship federally recognized and protected. All that great stuff the rest of the world hears about America: home of the free, land of equality for all? They've got some explaining to do," she said.

Kathy and Viki's problem is not solved yet. "Even if you are in the queue to get a green card, you are not there yet. Three to seven years is a long time to have to hold on to a job under any circumstances and economy. Bottom line: If I lost my job tomorrow, I'd have to start over," said Viki.

"We're hoping comprehensive immigration reform will speed up this backlog wait on the green card," said Kathy.

These women have not given up on being in the United States together. Kathy has spoken publicly on this issue for Out4Immigration many times. Her experience in working with the media and communications has led her to work with other volunteers in preparing their testimony to speak at the local and state level on UAFA and comprehensive immigration reform.

"I worked with our volunteers to get their statements in order to be presented to the

City of San Francisco to get the first resolution in support of Uniting American Families Act passed," Kathy said. "Later I helped volunteers get their statements in order to urge the state of California to support UAFA. It is the first state to issue a resolution in support of Uniting American Families Act. Both my city and state issued resolutions in support of UAFA. They put our Congressional elected officials on notice that their state supports equal immigration rights for LGBT Americans with foreign partners."

Kathy has written letters to the editor as well.

"In lending my communications expertise to Out4Immigration, I have overseen dozens of op-ed pieces, letters, and blog posts to newspapers and online sources about immigration inequality," she remarked. "I have worked with reporters, publishers, producers, and some of the leading LGBT bloggers in getting our story out there in print, online, video, radio, podcast, and TV."

She smiled and added: "The outcome of these efforts has been very good. Since Out4Immigration began in 2006, we have raised awareness about this issue one hundred-fold."

No one knew about the problem in 2006, according to Kathy. "It wasn't until you were in a same-sex binational relationship yourself that you realized this was a problem," she said.

"We started right here in San Francisco, writing op-eds to the *Chronicle* and the *Bay Area Reporter*," she said. "The *BAR* has been on top of gay and lesbian binational couples' stories and UAFA and LGBT immigrant issues in general since we 'raised awareness' with them about this issue in 2006," she stressed.

Kathy has contacted her federal legislators about the solutions needed. In her case, that is Senator Barbara Boxer (D-CA), Senator Dianne Feinstein (D-CA), and Representative Nancy Pelosi (D-CA-8). "The initial reception from the staff in these offices is very good and empathetic," she said, "but there is no follow-through." She said Out4Immigration volunteers get asked to provide more information, and do, but they don't see any results.

"Nancy Pelosi's people claimed that as Speaker of the House she couldn't co-sponsor legislation, for example," she said. "Dianne Feinstein simply wouldn't budge here. It's very frustrating."

Kathy's work with Out4Immigration includes spearheading the weekly letter-writing campaign with other O4I volunteers.

"We have been sending weekly letters to Congress seeking UAFA co-sponsors since the bill was re-launched in 2009," she stated. "Over the past two summers we organized a 'visit your representative' toolkit and several of our members made visits to their representatives' local offices."

In her work on this issue and with O4I, Kathy knows the people behind each of the three organizations working solely or primarily on gay and lesbian binational families' immigration issues.

Out4Immigration was started by a group of people in gay and lesbian binational relationships. "We had little or no political or even activist experience," Kathy said. "We were just frustrated that the law was not changing, and we were tired of watching our friends be forced into exile or have to make unbelievably unfair choices."

Today the group remains a loose coalition of volunteers around the world who step up and take action—getting resolutions passed in support of UAFA in their city, visiting their representatives, paying their own way to go to Washington, D.C. to meet with Congressional staffers and reps, writing blogs and op-ed pieces, speaking in public, and working with other LGBT and immigrants' rights groups.

Kathy and Viki are happily living in San Francisco and would like to stay there. They hope to continue to be able to live together in America.

Kathy's parents are in their 70s and live in Connecticut, a five-hour flight away. Viki's family is in Australia, a flight three times as long. "It would be easy for me to get to my folks if something happened," said Kathy. "But doing it from Sydney would be far more difficult."

Viki has had a harder commute to be with family. In 2006, her mother became very ill. "I made a number of trips back and forth," she said, "and when she died, we were both on the next plane to be at her funeral."

"It was embedded in our brains by that time how lucky we were to be able to travel freely because Viki has a visa," said Kathy. "It's something most people would take for granted, particularly a straight binational couple."

I asked Kathy how her family deals with her immigration problem. "Let's say we continue to 'raise awareness' with them," she said. "In the beginning they had no clue what we were dealing with. Like most Americans, they simply thought us being in a committed relationship meant we had the same rights. Through my work with O4I, through our struggles with Viki's visa and green card process, they have come to understand that immigration in the U.S. is a far more complex problem than what is sensationalized on the nightly news."

"My parents get angry when we talk about how Viki has been in the country legally, on a work visa for so many years, and has been paying taxes and contributing to the economy and she still doesn't have a green card," Kathy said. "My dad says the last real Democrat in his book was Harry Truman. My mom won't tell us who she votes for because it could ruin Thanksgiving dinner. They believe in an America where if you work hard and obey the law, then you get an equal chance. All of their grandparents came to America through Ellis Island. This has been an eye-opener, crash course on civil liberties for them."

Kathy remains most concerned with the fact her country's government does not recognize her relationship at the federal level.

"Despite being domestic partners and being married in San Francisco at City Hall in 2004, the federal government considers us 'legal strangers,'" she said. "It bans us from recognizing 1,138 federal rights available to heterosexual married couples, one of which is immigration, or my right as an American citizen to sponsor Viki for her green card."

Viki and Kathy know they have been fortunate to have many options open to them as a lesbian binational couple, many more than most. "In spite of this, our quest to stay together in the United States permanently has had some very difficult patches!" Viki exclaimed.

Kathy agreed: "Things like changing jobs, buying a house, moving to a new place by choice, losing a parent, illnesses—these things all happen and are a part of life. You deal with them, and you don't often 'choose' them. Yet being forced to leave your country to stay with the person you love—that's just unconscionable."

CHAPTER FIFTEEN

SHIRLEY AND JAY:
SPECIAL LEGISLATION KEEPS
TWO MOMS AND THEIR SONS
TOGETHER—FOR NOW

A binational lesbian couple in California had a very severe and life-threatening situation that was solved, for the length of term of the 111th Congress, by a special bill from Senator Dianne Feinstein with the help of Congresswoman Jackie Speier. Jay Mercado and Shirley Tan have been together since 1986, when they met and fell in love. Shirley was visiting the United States with her father and met Jay in San Francisco. Today they have teenage twin boys, Jashley and Joriene, and are outstanding members of their church and community— called "the model couple" by their friends, mostly straight parents with children.

They faced a deportation threat in 2009 that would have torn Shirley away from her partner and sons. At their house, ICE agents handcuffed and removed Shirley early in the morning in a surprise attack. But the family got relief when their federal legislators heard of their case and took action.

Karin and I met Shirley, Jay, Jashley, and Joriene in Washington, D.C. June 3, 2009, at the same event where we met others you will read about soon: Gordon, Carmen, Steve, Martha, and Lin. Shirley testified at the U.S. Senate Committee on the Judiciary about her family's serious immigration situation.

As recorded on the U.S. Senate Committee on the Judiciary website, she began her testimony with her personal details:

"I am a 43-year-old mother and housewife from Pacifica, California. I am grateful for the opportunity to share my story with you, and grateful, too, for Chairman Leahy's leadership on an issue that is so critically important to my family and the tens of thousands of others across the country."

"I did not know it, but my appeal had also been denied. All the while, Jay and I went about building our life together. I gave birth to Jashley and Joriene, the biggest joy in our lives, and became a full-time mom."

From the top, clockwise: Jay Mercado, Jashley Mercado, Joriene Mercado, Shirley Tan.
Photo by and courtesy of Jerry Wang, http://jumpclickclick.com

"Our family has always been like every American family, and I am so proud of Jay and the twins. The boys attended Catholic school through 6th grade and are now in Cabrillo Elementary School. They excelled in their classes and have always been in the top of their class. I volunteer in every activity at their school, and when the school needs a parent to pitch in, I have always been the first one they call. Jay was a member of the school board at their Catholic school. I am a Eucharistic minister at Good Shepherd Church, where Jay and I both sing in the Sunday mass choir."

"Our family is fortunate. We have never felt discriminated against in our community. Our friends, mostly heterosexual couples, call us the "model family," and even said we are their role models. We try to mirror the best family values, and we attribute the fact that our children are so well adjusted to the love, security, and consistency that we, as parents, have been able to provide. Jashley and Joriene's classmates at school know they have two moms, and it has never been an issue."

She explained the terrible event that changed their lives.

"Our lives, I can say without any doubt, were almost perfect until the morning of January 28, 2009. That morning, at 6:30 a.m., Immigration and Customs Enforcement agents showed up at my door. They were looking for a 'Mexican girl,' and, having nothing to fear, Jay did not think twice about allowing them into our home when they asked permission to search it. It turned out they were really looking for me."

"The agents showed me a piece of paper, which was a 2002 deportation letter, which I informed them I had never seen. Before I knew it, I was handcuffed and taken away, like a criminal, as Jay's frail mother watched in hysterics. I was put into a van with two men in yellow jumpsuits and chains and searched like a criminal, in a way I have only seen on television and in the movies."

She testified to her concerns while being lead away:

"All the while my family was first and foremost the center of everything on my mind. How would Jay work and take care of the kids if I was not there? Who would continue to take care of Jay's ailing mother, the mother I had come to love, if I was not there? Who would be there for my family if I was not there? In an instant, my family, my American family, was being ripped away from me. And when I did return home, I had an ankle monitoring bracelet. I went to great lengths to hide it from my children."

Her dismay echoed that of so many. "I have a partner who is a U.S. citizen, and two beautiful children who are also U.S. citizens, but not one of them can petition for me to remain in the United States with them. Because my partner is not a man, she cannot do anything to help me. Nor can my children, who keep asking why this happened to us and what will ultimately happen to our family."

She pleaded: "Passage of the Uniting American Families Act, UAFA, will not only benefit me but the thousands of people who are also in the same situation as I am. And so I respectfully submit to the committee today that changing the immigration laws of this country to include permanent partners will serve in the long run to keep families like ours together. Americans will be able to live at home with their partners rather than living in fear or in exile."

She stressed: "After 23 years building our life together, Jay and I know that our family is still at great risk of separation. We have a home together. Jay has a great job. We have a mortgage, a pension, friends, and a community. We have everything together, and it would be impossible to reestablish elsewhere. We have followed the law, respected the judicial system and simply want to keep our family together.

"For my children, and couples and families like ours, it is critically important that we end discrimination in U.S. immigration law. So I ask that you please look closely at UAFA and how important its passage is for the thousands of couples who are affected by the unjust discrimination we are facing in the immigration process."

She also gave thanks.

"Before I close, I would like to take this opportunity to extend my gratitude to Congresswoman Jackie Speier and her staff, who have shown so much compassion especially for my children. Congresswoman Speier has been supportive throughout this ordeal and went out of her way to help me and my family. And I would like to extend a very special thank you to Senator Dianne Feinstein, a member of this committee, for everything she also did for Jay, myself, and our children. Because of Senator Feinstein's efforts and the efforts of her staff, my deportation has been temporarily delayed until 2011. It is because of her great compassion that I am able to be with you today.

"Chairman Leahy, and members of the committee, it is a great privilege to be here with you today. I was honored to receive your invitation to appear before you today not only because of my own family but on behalf of the thousands of permanent partners who deserve equal treatment and to be able to remain with their loved ones and their children."

She concluded: "I humbly ask for your support of the Uniting American Families Act which would allow me to remain with my family and to strive for citizenship in this wonderful country that has been so good to me and my partner and such a blessed home to our children."

I had an opportunity to see this family again in July 2010, when we testified at a committee meeting in Redwood City, California, to educate members of the San Mateo County Board of Supervisors about the need to support UAFA and urge them to adopt such a resolution. That day they shared details of their life—married, twin boys, hardworking community members of Pacifica, a San Mateo County community, a strong and loving home that also includes Renee, Jay's mother.

Achieving notoriety because of the ICE raid, Shirley and Jay have gotten lots of press attention. Because of the boys, their struggle is more horrifying than the concept of two adults being separated or having to move away from America.

"They are exactly the kind of people you want living in this country," Immigration Equality's executive director Rachel Tiven told *People* magazine in their April 20, 2010, profile of Shirley and Jay and their family's plight.

But lesbian and gay couples—regardless of how long they have been together or how many children they may have—are forced to make an unacceptable choice between family and country. Why? Because the U.S. government does not see LGBT people or same-sex binational couples as equal citizens. The proof is in the current laws for marriage and immigration, among others.

The Uniting American Families Act would at last treat all couples equally under immigration law, eliminating the heart-wrenching scenes like the one in Pacifica, California. But, despite calls from media like the *Washington Post* and the *San Francisco Chronicle* and a long (and growing) list of civil liberties and immigration organizations, the bill has yet to really move forward. And all the while, mothers and fathers face being torn away from their children, and families are brutally discriminated against by their own government.

Shirley and Jay's family is being put through agony at the expense of American taxpayers. I'd rather see the money spent in other ways myself. By amending immigration law to include the phrase "or permanent partner" everywhere the word spouse appears, Jay and Shirley would not have the fear of deportation and relocation and all the rest of us could live in America with our permanent partners, where we want to live!

If Shirley is deported* the couple will have to decide between separating two sons from one of their mothers, or moving the family to a country they have never known. Neither is a good choice as far as Karin and I are concerned.

Shirley was given a reprieve in late April 2009, via the private bill from Senator Dianne Feinstein that allowed her to stay in America until the end of the 111th session of Congress. It was scheduled to be reintroduced by Senator Feinstein at the opening of the 112th Congress or until the Uniting American Families Act passes. That is something that rarely happens. And sadly, most couples and families cannot depend on legislation like that.

"Without the bill," Senator Feinstein said, "this family will be separated, or they will be relocated to a third country where Ms. Tan's safety and her children's well-being may be at risk."

Shirley and Jay have contacted and/or worked with the three major groups working on LGBT binational families' immigration challenges: Immigration Equality, Out4Immigration and Love Exiles. They have also worked with Melanie Nathan, who has a private court firm that deals with immigration issues.

Twins Jashley and Joriene help with the cause, too, and have become very polished speakers and advocates. They have testified, attended meetings, and appeared at media events. They have also done some lobbying at both the House of Representatives and Senate.

The Tan/Mercado family has also been invited to speak by National Queer Asian Pacific Islander Alliance (NQAPIA), Asian Pacific Islander Legal Outreach (APILO), and Marriage Equality at their functions. They have been on panel discussions at conferences and on television shows as well as in *People* magazine.

While all this is going on, Jay continues her career with Biddle-Shaw Insurance, where her boss is very supportive of the family's situation. Shirley, a former real estate agent for three years, when she was given a work permit by immigration until they stopped renewing it, has always been a full-time homemaker.

---

*   See Pertinent Definitions and Information, Chapter 37.

This story includes elements many others don't. Since Shirley was nearly deported, they got a strong taste of the downside of what gay and lesbian binational couples contend with. And they saw, for real, what happens to people if they are out of compliance.

Since they have sons, they got a frightening look at what families with gay and lesbian parents face. Since they have a multigenerational household, they also faced the problem with potentially relocating Jay's aging mother, who lives with them. None of that should happen to an American family!

You can view Shirley's testimony at the Senate hearing at
http://www.youtube.com/watch?v=9cTojNqjnP4

CHAPTER SIXTEEN

THOMAS AND TONY: WE ARE CONTEMPORARY NOMADS

Karin and I have spent time together out of America, but nothing com-
pared to what other couples have done—at least not yet. Two men who
have been together since 1993 have been on the road a lot of their time
after they tried to live in Germany, Thomas Arnold's home country.
That was after they had to leave America, Tony Eitnier's home country.
They spent six years together in the United States and four years together
in Germany. The rest of the time they have been moving around, in a
total of 12 countries at the time I interviewed them.

Tony and Thomas moved to Germany because Tony could not sponsor Thomas for immigration to America (a very familiar story by now, I'm sure you'll agree). Thomas tried the green card lottery 15 times with no success. The couple's story has been turned into a documentary called *Excluded*, which tells their compelling story of years on the road in exile in multiple countries so that they can be together. The film was produced and directed by sociology professor Dr. Lisa M. Nunn, University of San Diego, San Diego, California.

Thomas, 41, came out to his family in 1996. Tony, 40, came out to his family the following year. They met in April 1993, and have been together since. Since they were traveling so much, and we had no guaranteed internet connections, much of my interview was gleaned from information on their DVD and the rest from answers to other questions on my interview questionnaire by e-mail when they had access to it.

It was an interesting experience, sending them e-mails and not knowing which country they might be in when they answered. In one two-week period, I got messages from them from two different countries. And then we had problems with text getting garbled traveling to different places with different software. I was at my dining room table with my laptop, and they were in internet cafes in exotic locations.

The story of two men who are life partners but whose status is ignored and denied by the United States government is the basis of *Excluded*. Thomas and Tony, their fam-

Thomas Arnold, left, and Tony Eitnier, right, in India on their continuous travel.
Photo from their private collection. Used by permission.

ily, and everyone they know consider the men life partners. But Uncle Sam doesn't see it that way, so they were forced to go overseas.

That meant Tony had to leave his family in San Diego when they tried to live in Germany, and Thomas had to leave his family in southern Germany when that didn't work out for them.

From Germany to Cambodia, they've yet to find a place to call home. But they won't give up their relationship, that's for sure.

"Tony's my life," said Thomas.

"We are married as much as anyone else is married," said Tony.

"You don't know what it's like sitting around, waiting for people to give you equality," continued Tony. "It's maddening, it's maddening!"

"People say gay and lesbian couples shouldn't be allowed to marry," said Thomas. "You know, we're so committed. There's so many gay and lesbian couples who are so committed to each other. A lot of straight couples aren't that committed."

This couple wonders if they had known in 1993 how things would turn out "would we have stayed in the relationship," said Thomas.

They traveled in Africa for a year and a half after they met, then they sat down in Namibia one day and asked themselves the hard questions.

"What are we going to do?" said Thomas.

"Are we going to stay together?" said Tony.

"Because it's going to be a long fight," they both agreed.

"We had no idea," said Tony. "I'm an American. I should be able to live in my own country with my partner."

But they wanted to stay together, and did. They spent the first four years of their relationship traveling extensively and living in each other's country.

In 1997, Thomas moved to the United States and enrolled in school the next year to qualify for a student visa. He studied chemistry and eventually graduated valedictorian at his community college. But then he had to leave America because he and Tony didn't have the money for him to pay out-of-state or international student fees at a four-year school to continue his studies. "For five years, Thomas paid out-of-state tuition, eleven times as expensive as a California resident," said Tony.

Trained as a banker, "Thomas had to give up his career to be together with me," shared Tony.

"Our life has been affected by financial constraints," shared Thomas. "I couldn't work in the United States. We lived on one salary. Tony worked really hard teaching English as a Second Language."

Tony also worked at home on their website, which brings in some income, "but it doesn't supply enough money for us to live a comfortable life," says Thomas.

He added, "When we tell people we are a binational couple, and the problems we have, everyone is surprised."

When they moved to America together, they knew Thomas's time there would be limited.

"We didn't know how long we were going to be able to stretch this out," shared Tony. "We were hoping for about four or five years."

The couple was hoping that during that time they would find some other way to keep Thomas in the United States legally.

They explored the option of Thomas marrying their good friend Laurelle, but the reality of the penalties for that sort of marriage made the decision not to go that route easy. Laurelle confided that a semi-serious conversation did indeed take place, but that the serious implications made them realize they should not take that option. For one thing, the marriage would have to be kept secret, and "it would be odd and obvious that all of a sudden Thomas was staying here, and we wouldn't be able to explain it," she said.

Contrasting with the couple's plight, Tony's mother Freda met her husband Ken while traveling. Though Ken, from Malaysia, was not a U.S. citizen, Freda was able to bring him to California on a fiancé visa and marry him—something that Tony can't do for Thomas. And when Tony and Thomas had to leave California, they left their best friends behind: Freda and Ken and Laurelle.

They have traveled in 55 countries together to date, with Thomas having traveled in 60 total and Tony 80 total. But that will change! They were in the Philippines when I first exchanged e-mail questions and answers. We had an exchange from Vietnam. The last time I checked in with them they were in Thailand. That was in a three-month period.

Tony and Thomas have received traveler's visas for a wide range of countries, including India, Sri Lanka, and Cambodia, but the one visa they want—the American one—is the one that's been denied many times.

Both Thomas and Tony are extremely frustrated. "We feel we have tried virtually every way we can to get Thomas into the country, stopping just short of marriage fraud," complained Tony. So far nothing has worked but they're still hoping.

Germany passed the Lifetime Partnership Act in 2001, so Tony and Thomas tried living in Berlin but were not happy being there. Thomas described how depressed Tony got, and Tony shared how Thomas could not crack the job market at the ripe old age of 37. "We thought all the problems we had in the United States would be solved when we moved to Germany," said Tony, "however we had a new set of problems."

These men know the consequences of being ripped from their countries—torn apart from family and friends in order to be together. "After spending my whole life in California," Tony said, "I moved with Thomas to Germany, where we could get recognition for our relationship."

But the move turned out to be more difficult than they anticipated. Tony found that his education in California didn't translate well in Germany, and he had no contacts or resources.

"We didn't have to deal with any kind of immigration issues there," shared Tony. "I'm legal in Germany. Neither of us had to worry about deportation."

But Tony and Thomas realized that they had raised their level of expectation about how Germany was going to change their lives, "I guess to a level that was unrealistic," commented Tony.

For the first time in their 10 years together (at that time), they would be equal in Germany. Both would be working and sharing chores and incomes. In the past, one or the other had been working and the other had been doing the chores. But new problems emerged in Berlin.

Thomas shared that Tony couldn't sleep for the first two weeks there, so he couldn't sleep because he was worried about Tony. Tony agreed that it was because he was depressed and anxious. "It was a massive amount of change at one time," he added.

"If you don't choose to do something," Tony said, with amazing insight, "if you're kind of forced into it, it gives you this kind of victim mentality that is damaging."

Another key point from Tony is this: "I just feel exhausted by life, by how many places we've lived and how many times we've moved and how many people we've known."

Another crucial point from Thomas is this: "We build a life somewhere, just to leave it again."

We also are aware of what this couple must be aware of: Living the life and documenting it at the same time brings double pressure for us. But it brings double value—or invaluable information—for others. Karin and I really appreciate the work Tony and Thomas are doing with their website (*www.contemporarynomad.com/*) and their blog (*www.contemporarynomad.com/blog*) to share the reality of their nomadic lives for everyone and to help stop the reality of what we all face in terms of non-acceptance in the United States.

In Germany, Tony felt like a refugee and felt treated like a child because of his language skills, though he was 35. At the same time, Thomas, a German citizen with a newly completed bachelor's degree from Germany, was considered unemployable at age 37 by local firms. So they left.

"Our solution to live in my country didn't work out well," Thomas said. "We decided we could no longer stay in Germany." Their truly nomadic lifestyle began in 2007, and though traveling the world has allowed them to stay together, it's not what they really want long term.

They couldn't go home to California because UAFA had not passed. So they decided to "go nomadic" and perpetually travel the world until they could return to San Diego and their family. Home became two backpacks each as they set off to "surf a wave of visas" in an ironic twist to their lives as they don't/can't stay in places—the opposite of what they had wanted to do in San Diego.

Most recently, they have been nomads in Cambodia, Hong Kong, Macau, China, Tibet, Nepal, India, Sri Lanka, Thailand, Myanmar, Laos, the Philippines, and Vietnam. At the time I was finishing this book they were in Thailand and planned to be in Indonesia next.

What Tony and Thomas want is really the same thing Karin and I want: to be in California and to live "a normal life" with family and friends—and to be able to visit family and friends elsewhere when and why and how long we want.

The first time Karin and I left America together, in 2009, we lived out of two suitcases each and Karin's car, staying in hotels and hostels, bed-and-breakfast places, a rented flat in France, and other lodgings in Spain, England, and Scotland for six months. We really wonder how Tony and Thomas can live like this for so long with "home" as two backpacks apiece—and we wish them well!

If you want to follow Tony and Thomas on their journey, visit them at *www.ContemporaryNomad.com*, or join them at *www.facebook.com/ContemporaryNomad* and keep track of their epic travel so they can be together.

To view *Excluded* online, go to *www.excludedthemovie.com*. To find out about free distribution of *Excluded*, see Media, Websites, and Sources, Chapter 36.

CHAPTER SEVENTEEN

GORDON AND RENATO: I GOT A WORK TRANSFER SO WE CAN LIVE IN NEITHER OF OUR COUNTRIES

Another gay couple who are living outside the United States in order to be together are Gordon Stewart and his partner Renato. Renato is from Brazil and was denied entry to the United States on a student visa, precipitating their relocation to the United Kingdom. Karin and I met Gordon in Washington, D.C. in June 2009 when he testified at a Senate committee hearing and attended Immigration Equality's press briefing on LGBT issues and legislation. We saw him again the following June at Immigration Equality's Safe Haven Awards, where his company, Pfizer, was honored for its work on our issue.

Gordon and Renato met in Rio de Janeiro on New Year's Day of 2000. They ran into their immigration problem in Sao Paulo, at the U.S. Consulate, where Renato, a lawyer in Brazil, had applied to have his U.S. student visa renewed to continue his studies in the United States. On that occasion, Renato's visa renewal was denied, and since Gordon and Renato could not be together in America, they relocated to London in 2005, where they live together now. "But I work most of the time in New York," said Gordon, "so we live together in one country, but I am working in another much of the time." And where they live together is neither one's home country.

Gordon, 50, works as a board member for Immigration Equality and speaks on this issue as often as he can. He works with Congress on UAFA, and meets with employer representatives and company contacts to educate them on the impact of current U.S. immigration law and how it impacts same-sex binational couples like his. Renato, 46, stays in London and prefers not to share his full name or other identifying factors.

Gordon shared his personal story with the U.S. Senate Committee on the Judiciary at their hearing on UAFA on June 3, 2009. The following is his testimony:

"I am an American living abroad, simply due to the fact that our country's immi-

Gordon Stewart at Immigration Equality Lobby Day, September 30, 2010.
Photo by Judy G. Rolfe. Used by permission of Immigration Equality.

gration laws have forced me to leave the United States in order to be with my partner, Renato, the person I love."

He continued his testimony with these details:

"I am here today because, like so many other Americans in similar situations, I believe it is imperative that we fix our broken immigration system, and specifically that it is long past time we treat lesbian and gay Americans and our families equally under the law. I traveled to be with you today from London, where I work for Pfizer."

"I am fortunate to have worked for more than 14 years for Pfizer. Pfizer is a company that recognizes domestic partnership. Unfortunately, the U.S. government does not recognize Renato, my partner of more than nine years. For two years, Renato lived with me in the U.S. as a full-time student, studying English and pre-Law. He is a trained lawyer in Brazil."

"In June 2003, while enrolled in a full-time, accredited academic program in New York, he returned to Brazil for what we thought would be a routine second renewal of his student visa. The renewal was rejected and he has never been able to return to our home in the U.S. For weeks, I left his things exactly as they were the day he left, hoping that soon he would be able to come home. He never came back to the U.S."

He shared more about that wrenching incident.

"Renato wanted to live and study in the United States. Yet because the immigration laws did not recognize him as my family member, nothing I could do would bring him back to our home."

"So to be with Renato, I commuted to Brazil every other weekend for more than a year and a half. This commuting took a huge toll on me emotionally, physically, and financially. Eventually, I was fortunate to find a position with Pfizer in the UK, where we can live together again. The UK government has recognized us as dependent partners, and we both have the right to live and work in the UK. While we are grateful for this solution, it means separation from our family and friends and puts significant limitations on each of our career opportunities. And we were forced to sell our apartment in New York."

His story included this statement: "The United States' discriminatory immigration laws have also affected my extended family. I am lucky to have five siblings. In August, I will attend my niece's wedding in California. It will be a big family reunion, but my partner will not able to join us. Renato cannot even get a tourist visa to visit the U.S. Imagine what that means."

"If I want to be with my family for important occasions such as weddings, graduations, Thanksgiving, Christmas, and the recent baptism of my godchild, I have to travel alone and leave Renato in London. Or if we want to celebrate an important occasion together, it is usually the two of us alone, far away from our family and close friends."

Gordon shared this sad news. "Recently, when my sister was diagnosed with cancer, Renato could not travel with me to visit her, and I could not spend as much time with her as I wanted because I live and work in London. That is the reality of our life together."

"Last year, I reluctantly and sadly sold our family farm in Goshen, Vermont, because I cannot vacation there with Renato. Our family had the farm from when I was six years old, and our parents both died and were buried there. Imagine what it is like to own a property to which you cannot travel with your partner. It is impossible to maintain a 19th-century farmhouse from the other side of the Atlantic. That is the reality of American immigration law for couples like us."

Stewart stressed: "I am deeply disappointed that my country has treated Renato this way, and I am furious that we cannot visit or live together in the U.S. Despite the fact that I am a tax-paying, law-abiding and voting citizen, I feel discrimination from my government."

He did include some positive news: "Fortunately, my company, Pfizer, has been very supportive from that awful day when Renato's visa renewal request was rejected in

2003. The UK has allowed both Renato and me to move there, based on my temporary transfer from Pfizer. The UK recognizes permanent partners for immigration purposes, as do 18 other countries. Renato has a permanent partner visa. The U.S. should offer the same."

"The decision to move to the UK was the best decision I could have made at the time. But I would like to be able to come home; I should have the right to come with my partner to visit or to live, but we can't. That is the reality of U.S. immigration law."

He urged action.

"Thousands of other lesbian and gay families are separated like we are. Unlike us, however, they do not have the support of a company like Pfizer to help find a solution to this impossible situation. The Uniting American Families Act needs to be passed now. I hope today's hearing will be a step in that direction."

And he shared thanks.

"I would like to extend my sincere thanks to Senator Leahy for the strong stand he has taken on supporting families like mine. Let me thank all the senators for taking the time to listen to my story. I am the voice of many wonderful Americans who have been forced to make the difficult choice between family and partner and country and partner."

At this point, a letter from Pfizer was read into the Congressional record.

"Pfizer submitted a letter for the record at the June 3, 2009 UAFA Senate Judiciary Committee hearing. In that letter Pfizer laid out the firm's commitment to UAFA and made a compelling business case about why UAFA's passage is important," noted Steve Ralls of Immigration Equality. "Pfizer is also a leading member of the Business Coalition for UAFA."

In addition, this story was in *The Advocate* online September 21, 2010:

The Best Companies in the U.S.

With all the talk of boycotting those companies that don't stand strongly behind gay rights, here is a list of 25 of the best companies in the U.S. when it comes to gay issues.

By Advocate.com Editors

Pfizer — The pharmaceutical giant has been a proponent of volunteerism and philanthropy, and there's no exception where gay causes are concerned. Pfizer has been a big donor to the LGBT Caucus of Public Health Professionals and has backed HIV/AIDS research across the country and around the world. In 2009 the company teamed up with GlaxoSmithKline to form a pharma firm focusing solely on HIV/AIDS.

Gordon's testimony continued: "Allow me to add that my company, Pfizer, has earned, for the fifth consecutive year, the top rating of 100 percent in the 2009 Corporate Equality Index, an annual ranking published by the Human Rights Campaign Foundation that evaluates businesses on their treatment of LGBT employees, investors and customers. Pfizer Chairman and CEO Jeff Kindler has said Pfizer supports its LGBT colleagues because 'doing better in recruitment and retention, in understanding diverse markets and in making Pfizer a better place to work does ultimately drive up our value.' However, he said, we mainly 'support our LGBT colleagues because it is the right thing to do.'"

Stewart concluded: "America also should support its LGBT citizens and families. Because it is indeed the right thing to do."

Interviewing Gordon, I learned that he has a large extended family in the United States, five siblings, eight nieces and nephews, two aunts and an uncle. He has their support on this issue. His family supports the work of Immigration Equality with regular donations. His nephew joined him when he testified at the Senate hearing.

Gordon worked for Pfizer, Inc. before he met Renato, but since they got together and had to leave America, "the situation has somewhat limited my career options," noted Gordon. Though Pfizer is extremely supportive as shown in his testimony before the Senate hearing, and has been recognized for their support at the Immigration Equality Safe Haven Awards June 8, 2010, it still affects Gordon's career path. "Pfizer has helped Immigration Equality set up a business coalition," said Gordon. It is something that will help advocate for the solution same-sex binational couples need and lend nongovernmental support to the issue.

You can view Gordon's testimony at *http://www.youtube.comwatch?v=GmiVawXrozc*

CHAPTER EIGHTEEN

STEVE AND JOEY: LOST THE JOB, LOST THE WELCOME— CANADA, HERE WE COME

Karin and I met this wonderful couple, Steve and Joey Ormana (not their real name, by request), in Washington, D.C. when we attended the June 3, 2009, Senate hearing. We spent time at dinner visiting with them and another same-sex binational couple. The six of us at the table shared three different versions of immigration challenges!

Steve Ormana, 59, and Joey Ormana, 49, shared their employment concerns and worries about their future as the economy was dipping and it was not a fun thing to hear. If Joey lost his job, he might not be able to stay in America.

As it happened, Joey did lose his job. He was forced to leave the United States four months later. He is still unable to return because when he lost his job, he lost the work visa that went with it. Sadly, at the time Joey lost his job, he was two-thirds of the way toward getting his green card and permanent residence in the United States.

The litany that is so familiar to me included this for them: Steve is an American citizen, but Joey is not. They met online in the United States in 2001, when Steve was living and working in Pittsburgh, Pennsylvania. Joey was working on his Ph.D. there, after getting his master's degree at a university in another state. "After chatting several times, we agreed to meet in a coffee shop in Shadyside in Pittsburgh," Joey said.

Steve was very out, "about as out as you can be in Pittsburgh," he laughed, because he was the first paid employee for GLSEN Pittsburgh, a chapter of the Gay, Lesbian and Straight Education Network, where he worked until he relocated to be with Joey and Joey's new job in Washington, D.C. As a trainer/program coordinator for GLSEN Pittsburgh, Steve had talked to more than 10,000 people about LGBT issues and made 70 presentations a year—more than 300 total while he was there.

He talked to teachers and teachers-in-training and college and university sociology and education classes in western Pennsylvania trying to make schools safe educational environments for all students. Meanwhile Joey, who had a first same-sex relationship while getting his master's degree, had never even been to a gay bar before he met Steve.

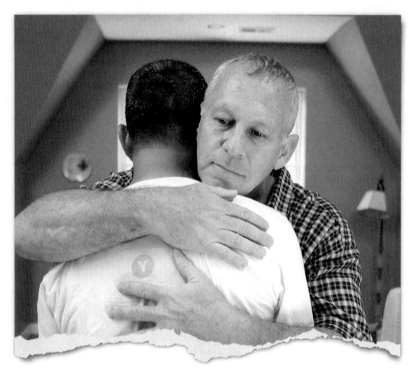

Photo of Joey Ormana (back to camera) and Steve Ormana taken by and courtesy of
Todd Franson, *Metro Weekly*. Used with permission.

After getting to know each other and realizing that they were meant to be together,
Joey moved in with Steve after six months of dating.

While Steve is very out about being a gay man, Joey, a Muslim from a southeast
Asian country, is not out to his family, who would disown him. That has made the solution of moving back to his home country less than comfortable for him. In America,
Joey came out to a few people after he met Steve and they were together. But he never
came out to his family and cannot. "I left America and had to be separated from the
most important person in my life," said Joey. "I am back into the closet because I am
not out to my family. They are really religious. It's harder for me to be me after going
home to my country."

Steve continued to work at the GLSEN position he loved for two and a half years,
after Joey went to Washington, D.C. for his new job with a prestigious engineering
firm. Each weekend, one of them would make the drive between Pittsburgh and Washington, D.C.—hard as that was. After Joey got approval for his green card, the couple
thought they were home free, so Steve left the work he loved so much in Pittsburgh and
relocated to Washington to be with Joey. After renting for a while, they wanted to own

their own place and bought it—but disaster struck when Joey lost his job and with it, his work visa, turning their lives upside down again.

Steve and Joey had to sell their home in Washington, D.C. one month after they bought it. They had checked with Joey's employer before buying a place, because they needed to be sure his job was certain as the American economy was sliding. Assured that there were no issues to his job safety, they bought a place together and settled in. But just a few weeks later, they were faced with selling their place and being separated from each other, then having to both leave the country in order to stay together. What a hit they took!

When I interviewed Steve on Skype on September 4, 2010, the plan was to move to Canada together. The couple hired a lawyer and is going through the required processes to move to Canada so they can be together again. Steve told me he was excited to get the news that the next step for them was to have physicals required by the Canadian immigration rules. Sadly, it meant one more step away from being in America together. But happily, it meant one less obstacle to being together again finally in Canada. What an emotional roller coaster for them!

He was trying to be optimistic about moving to Canada—which wasn't confirmed at that time—while he had been separated from Joey for nearly a year. "I dropped Joey off at the Denver airport on October 21, 2009," he said. "It just feels like everything is on hold. You can't make any plans. We're apprehensive if Canada doesn't come through. We don't know what we'll do if that doesn't work."

The worst day of their lives was when they had to separate at the Denver airport. "Watching Joey walk through those doors was like watching the person you love most drowning and not being able to do anything about it," Steve said. "It was so painful watching him go through those airport gates, not knowing if we were ever going to be able to get together again. That was just pointless! It was senseless! There was absolutely no reason that this had to happen." But it did.

"We aren't going to live with Joey being noncompliant, going illegal," Steve said. He knows how hard Joey has worked on his career, and "we weren't going to jeopardize that," he stressed. This couple could only stay in the United States together if Joey got his green card. They can't afford to not work, and "Joey's country is not an option for us," Steve stressed. "I wouldn't be able to work there, and being gay there is not a great idea. Neither of us would feel comfortable with that."

Unfortunately for them, asylum is not an option because in order to request asylum, Joey would have to be out as a gay man in his home country and then be threatened or worse. They don't want to go into harm's way for a chance at asylum, so they will move to a third country to be together.

Joey's skills as a structural engineer are desired in Canada. Joey is a professional skilled worker in the eyes of the Canadian government. Steve can join him there, since Canada recognizes Joey and Steve as a family, something they can't get in America, even though they were legally married in Connecticut July 12, 2009.

Joey was sad as he recapped his story. It made me sad, too. "My partner and I were together for almost 10 years before I had to leave the United States because I was laid off due to the economic situation," he said. "I am not a U.S. citizen. Although we got married, my partner cannot sponsor me to stay in the country because our relationship is not recognized by the federal government."

"When I got laid off, my work visa automatically was not valid anymore," Joey said. "My company sponsored my work visa. I was in the middle of obtaining a green card. I had passed two stages out of three to get it; in fact, I was waiting for an immigration number to be a permanent resident in the U.S. when I lost my job."

Joey is another victim of the backlog of immigration cases the U.S. government works on. Without the one- to three- to seven-year delay people face, he would have his green card and this story would have ended very differently.

He regretfully shared this fact: "I graduated with a Ph.D. in structural engineering from a U.S. university with a full academic scholarship. But I can't stay to pay back America by working and contributing my knowledge and paying taxes because we don't have the same rights as heterosexual couples do."

What Joey and Steve want is to live in America together. They have not given up on that option—and won't. They want to be near Steve's aging parents and extended family. Joey said, "What my family doesn't know won't hurt them," describing why it would be okay to not live in his country where his mother and siblings are.

They have advocated for this issue by sharing their story at events. Joey told his story at a fund-raising event for Immigration Equality in Washington, D.C. This is the group they contacted for help when they had their crisis. They were interviewed for a story in their hometown before they had to leave. Steve testified at a meeting for Congressional staff members, where his father also shared his thoughts on the issue and his wife's thoughts, too, in the letters included in this chapter.

While the details are unique to this couple, the basic story resonates with so many others. Joey sums it up with this comment: "My partner cannot sponsor me to be a permanent resident. If we were a heterosexual couple, my American partner would have the right, according to the law, and could sponsor me to be a permanent resident, no questions asked."

Sadly, as active and open as Steve and his family are, Joey cannot get support or help from his family because he cannot talk about his immigration problem with them; he is not able to be open about who he is.

Joey is, therefore, now self-employed in his home country, waiting for his move to

Canada. Steve is living and working with family in New Mexico, waiting for his move to Canada. There they will be together and employed and recognized as family.

As hard as it is to hear Steve and Joey's story, what made me cry was the touching testimony Steve's father gave in Washington, D.C. on October 23, 2009. Here, with Steve's permission, are the letters from his father and stepmother that were entered into the proceedings. This is family love and support of the highest order.

"My name is Allen," (I cannot use his last name, by Steve and Joey's request). "I am Steve's father and the father-in-law of Joey. My wife, Doris, was unable to make this trip but requested that, in addition to my statement, I read a message she wrote. Doris and I have been married 38 years and have a blended family of nine children and 14 grandchildren. Joey and Steve became a couple about nine years ago. Recently they were married at a small ceremony at our oldest daughter's home in Connecticut. Approximately eight months ago, Joey, a structural engineer with a Ph.D., was let go along with several others. Inasmuch as he had not yet received his green card, he was told he had to leave his adopted country by October 31 if he did not find another position in his field by then. However, no one would hire him because he did not have the green card."

"This has been devastating for Steve and Joey and very sad for the entire family. We all love Joey very much. The two of them bring such happiness to every gathering, cheerfulness to every event, as well as concern for anyone who is having problems. They are favorite uncles for the young people in our family. A loving, devoted couple, they bring much joy into our lives."

"We can't help feeling that their current situation is so unfair. If they were heterosexual, Steve could sponsor Joey for citizenship. I understand there are approximately 36,000 binational, same-sex couples who face the same dilemma each year. Thank you."

"And now I'd like to read Doris' message:"

"Our son-in-law, Joey, has endeared himself to our family and to many others. He came to this country alone, went to college, and eventually achieved a doctorate in structural engineering from the University of Pittsburgh, mostly through full scholarships. Isn't it ironic that the same country which made it possible, now insists that he leave?"

"He has been an exemplary citizen, without the benefits of citizenship. He loves America and has done all the right things to become a legal citizen, but this has been denied him simply because he is gay."

"The fact that, just two days ago, he had to leave this country is a tragedy for him and our son, Steve, as well as the rest of our large family. But it also is America's loss. Joey would be a great asset to our country. It is especially poignant at this time of year, because the last thing Joey said to me as he was kissing me goodbye, was, 'Save my place for me at the Thanksgiving table.'"

"But this is not just Steve and Joey's story; it's the story of tens of thousands of others caught in the same situation. Those with children have it much worse. If the spouses were not gay, many of these obstacles wouldn't exist at all. The fact is, that discriminatory laws are tearing these families apart. I hope that when Congress realizes this discrimination is bringing such pain to families like ours, they will act to remedy the situation."

"Our family needs our missing spouse/son/brother/uncle back at the Thanksgiving table where he belongs."

When I interviewed Steve, it brought back all the pain of late October 2009. The day after Steve took Joey to the airport and said goodbye, he flew to Washington, D.C. The day after that, he testified about the issues of same-sex binational couples at the meeting where he invited his father to participate as well. "I was raw," Steve said, choking up.

More than a year later they were still in separate countries, waiting to be together in a third country, Canada, where neither of them have lived. Last I heard, Steve and Joey should be reunited in Canada about the time this book is available to the public.

CHAPTER NINETEEN

MARTHA AND LIN: WE MET IN THE NETHERLANDS AND NOW WE LIVE THERE TOGETHER

Martha and Lin McDevitt-Pugh live in The Netherlands today, which is neither of their home countries. But this lesbian binational couple didn't move there to be together—they met when they were both there, and their lives merged after many years of friendship and a decade of geographic separation when Martha went back to America to live. Unlike the other stories, sometimes gay and lesbian binational couples don't have to move away from America together to be able to be together. They find each other outside America, then have to stay overseas in order to maintain their families.

"Martha, then 23, was in college, doing a period of study in Amsterdam," shared Lin. "She was working as an intern in the office of a friend of mine, who became our mutual friend." Lin, aged 27 at the time, had left Australia to work in Amsterdam for an anti-nuclear group and was going to her friend's office to use the electric typewriter to work on her organization's magazine.

She found Martha there alone, and it was "friend at first sight," they say.

Lin had found Amsterdam to be interesting while traveling around in the late 1970s, exploring the work of anti-nuclear groups. She took a chance to work for a group and then realized she didn't know how much that choice would change her life. "I had to figure out how to get there legally and stay there legally," she remembered. "I didn't know anything about immigration at the time."

She figured it out and worked there and met a partner and had a son, right around the time she and Martha met.

"Martha knew Koen, my son, from the first days of his life," said Lin. "That's really important to me." Martha, single at the time, met a girlfriend and they moved together back to America. "She was in the Air Force," Martha recalled, "and I thought it was important she get out of the Air Force. It was before Don't Ask, Don't Tell (DADT)."

So Martha spent 10 years in America, away from her friends. She and Lin's family saw each other on visits and kept in touch over the years. "Then when I

Martha, left, and Lin, right, McDevitt-Pugh in The Netherlands.
Photo by Dineke Stam. From their private collection. Used by permission.

was a publisher," Lin shared, "I was able to go to America and visit again."

Martha worked in the high-tech industry in Silicon Valley, while Lin led her life in Amsterdam. "I was able to go to The Netherlands," she said.

"That and a few telephone calls," said Lin, "and we kept in touch and were really close."

"Don't forget e-mail," reminded Martha.

"Martha got me connected with e-mail when it was very new," remembered Lin. "I had to ring into Manchester for connection. Martha always managed to get really great jobs. She'd come over and visit us. We stayed close throughout the 10 years."

When her son was about 12, she said, her relationship with Koen's mother dissolved. Martha and Lin became aware in 1998 that they wanted to be more than friends. As exciting as that was, their challenge then became how to be together in the same country. "My son was 16 at the time and I didn't really want to move him from his friends and his other mother," said Lin. "And I thought that was a bit young for me to leave him," she added. He was living with both mothers part time. He is now 28.

"We visited each other for about a year and a half between The Netherlands and

California, which is quite a long distance," remembered Martha. "I had a really good job, so I was able to pay for her to come visit, and I would sometimes go over there, so we saw each other every six weeks. We had friends who had a relationship between Santa Cruz and Maine," she recalled, "and they told us about the six week rule." The friends told them, "If you don't see each other after six weeks it becomes really hard."

"When Lin asked me if I would move to The Netherlands I said yes. It seemed like it took quite a while," Martha continued. "I said yes, but not every part of me meant yes."

"It took a lot to give up my life in California," remembered Martha. "I have all my family in the San Francisco Bay Area, and my nieces and nephews were small, and my Mom was 71 when I left, so I didn't really want to be leaving her." Martha also had a really great job that she didn't want to leave behind. "I knew I couldn't get a job like that in Europe," she said. "It was hard!"

"I thought we could live for two years in the Netherlands and then move to the United States," Lin said.

"I somehow knew that wasn't going to happen," shared Martha. "I knew how immigration worked." She knew in The Netherlands there is no difference between couples: gay, straight, married, unmarried. "They also looked like they were going to be opening up marriage," Martha said. "I knew that here [the United States], there was no way. That's what I told my boss when I left."

Her boss said, "Don't leave, don't leave."

"I told him, 'Well, my partner is Australian, and I can't bring her in,'" she recalled, "and he said, 'Oh, right' and that was it."

"Somebody said to me later, 'Why didn't you ask your company to transfer you to Europe?'" Martha said. She hadn't thought of that. Her firm had an office in The Netherlands, but her job was based in Silicon Valley. "My job wasn't something I could do from there," she said, "but I didn't look at what they could do for me. I didn't give them the opportunity to keep me."

"I think that's a big part of this story," continued Martha. "I think a lot of us don't know how it works and don't look at what could be possible. We don't look at whether it's our families, our company, whatever support is available."

At the time, Martha was managing technical communications for her company, and the staff was based in America. "Some of them were remote, but I didn't know; I assumed that there wasn't an option to stay with the company," she added. "I didn't think there was anything else I could do for the company."

Martha had a Dutch colleague based in Silicon Valley. "He went over to The Netherlands for a year because he wanted his kids to have an experience living in The Netherlands. "After I left he said, 'Why didn't you ask?' and I said I didn't think to ask what they could do for me."

Martha was sanguine about how things turned out. "It wasn't a bad time to get out. I was working in a software company, and I moved in 2000 before everything crashed. I got out of Silicon Valley at a good time."

On the other side of the Atlantic, there was no Silicon Valley and she couldn't find an equivalent job. "Lin would always clip things out of the newspaper that read: "We're looking for young, executive managers under age 25, up to age 30." That's The Netherlands, they're allowed to discriminate based on age.

Martha faced the same employment situation that Thomas Arnold faced, when he and Tony Eitnier tried to live in Germany after Thomas spent years in college in America.

Martha persevered. "You have to find your own opportunities," she said. "I now have a job, and it's just as good of a job as I had—of course, it's taken me 10 years…"

"I've had good jobs," said Martha.

"You've had great jobs," agreed Lin.

"But it took a long time," continued Martha. "It took letting go of what I had here [the United States] and looking laterally, looking outside my field, outside my comfort zone."

"There has to be a part of the story about me, too," said Lin. "Was I willing to come to America? I didn't have a huge ambition to be living in The Netherlands, apart from my son living there. I've got aging parents in Australia; I've got a Dutch son and an American wife."

"I've got so many places where I could be," she went on. "I don't have a real urgency to live in The Netherlands, but there I am a first-class citizen. I'm really treated well. It is of absolutely no relevance that I am gay. I can go places, see people, be who I am, do what I want to do, because I am me. I am not stopped anywhere because I am gay."

"For the longest time, I kept my Australian citizenship because about as long as The Netherlands, they have had the same rule that you can bring in your same-sex partner. So I thought if I ever was going to go back to Australia, I'd need my Australian citizenship to be able to bring my partner in.

"It wasn't until 2001 when we got married that Martha said: 'Look, you've been in The Netherlands longer than you've been in Australia. You're very politically active, and it's strange that you're not able to vote.'"

So Lin got her Dutch passport and lost her Australian one in the process, and later got it back. "I have two nationalities, and it was really important for me to regain the Australian passport because I wanted to have the opportunity to bring my partner into Australia if that was to be an option ever, in the future. I think it's really important. We are living in a globalized world. The fact is, I have a Dutch son. The fact is, I have an

American wife. The fact is, I have Australian family. We need to be able to freely choose which one of those countries we want to be in."

"It was also very important to your parents that you have your Australian citizenship," added Martha. "It was really hard for them that you weren't Australian any more and you were fighting for your right to come into the United States." Lin's parents felt that she was rejecting her Australian identity and "they felt very bad about that," she added.

"They also felt like when I moved to The Netherlands, I didn't really migrate, I just sort of went over there for a three-month trip and never came back," she recalled. Her parents "had to come to the conclusion that I wasn't coming back," she mused. "I also had to come to that conclusion myself."

For Lin, it took a long time to come to that conclusion. "It wasn't until my son was five," she said, "that I really knew I couldn't rely on going back there. I couldn't put him through that migration process. His other mother wasn't planning on going there, so that's when I really realized that I'm in Holland for the long run."

When people ask Lin if she would really want to live in the United States, she stressed: "It's a really hard thing. I'm not a first-class citizen there. What would make me want to be there?" There was one exception: "It was really, really important for Martha to be there."

"Yes, family," declared Martha.

"That would be it," agreed Lin.

Karin was present at this interview. She wanted to know: "If things change in the next year or two, say, would that make a difference to you?"

"They'd have to change a few things," Lin replied.

"You know, like marriage," stated Karin, "and immigration."

"Our marriage is recognized here in California," said Martha.

"But the federal stuff would have to change," added Lin.

Yes," agreed Martha.

While their Dutch marriage is not formally recognized by the federal government for immigration, "at immigration, an officer of the federal government recognizes it when we come to America for a visit," Martha said.

"I think that we both have a dream that in our old age we will be living in this country [America]," stated Lin. Karin wanted to know why that was what they might want to do. "I think it's really hard to say that," mused Lin. "But I think it's the nature of Martha's family that would have us living, probably, in California."

"Why would I not be living in Australia? We might be, but then we might be living in The Netherlands." Martha added, "We live in a country that's neither of our countries right now, but we will be having grandchildren, so that's going to have an impact."

I teased them about anchor babies, and we all laughed.

Karin shared a fact about our family with them: "We've got grandchildren, and we will have great grandchildren, probably in the next few years."

"It's a factor, isn't it?" said Martha.

"Oh, very much so," agreed Karin.

"I also find that the longer I'm in The Netherlands," elaborated Martha, "the more remote the possibility feels that I'd have to have a really good reason to uproot myself. But I think that might just be the effort it would take to move."

I reminded her that it was habit, effort, day-to-day life, and she agreed.

"But we're really sitting on the fence," Martha added. "We've been there 10 years, and we haven't bought a house. We're renting, and it's a really good deal, but we don't really want to be in Amsterdam."

"When we think about buying a home—we're both in our 50s—it's like we can buy something, but then, you know, does that really anchor us somewhere in case we can't sell it easily or whatever," she confided. "So where should we buy? You know, where do we want to be possibly for the next 10 or 20 years?"

It's hard for them to imagine having a property where they might have to leave it behind.

Karin interjected: "You have to think about health care for the future, old age pension, caring for the elderly, where will that really work for you?"

"Yes," agreed Martha, "I really feel like we have something built up in The Netherlands, and so that would be the easiest and the most practical option, but I'm not sure."

She added: "I'm sure you're really right, Lin, that family here in California will really call us, will make us want to be here."

"But I also want to say," added Lin, "that I really, really, really didn't want to live in America during the Bush years. It was just so horrible." She shared that in Holland, she "had nightmares about this place," and we agreed that we still do sometimes.

"After the election of Obama, I felt for the first time ever the idea that maybe this is a place we could live. Maybe there is hope for this country," Lin said, adding that it will take a long time to make the changes we need because American government takes so long to do things.

Living outside the United States, Lin and Martha's perspective has changed about America, and they were glad to see a population willing to vote for a president who "is willing to make change happen." Lin said she noticed with the elections "that there was a willingness to change, so that means a large population of people are saying, 'We've had it!'"

She continued: "I'm noticing that the way people are thinking about gay marriage, for example, it's changing, it's moving all the time. So America is moving forward, it's becoming more and more a place where we could be."

Lin recalled a family picnic on a previous visit and how all Martha's siblings got into their cars with their kids and drove home at the end of the day, and it was normal. She and Martha got into their car to go home, and it was different. It didn't look or feel as normal as she wanted it to be.

"Martha is an amazing person, such a wonderful person. She deserves to have that degree of ordinariness that everybody else does, but she doesn't even get that." She added, "It seems to be a really weird thing to be going for, but now I think we have achieved something of a degree of ordinariness that other people have,"

And take for granted, I added.

"And take for granted," Lin agreed.

"But the way I look at being in exile is that it gives you an extraordinary life," said Martha. Turning to us, she said, "I look at what you guys do for six months and think it's so amazing!"

Karin laughed and said she agreed. I added, "We don't get any sympathy…"

Martha agreed that it could be hard and there were challenges to being a love exile, but looked at her move and the timing and said: "I could have stayed here. I could have done my career. But I was really forced completely out of my comfort zone to go into an industry that I didn't know. I work in a bank now, and I just started a new job two months ago and it's something I thought I would never do."

She is managing a communications team within the bank's IT department. "It's really challenging and fun," she declared. "My team makes videos and digital magazines and lots of really cool stuff." She wondered out loud how that had happened.

For me, Martha nailed it when she said: "You know I got here out of adversity, and I think how extraordinary it all is."

But there is a lot of ordinariness to it, too, I reminded the four of us. In spite of how normal gay and lesbian families are to us, we agreed that America isn't far enough along yet.

Whether Lin and Martha will live in the United States remains to be seen. In order to be together, Martha left her job here and moved to The Netherlands. "I had my employer sponsor me for my visa over there," she said, "so that was how I went about it. I got moved and everything, so that was all taken care of."

"And then Lin became Dutch, so I was able to become Dutch because I was married to a Dutch person, yet I could keep my American citizenship. Then Lin was able to become Australian again because she was married to a Dutch citizen," she added.

"These are the kind of interesting little quirks in the law," mused Lin. "United States law doesn't recognize our marriage. But because we're married, Martha was able to keep her U.S. passport. That's interesting, isn't it?"

"The Netherlands doesn't allow dual nationality," stated Martha. "The exception is if you are married to a Dutch citizen." She added: "The U.S. doesn't block dual nationality." And when Lin went to get her Australian passport back, she was able to register under her current married name, even though Australia doesn't recognize same-sex marriage. She got it because of her marriage in The Netherlands. Her marriage license showed her hyphenated last name, so they recognized her as married.

"Our story is important because there are always circumstances in life, and we don't choose them," said Martha. "The fact that we can't live together in my country is a federal legislative issue that affects our lives—and it's just a circumstance we have to deal with. We've taken a circumstance that we didn't choose and we don't like, and we've not let it run our lives."

"You never know how the future is going to go," Martha said, thinking of her 1980s friends from South Africa fleeing from apartheid and the Berlin Wall falling as examples. She cited a newspaper item that day that showed a federal court judge saying Don't Ask, Don't Tell was unconstitutional, and remarked how a Democratic Party President had brought it in and Log Cabin Republicans had challenged it in court.

"We don't know how and when things are going to change," she said thoughtfully. "But let's just look every day and say, who do we want to be, and how to have integrity with ourselves and situations and the people we love, and what's the next step we can make to make this a more workable world?"

Martha reiterated: "We need to see how to make the world today more workable, rather than hope for the future or say the past was really bad and we're stuck with it." That's where their group, Love Exiles Foundation, comes in, she said.

"I'm probably not going to wake up tomorrow and have the freedom to bring Lin into the United States," she declared. "However, what could I do now that will help? Love Exiles came out of recognizing that the most amazing people I've ever met are the people in this community. They've traveled across the world to be with the person they love, whatever obstacles they've met, and have built up lives in adverse circumstances. If they're not facing adversity now, it may be down the line."

Love Exiles is designed to empower gay and lesbian families to deal with the adversity they face in being together. "We had potlucks for years, and they were so great because the Americans would talk about all their issues, and Dutch partners could share information with each other about how they kept in contact with families elsewhere, got services in The Netherlands, all sorts of things."

Lin pointed out that those sorts of things were the same for any binational couple, and while they certainly helped LGBT families living in other countries, it comes down to "a very simple story—we just don't need to be different." That's why she said it is important to pass Uniting American Families Act (UAFA).

Lin was realistic in her expectations. "If it does pass, it won't change that much for us right away," she said, "but it will help so many others that we must see it passed."

When Martha moved to Amsterdam, she found there was a chapter of Lesbian and Gay Immigration Rights Task Force (LGIRTF), the precursor to Immigration Equality there and connected with it. "They weren't working on changing the law," recalled Martha. "But they met and socialized."

She found them online and then went and met really incredible people there. "I felt like when I moved from America I fell off the map," said Martha. "I couldn't engage. I couldn't belong to anything. I couldn't do the things that needed to be done to make the change we wanted. And then I found that we could through a group."

"We just don't need to be different," emphasized Lin. "UAFA, or RFA, or another law needs to make us the same as everyone else."

"We found out there was a community all over the world, and we found that we could engage, we could do the things that needed to be done," said Martha. "We're part of this, too. At the time, no one was talking about love exiles and no one was talking about the people leaving the United States. We kick-started that conversation."

Some people have no country they can be in, and Love Exiles helps them investigate their options, shared Martha. "Like, for example, Canada is a good option and people don't always know that." So that's a way that Love Exiles helps. "People have no idea of their options," continued Martha. She said that if one of the two partners is European, they have options of moving to a European country where their relationship is recognized. "The day before we launched Love Exiles, we got somebody calling and saying 'Oh, I'm in London, and my partner's from Los Angeles, and our lawyer just called us and said we need to start a chapter in the UK. They were a Dutch/U.S. couple, and it didn't work for them to live in The Netherlands, so they went to the UK."

"One of the things we want to do is to give people a piece of safety, a lifeline, so they know they have more options than they think they have," continued Martha. She warned that some people think that something dire will happen to them, but they don't know what, or they think they only have one option that they don't really like, for example. "We give people pathways so that they can see what they can do," she told me.

"I'll be having a phone conversation in a couple of days with a woman in New York," she said. "Her partner's from Germany, and they don't want to go there, so she's asking, 'What else can we do?'" Martha stressed that she is not a lawyer, but with a couple like that she can share what other people have done and what would be involved in that.

"That's bigger than your story," I reminded her.

Martha and Lin agreed that they do impact the cause in a bigger way then just their story. "We build community, we make sure that it's visible, the fact that there are people outside their country, and frankly, our work has been taken over by many other people. Journalists, for example, come to us.

In 2009, the *San José Mercury News* was planning a story on Martha and her family and the way U.S. immigration law affected them. Reporters spent three months on the story. They interviewed Martha and her sister Amy, when Martha was visiting in January. They came to the airport to meet Lin, when she arrived in March, a few days after Martha. They came to the house to see her with her niece and nephew. They interviewed Martha's mother on the telephone. They also interviewed people in the love exiles community in Canada.

During the course of that project, Martha met Melanie Nathan. Melanie was working on her own immigration challenge and had found out about Jay Mercado and Shirley Tan. She wanted to help them before Shirley was deported. So Martha asked Melanie to meet her and Lin for tea and discuss the issue. Jay and Shirley came, too.

"To be honest," Martha said with a smile, "I like to be in charge. And when I hear a story of an asylum seeker who's been through what Shirley's been through, having her mother and her sister murdered, being shot in the head herself at the age of 14, feeling unsafe in her own country, fleeing to the United States, and then the whole bureaucratic issue of not getting asylum after years, that makes me feel really powerless. I try to make a difference for people who are in immigration situations, but I really don't know what to do around asylum seekers. It's out of my depth. It's very emotionally upsetting to me."

She felt bad at the time because she didn't think she could help, but she promised Melanie and Jay and Shirley that she would make a call to Senator Dianne Feinstein's office.

"I had just done this amazing class, a 10-month class called Partnership Exploration," she remembered. "One of the things it was about was knowing that 'I don't know' is a very powerful place. All my life I had avoided the place of 'I don't know.' I work in information technology—I like to know things."

"So Lin and I had tea with them, and I kept thinking, *Hmmmmmm, 'I don't know' This is a good thing, 'I don't know.' Let's not get upset about this, let's just be in 'I don't know.'*"

"Lin said something very powerful," recalled Martha. "Shirley and Jay were talking about how their previous lawyer had really messed up the case. And Lin said, 'You need to stop being angry at that lawyer, because that's in the past now so just let it go.'"

"That made a difference in the conversation," Martha remembered, smiling.

"When I was sitting with 'I don't know,'" she continued, "I said, 'Do you have pictures of your kids?'"

Well, of course Shirley and Jay had pictures. And since their sons are twins, they had two pictures of this, and two pictures of that, and pictures with the boys together.

"So all these pictures were out on the table," Martha said with a grin. "And all of a sudden there were completely different people in front of us. We're mothers, Melanie is a mother. They're mothers. So we suddenly had this fundamental human connection in front of us, and we saw who they really were. They were not just upset, sad people, but they were people who had huge commitment to family, and that was what this was all about."

So since the *Mercury News* story had not been published yet, Martha told Melanie to hook the paper up with Shirley and Jay, which she did. "First, they decided they didn't want to go public with their story," remembered Martha. "But then they did go public, and their story was the lead in the story in the *Mercury-News*," she said.

"If we hadn't been working on that story for several months, Jay and Shirley wouldn't have hit the press in time," Martha said. They were facing Shirley's deportation 10 days after that fateful tea appointment in San Francisco. Martha's phone calls to Senator Feinstein's office and an e-mail to a staffer helped in the situation. At the time, Martha didn't feel like she had done anything, but when she got back to Amsterdam, the Love Exiles Foundation wrote a letter to Dianne Feinstein, and she referred to it when she did the private bill to keep Shirley Tan from being deported and tearing her family apart.

"Those are very simple things I did, and that we can do to make a difference," Martha said.

Karin and I agree. You can do what seem like simple things, but those things can make a real difference. Share your story. Share someone else's story. Write a letter. Make a phone call. Make a difference!

Things are happening, the issue is reaching critical mass, we all agreed. "Sometimes I do things I wouldn't usually do, and they make a difference," confided Martha. Her phone calls to Senator Feinstein's office is one example. And it helped. "It's also about people going beyond the ordinary, to reach out, to help," she said.

When Martha and Lin met Melanie and Jay and Shirley, they were in California visiting family. "We were on vacation," Lin remembered. "It's not ordinary to do work like this when you are on vacation in America."

"We had also done work the week before," added Martha. "We had met with Amos and people from Out4Immigration. Mickey, Wendy, Belinda, Kathy. Their little kids were running around. Lin said in the middle of a chaotic meeting, 'What do you guys want?' and I said, 'I want a Congressional hearing before the summer.'" That was in March, a week before they met Jay and Shirley. "I thought that there was a snowball's chance of that," remembered Martha. "But the hearing came in June."

"What's powerful is saying what you want," said Martha. "My personal agenda is to empower people around this issue because, by its own nature, it's a disempowering issue when you're stuck and you don't have a country where you can be together."

"What happened when we met Melanie, and what happened when we met Shirley and Jay, and what happens when we meet anybody is: if you listen to people, so they get out of just being upset, they get that they have a reason to be upset, and they get listened to. What emerges from that is people can then look to see what action they would like to take and what would be empowering for them through their own self-expression, and that's different for everybody," she said.

"I'm not good at walking the halls of Congress and knocking on doors," she continued. "I don't live in Washington. I don't live in the United States. And it's not that fun. But we ran around in the Senate Office Building with Jay and Shirley and Joriene and Jashley after the hearing in the Senate Judiciary Commission in June 2009, and those kids loved doing that! They loved running down to the next office, the next flag. They were great, and powerful. 'Let's go talk to Jeff Sessions. I have a question for him,' Joriene said. Hours after, Sessions spoke out against immigration rights for same-sex couples at the hearing at which his mother spoke, describing her horrible situation."

Martha thinks it's important to let people know they are part of a bigger situation than just their own issue. "They can start to see that there are some things that can happen," she said. "There's work to be done, and they can choose for themselves how to engage, how to get involved."

She said to me: "Your self-expression is writing a book."

And I had to agree, adding, "I never thought I would be doing that."

Karin jumped in and talked about how the hand of spirit was showing itself again in this immigration solution process, with Findhorn Press being part of the process by publishing this book.

"Thierry [Bogliolo, publisher of Findhorn Press] is completely behind this issue and this project," Karin added. "When we talked to him about this book, he didn't say, 'Wait until I think about it'; he said, 'YES!'" She added that something that normally takes months, even years to do, we were doing in weeks, to get it out as quickly as possible. Our book is a handbook of the issues, designed to empower people to help, to empower them to pass the law by sharing stories and resources.

Lin and Martha reminded us that people need to know that they have a story to tell. "One of our Love Exiles board members, a lawyer from New York, has to remind his friends that he has no way to live in his country with his husband." stated Lin. "Even in the gay community, our situation is not well known."

She continued: "The other thing [is], around the world it's a very little understood phenomenon."

Lin and Martha have testified and written and sat on panels and done lots of work for this issue and recommend that everyone takes any opportunity to share their story and share how you are excluded by U.S. immigration law.

"That's how you raise awareness," said Martha. "And how I ended up speaking at a Democratic Party LGBT caucus."

"We realized we had access to the Democratic Party through Democrats Abroad. Martha had become involved in Democrats Abroad, and through that, we were pushing resolutions and planks for the platform," Lin said.

"Democrats Abroad passed a resolution to pass UAFA, that two of our board members were instrumental in drawing up," said Martha. "And when they did the San Francisco resolution [to support UAFA], they used our text." Prior to that Leslie Bulbuk worked with then-Assemblymember Sally Lieber on a California resolution.

Martha's family helps with meetings and rallies and other events when Martha and Lin can't be there. "It's great!" they said, "because it's a family issue—it's not just us; it affects them, too." It's not just Martha being expelled from the country," shared Lin. "It's them losing her, too."

"That's right," agreed Martha. "That's our Torn Apart piece—being away from family here."

She has encouraged her mother to help, too, and credits her making a phone call to Senator Barbara Boxer's office in support of UAFA as the call that made the senator announce the next day that she supported UAFA. "Who knows if it was," said Martha, "but we say it was because on the day after Mom called, Senator Boxer announced her support." That enforces the power of one person to make a difference.

Lin and Martha attend international events such as the Outgames and organize workshops there. "In 2006," Lin shared, "we organized a really great workshop and had the whole room in tears, in Montreal." She related how she asked the audience at the beginning of the workshop if there were any love exiles in the room. No one raised a hand. At the end of the workshop, she asked the same question. Lots of hands went up, as people realized they were love exiles.

"They didn't realize that just because they didn't want to live in the United States, that didn't mean they weren't love exiles," said Lin.

"Sometimes people just don't let themselves admit it is an issue," said Martha.

In 2009, this couple was involved in a lot more workshops at the Outgames. "I did a workshop with corporations," Lin shared, "on LGBT networks in corporations, and Love Exiles, and other workshops."

Lin said that people don't want to recognize that they are structurally discriminated against. "So we bring the bad news that we are actually discriminated against. Then we bring the good news, that you can do something about it."

"My biggest message in that workshop," said Martha, "is *DO ASK, DO TELL*." She explained, "if you meet a same-sex couple where the men or women are from different countries, ask about their situation. You have no idea what they're dealing with, and people aren't necessarily going to talk about it."

She said: "They don't know how much support is out there. They're probably sick of their own situation. But ask, and if you are a binational couple, share."

She added: "When you introduce yourself to new colleagues, share why you are living there—or whatever opportunity you have, take it. No one is going to care about our issue unless we talk about it. I think that's our biggest thing. I think if people had an idea of how big this is, and what an impact it has on companies and families and communities, something would shift. It's starting to happen. It's not just a person here and a person there."

She felt strongly that "if the issue could be encapsulated so that people could see the numbers, people would really pause and say 'what?' You still have to keep saying it, sharing the story, so we get lots of 'whats?'" she said. "We have to tip it, to get the discussion going."

Lin reiterated how important writing is to get the message out. She has done a lot of work over the years with the United Nations. "I've got some good connections with Unifem," she shared. "Whenever I'm in New York and they're having a party, I go." But her friend at Unifem never introduces her as "my day job," Lin said with a smile. "She always introduces me to everybody as part of Love Exiles Foundation. Martha was invited to write an article for a publication for an international human rights organization based in The Netherlands. She talked about all the issues all over the world, and now *Signs: Journal of Women in Culture and Society* are publishing about it, too."

"The other thing that I've done around the issue," said Martha, "is I work for marriage equality. You know, the Netherlands was the first country to get marriage, and I thought, okay, it exists here; the sky's not going to fall. How do I get it out there, the reality, which is the future of many other countries, so that people can get their future now?"

"One thing we did was have a very famous Dutch photographer take our wedding pictures," Martha said. "We were wondering what you wear, how do you look, there were no role models out there for us." They decided on white, and they had their pictures taken. "She's not a wedding photographer," Martha continued. "So Lin had to ask her a lot of times, until she got a Yes. Lin has a relationship with her because she had photographed Lin's son Koen while he was still in the womb. We knew she would take different kinds of pictures."

Martha and Lin told her they wanted the photographs to be sold to the media and published. "When we got married, I wrote an article for *The Advocate* magazine," said Martha. "They bought a picture." Their wedding photos have been used in magazines, on the cover of a book, and in gallery and museum exhibitions.

They got how great it was that they had marriage equality in The Netherlands, and they wanted "to get it out there so people could start getting used to it—see what it looks like, see that it's just a normal thing," commented Martha.

That same year they came to America to visit. "We had our wedding album and marriage paperwork with us when we arrived at the border," Martha recalled. "The officer at immigration asked us the usual questions and put us through the regular routine. We told him, we are married, and showed our certificate. 'Is that a legal contract?' he asked"

"Sure," they said, and asked if he wanted to see their wedding pictures. He declined. "That was when we learned that you could get through immigration very quickly—you could accelerate things. He wanted us gone," Martha shared.

Gay and lesbian marriage is not such a mystery today, since Mayor Gavin Newsom opened the doors to it in San Francisco in 2004, and it continues to be in the news.

Lin, now self-employed, completed an MBA to better prepare for a possible career in the United States in the future. Martha works for a large Dutch bank. Love Exiles is a major part of their lives, too. They continue to lobby companies through it to improve LGBT issues and the immigration process for same-sex binational couples.

Martha shared her story of riding a bus across the United States with 50 marriage equality activists. "I did a radio show about it called Love Exile on the Road," she shared. "It's a great community and it was a great experience. We had different shirts we were supposed to wear every day. In Denver, we were wearing Out4Immigration shirts, the giant pink triangle with the statue of liberty coming out of it. "Before I went on the bus trip I came home to the Bay Area, and I had a little party before I got on the bus. It was for people who had donated money to help make my trip possible. We had Love Exiles t-shirts. My nephew was in fourth grade at the time. I was wearing an Out4Immigration shirt and he asked if he could have it.

"I knew I was getting another one, so I gave it to him," she continued. "A few days later, I realized I was in the right time zone to call my family, so I called my sister to chat."

Her sister told her that Martha's nephew had worn the shirt to school. His father wanted him to be ready to answer questions if he was asked about the shirt. When people asked about his shirt, he said that he was sending a message to his elected representatives. It gave him an opportunity to help. And that helps us all.

CHAPTER TWENTY

AURELIO AND ROI: WORKING ON A HUMANITARIAN PAROLE TO BE TOGETHER AGAIN IN AMERICA

In 2004, Roi Whaley and Aurelio Tolentino met online in a support group for people with HIV/AIDS. Aurelio, recently diagnosed, was unsure of where to get help. He was glad to turn to his computer, where he could immediately talk to other people dealing with the same situation and get the helpful listening and informed conversation he needed.

Roi, who had been diagnosed in 1986, saw Aurelio online one night and contacted him in the chat room. Aurelio, a nurse, was working in Long Beach, California. Online, Roi counseled and encouraged Aurelio about his diagnosis and the future.

Roi helped Aurelio with his questions and concerns about his health. He also helped Aurelio deal with an abusive relationship he was in. They supported each other and helped each other with hard situations. As they chatted online, their friendship became a relationship. Aurelio, from the Philippines, had come to the United States on a work visa and had a job which sponsored him for American employment.

"I knew there was something special about Aurelio," said Roi, "and I knew that I had to help him. It didn't matter if he fell in love with me. I just wanted to let him know that I would always be there for him," he said.

"And he gave me the courage to get out of that relationship and never look back," Aurelio added. "There was something about his voice that just told me I could trust him," he shared.

Roi, a Gulfport, Mississippi resident, has deep southern roots. He worked for nearly 20 years as a supervisor at a well-known casino in Gulfport and weathered the devastation of Hurricane Katrina. Today he is still there, where most of his family still lives. But one important part of the family, Aurelio, is gone. And he's gone because the United States government ripped Roi and Aurelio apart because of their relationship, which doesn't match U.S. immigration and marriage law definitions.

New wedding bands on the hands of Roi Whaley, left, and Aurelio Tolentino, right, on their wedding day in Canada. From their private collection. Used by permission.

In 2004, the same year Roi and Aurelio met online, Aurelio applied for a green card. At the required physical, his HIV-positive status was discovered, so his application was denied. Although the situation is different now because of a change by the Obama administration, at that time the United States maintained a ban on HIV-positive immigrants and travelers.

The news was devastating to Aurelio, who was fearful of returning to the Philippines, where he had been targeted and attacked because of his sexual orientation. So he applied for asylum to stay in the United States. But that didn't work either, because of timing. To successfully apply for asylum, a person must petition within one year of arriving at the U.S. border. Because Aurelio thought he would get a green card to work as a nurse in his adopted country, he did not apply for asylum until later than one year after his arrival. His green card application was denied and his asylum application was denied.

Because he had failed at both attempts, Immigration told Aurelio he would have to leave. But that meant leaving Roi, the person he loved. That was a terrible situation for them, but Aurelio did what he was asked to do. He even left America earlier than required and went to Canada, where his mother is a legal permanent resident.

While Aurelio tried to apply for asylum in Canada, Roi was diagnosed with terminal cancer in Mississippi. Aurelio's application for asylum in Canada was denied, which means he will have to return to the Philippines, where he knows he will not be safe.

Roi, 46, only wants Aurelio, 39, at his side while he fights cancer and deals with his HIV-positive status. "I just want to be together," Roi said, "but the American government won't let us." The couple estimates they have spent $40,000–$50,000 on attorneys and filing fees and they are still living in different countries.

When I interviewed Roi on the phone, he had just returned from a trip. He visited his oncologist in Seattle and then went to Vancouver to visit Aurelio and his mother. But because of his deteriorating health, Roi won't likely be able to visit Aurelio when he has to return to the Philippines. That meant their visit in Vancouver in September 2010 might have been their last time together.

"We have followed every rule and complied with every request Immigration has made," said Roi. "But now it seems like we are being punished for following the rules. We've been inseparable from the start," he added, "and now we can't be together."

Aurelio wants to be in America with Roi but can't. "If Aurelio gets residency in Canada, I will become Canadian," said Roi. "If Aurelio has to go back to the Philippines I will go with him, but we can't work there, so we won't have our medicine or health care," he stressed. "I can go there until the law changes in America and then hope we can be together back home where we want to be."

Today the couple is hoping that Congressional intervention in the form of a humanitarian parole will help them. Half a dozen newspaper interviews have told their plight. They need help from their Congressional Representative, Gene Taylor (D-MS-4), but when Roi first called to ask for help, a staff member told him the Congressman might not intervene.

"If there were ever a case where a member of Congress should feel compelled to intervene, this would seem to be it," said Immigration Equality's Steve Ralls. "Aurelio played by the rules. He left the country when he was instructed to, he was 110 percent honest on every piece of paperwork with immigration, and now he and his partner are being punished for that. People who demand that immigrants play by the rules need to be the first in line to say Aurelio should be back in this country."

A governmental remedy for Roi and Aurelio differs from that of Shirley Tan and Jay Mercado, Ralls explained. The two men are requesting that the Department of Homeland Security grant a humanitarian parole, in which Aurelio would be temporarily allowed back into the U.S. to care for Roi.

Humanitarian parole requests are more viable when supported by a congressional representative. In June, 2010, Massachusetts Senator John Kerry successfully lobbied for a Massachusetts gay couple, for example, to be reunited for one year after one partner's asylum request was denied, forcing him to return to Brazil.

With the help of Immigration Equality in Washington, D.C., Roi and Aurelio have again asked for Representative Taylor's help. After more publicity about Roi and Aurelio's situation, "Congressman Taylor reached out to Roi and said his office wanted to work with him to see how they can best help him," Steve Ralls of Immigration Equality said. "We hope that Congressman Taylor will work with Roi's attorney here at Immigration Equality to find a way for Aurelio to be here in this country with Roi. It is a very positive step forward."

The problem now is paperwork, Roi said. "They're [his attorneys at Immigration Equality] waiting for forms and waiting for fees and bank statements," he said. These documents are included in an application for humanitarian parole because the U.S. government requires an affidavit of support as part of the application. In the affidavit, the sponsor, in this case Roi, must attest that the arriving parolee, Aurelio, will not become a public charge and cost the government a dime.

But when I talked to Roi on the phone again, there was a new snag. His attorneys at Immigration Equality advised them that Aurelio must apply for a tourist visa, because an application for humanitarian parole is highly discretionary. The status is intended for individuals who have no other means of entering the United States and who have exhausted all other options. Even if the likelihood of Aurelio obtaining a tourist visa is very low, it is another hoop they are advised to jump through just so they can be together.

"Aurelio now has to apply for a tourist visa, which he has never had," said Roi. "That means he has to pay $140, which we know is a waste, because they won't give him a tourist visa," Roi said, openly exhausted and irritated. The complexity of U.S. immigration laws and the money they have already spent to be together never ceases to amaze and upset this loving and determined couple.

"The fee for the humanitarian parole they desperately want is another cost of more than $300," Roi shared. In spite of these challenges, he and Aurelio stay optimistic about their solution and about the new legislation introduced by Senators Menendez and Leahy in the Senate.

"Aurelio and I hope to be together for the holidays," Roi said, "together in America." But the paperwork alone could take five months or more. They might miss being together in Mississippi for Christmas 2010 and New Year's 2011. Their fate rests with the Department of Homeland Security. Their request for humanitarian parole would allow Aurelio to reenter the United States on a temporary basis to be with Roi as he battles his illness.

Aurelio, who has not been barred from returning to the United States, would in the long term prefer to find work in the United States as a nurse, a field with a high employment demand. However, for the moment, he is concentrating his efforts on reuniting with his husband and life partner through the only means available for them right now, which is entering on humanitarian parole.

Neither Roi and Aurelio or Immigration Equality is ready to give up the fight. "We want the public to help us," said Roi. "We need people to ask Congressman Taylor to intervene and get Homeland Security to grant Aurelio the humanitarian parole that will let me be with the man I love."

The couple has already been forced to live apart for three years while Immigration Equality tries to get them reunited. That's not normal for them; they have been inseparable since they got together in 2005. That's when Aurelio learned how to drive and put all his belongings into a Honda Civic and headed east to Mississippi to be with Roi.

At one point because Hurricane Katrina destroyed Roi's apartment, the couple shared a 30-foot Federal Emergency Management Agency (FEMA) trailer. Roi's casino was destroyed, too, so he worked in construction while Aurelio found a job at the local hospital.

"We were perfectly happy living in that little trailer," Roi laughed. "It was small, but it was home and we were together. So it didn't matter where we lived."

But when Aurelio had to leave the country in July 2007, their life became phone calls to each other instead of living together. At first Roi would go to Canada every two to three months for a visit. But then he started having headaches and was diagnosed with toxoplasmosis, a common opportunistic infection associated with AIDS. Then a CT scan in 2009 showed that Roi had a benign tumor in his brain and a metastasizing tumor in his lung. His cancer was stage III and had spread to his pancreas and adrenal glands. Because of his low T cell count, he couldn't be treated with chemotherapy.

He has a new oncologist now and is in good spirits, but the prognosis remains grim. "My doctor tells me I've had several miracles so far, but that I shouldn't expect it to continue that way," Roi says.

While he has serious health issues to deal with, Roi is more concerned about Aurelio's well-being in Canada or whether he has to go back to the Philippines. Though a federal judge in New Orleans denied Aurelio's asylum request, ruling that he had failed to show why he would be in danger if he returned to his home country, Aurelio's sister there has been harassed about her brother's HIV status.

"She was told he'd be beaten and castrated, with his penis fed to a dog, if he returned there," said Roi. "If he has to go back, he's going to die there. He's not going to have a job. He's not going to have access to the medication he needs to live. He's probably going to be shunned by everyone in his family," he sighed.

"And Roi is just not going to be able to make a trip to the Philippines in his condition," Aurelio said. "We're in fear of getting torn apart again," he said, "except this time it's going to be across oceans."

As mentioned earlier, Roi's House representative Congressman Taylor has indicated that he may be willing to help, as reported in September 2010, by the *Dallas Voice*. In an e-mail to Roi, Taylor's constituent liaison wrote that the congressman's office had reached out to Obama administration officials and that an immigration liaison was researching whether there was anything that could be done to help them. Taylor's press secretary, told *The Advocate* that his office was considering how it might be able to assist Roi and Aurelio.

Hopeful for a resolution that could bring them together, Roi waits for Aurelio in Mississippi after his visit to Canada, where the couple wed in 2010. "We kept postponing this marriage," Roi said. "But life is short. So we finally decided to go for it, to live in the moment."

[At the time of publication, Roi and Aurelio's situation looked like they would be together for the holidays. Steve Ralls from Immigration Equality told me that although they wouldn't know for sure until Aurelio was in the United States, "the prognosis is very good. His tourist visa should allow him entry into the U.S., and given that he has never overstayed in the past—and has, indeed, left at the request of Immigration—there's every reason to believe he'll be able to come to the U.S. for at least a few months to be with Roi." That's terrific news and a great thing for this couple to look forward to. But a woman, Miriam, posted this sad reminder on the *feministing.com* blog November 15, 2010: "It's only a tourist visa, it's not permanent, and these men are the lucky ones." While in final proofing of this book, I heard from Roi about their plan to be together for the holidays. They were concerned about a confusion on the visa, so though he was exhausted mentally and physically, he said, he was flying to Seattle to see his oncologist and then going to Canada to visit Aurelio.]

CHAPTER TWENTY-ONE

LESLIE AND MARTA:
ASYLUM MEANS WE CAN STAY TOGETHER IN AMERICA

Shirley Tan's bid for asylum failed because the threat to her life in the Philippines came from a relative (who shot Shirley and killed her mother and sister over an inheritance) instead of from the government. Aurelio Tolentino's bid for asylum failed because the judge he saw in New Orleans ruled he had not convinced him of danger he faced by being returned to the Philippines.

But other same-sex binational couples have managed to stay together in the U.S. by winning asylum for the non-U.S. partner. This information from the Immigration Equality website gives background information for the issue:

> In 1994 former Attorney General Janet Reno decided that a Board of Immigration Appeals (BIA) case, Matter of Toboso-Alfonso would be considered precedent, meaning that the BIA, Immigration Judges, and asylum officers had to follow its ruling in the future. Toboso-Alfonso recognized persecution based on sexual orientation as a potential ground upon which to apply for asylum, paving the way for many successful asylum applications on this ground thereafter. Since then there have also been some (though much fewer in number) non-precedential cases granting asylum based on transgender identity as well as some cases (also fewer in number) granting asylum based on HIV status.

The site goes on to explain aspects of life under asylum and gives links for more information, reminding asylees and others that:

> Winning asylum in the United States is a difficult and often stressful process. Asylum is a very good status to have in the United States, but it is important for asylees to understand certain limitations and responsibilities which come with the status. Links to information on procedures to follow, information on

Leslie Bulbuk, left and Marta Donayre, right. Photo from their private collection.
Used by permission.

how many asylum cases are allowed, travel restrictions and other aspects of
asylum are spelled out at
http://www.immigrationequality.org/template.php?pageid=163"

One lesbian couple together in America because of an asylum ruling for the non-American partner is Leslie Bulbuk and Marta Donayre. Their story mirrors the pioneering work they have done for other same-sex binational couples' immigration challenges through their organization Love Sees No Borders (now defunct).

Marta and Leslie met in 2000.

"We met on February 27," said Leslie.

"Our first date was on March 4th," remembered Marta.

These two activists were attending a training for the Lesbian Gay Bisexual Awareness Project (LGBAP), an organization that is no longer in existence. "Members of their speakers' bureau would go to high school, college, and community college classes that had requested speakers," said Leslie. "Our mission was to simply answer questions students had about the LGBT community." She added: "Marta and I met at an annual training meeting, where speakers were prepared to expect any possible scenario in the classroom, from hostility to getting asked questions that were quite personal in nature."

"We had our first date the week after we met," said Marta. That date led to others. They dated exclusively and became a couple in a short amount of time. The new couple faced a crisis the next year in April, when Marta lost her job from a layoff in the dotcom crash.

"We had been a couple for about a year at that time," said Leslie. "She had an H1B visa, and her employment visa was tied to having an employer. I had no ability to sponsor her for immigration. Marta had to either find a new job or leave the country."

Once Marta was laid off, the couple began the process of trying to find out how long she had before she had to leave the country. "We also began trying to find a new job, so I could hopefully remain in the United States," Marta said. "In speaking with numerous people, including human resources managers and attorneys, we found a wide variety of answers regarding how long I had before I had to find a new job or leave the country—they said anywhere between 10 days to a month to indefinitely."

Marta's situation was similar to that of Joey Ormana, whose story appeared earlier. When she heard the layoffs were coming at her company, she talked to her manager and was assured that she was fine—not in danger—because he was going to do all he could to keep her in the company. "And he did," Marta shared. At that time she started looking for jobs elsewhere for her friends who were in more danger of layoff than she was.

"But I was let go in the layoffs," recounted Marta. "I used the contacts and connections I had made for my coworkers for myself and I found a new job that kept me in the country."

For this lesbian couple, the best solution did turn out to be asylum. Marta is in the United States permanently now because her situation in her home country of Brazil would make life dangerous for her as a lesbian. "Marta was granted asylum in February 2002," said Leslie, "due to the fact that the situation in Brazil is dangerous for LGBT people."

Having an immigration issue "is an awful situation to find yourself in," Marta shared. The women, who have been out since the mid-1990s, pioneered work on the immigration challenge gay and lesbian binational couples face. When they faced their crisis, there was little information about the situation or solutions.

Said Marta: "We were affected by immigration problems because same-gender couples, no matter how long they've been together, or how serious their relationship is, or whether or not they are married, are not recognized as family by the American government."

"Due to the Defense of Marriage Act (DOMA)," added Leslie, "I was powerless in keeping Marta here in this country, despite our commitment to each other."

The couple, who are in their 40s, live in Sunnyvale in the San Francisco Bay Area, California. They have been activists for LGBT issues in general, and have been working on the immigration issue for more than a decade.

"Ours is the story of the struggle to overcome biased and discriminatory immigration laws that exclude same-gender couples," said Leslie. "Our nation is losing thousands of Americans, with work skills learned here in the U.S., to other nations that allow same-gender couples to immigrate there—most specifically to Canada," she added.

"The U.S. has a shortage of skilled workers, and yet is doing nothing about retaining those workers," said Marta, "therefore, our loss, in many cases, is another country's gain."

At the time Marta and Leslie were going through their issues with immigration, shared Leslie, "we began the process to immigrate to Canada." If they had gone, the United States would have lost two skilled workers.

Marta and Leslie started a group called Love Sees No Borders and became active and visible in the community. As a result of Marta's activism, an immigration lawyer shared some news with them that helped Marta's appeal for asylum. "Due to Marta's high profile and visibility," Leslie shared, "we found out she could be eligible to apply for asylum, since it would most certainly be dangerous for her to go back to Brazil and be as open as she was able to be in the United States."

Nearly a year elapsed between the time Marta lost her job and was granted asylum. During that time, the couple had begun the process to move to Canada, since under the Canadian system at the time both Marta and Leslie qualified to be accepted there.

"Since there was no way to predict whether Marta would win her asylum case," said Leslie, "we had to work on the Canada option as well, in order to ensure that we would be able to be together, no matter what."

In addition, they had two different companies working on Marta's work visa. "It felt very much like a game of chess, where all we focused on was the opponent's and our next moves," said Marta. By opponent, she meant the dire situation they were in. "We never disclosed the asylum case to anyone," Marta shared, "because we feared that the companies would withdraw their applications and we would be in a bad situation if the asylum claim got denied."

"There are no words to describe the stress at the time of not knowing whether Marta and I would be able to remain together in the United States or whether we would need to move to Canada," reiterated Leslie. "It was nearly a year of the most intense stress and emotion that I've ever experienced."

"Once I was granted asylum," said Marta, "it felt like the stress remained with us for a long time. We felt we could liken the experience to having post-traumatic stress disorder (PTSD."

"Both of us, especially Marta, have had our health impacted by this unpleasant journey," Leslie confirmed.

The outcome of the asylum case was positive. "I was granted asylum here in the U.S.," said Marta, "and now I have a green card."

Leslie and Marta did not just work on their own case; they tried to find a solution for other couples facing immigration challenges. As the founders of Love Sees No Borders, they were very active in raising public awareness of the immigration issue as it related to the LGBT community. "We put together town hall meetings. We wrote articles. We approached newspapers, magazines, TV, and radio stations to do stories on our situation and on the plight of same-sex binational couples," said Marta.

"We attended and presented at conferences," added Leslie, "and worked in coalition with immigrant organizations to raise awareness of our need for a solution in the unfair immigration system." They tried to raise awareness of immigrants in the LGBT movement. They spent their own money to fly to Washington, D.C. and to meetings and conferences in other parts of the country to lobby members of Congress about the Permanent Partners Immigration Act (PPIA), the precursor of Uniting American Families Act (UAFA).

"We did a hunger strike in San Francisco for immigrant rights," added Leslie. "And Marta was the only person representing a non-union LGBT organization on the 2003 Immigrant Workers Freedom Ride, where she spoke about the lack of recognition for immigration purposes to audiences and media throughout the nation."

"I also had to educate my fellow Freedom Riders," remembered Marta, who represented Love Sees No Borders and the National Center for Lesbian Rights during the trip.

The couple worked with former California State Assemblymember Sally Lieber to draft and pass the first-ever statewide legislative resolution in support of PPIA. Since then, other governmental bodies have issued similar resolutions. California's State Legislature passed another resolution in 2010, this one in support of today's version of PPIA, Uniting American Families Act.

One of the most critical parts of this story is this: "At the time, we were one of only several binational same-gender couples that were public about our immigration issue," said Leslie. "It was, and still is, a risk for couples to come out publicly due to the U.S. government sometimes refusing a visa to an immigrant who is coming here to visit his or her partner."

That's what Karin and I face. And others who have shared their story have faced this, or might do so in the future.

"They know we have no options to remain here legally," Leslie reminded us.

"Perhaps the thing we're most proud of from our time doing intense advocacy work," said Marta, "is the fact that we were to a large degree working in and with the immigrant rights and labor movement communities." She continued, "one of the interesting facts is that many people working in the immigrant community identify as LGBT, yet their advocacy is primarily for immigrant rights, and many are likely to check their LGBT-immigrant identity at the door."

"Many don't talk about their own orientation," said Leslie, "almost certainly due to frustration with the visible mainstream LGBT community's focus on only LGB (and sometimes T) (read: white) issues."

Through their work with Love Sees No Borders over the years, Leslie and Marta have written many letters to the newspaper. "We became a de facto public relations firm for the PPIA, now UAFA," shared Leslie. "Many of our press releases were carried verbatim in many local and LGBT papers around the nation." She added that they also received international coverage, especially in Brazil, since the media there was interested in a Brazilian being involved in that kind of visible effort.

Their efforts paid off. "We have two large, large boxes at home holding the press coverage we were able to garner," said Marta. "We were instrumental in getting the issue in the face of the immigrant and LGBT movements."

Leslie and Marta's notoriety helped the issue move forward. "At the time we started Love Sees No Borders," shared Leslie, "we were one of only a few couples in the United States who were public about their issues with immigration. We put ourselves out there in order for the LGBT movement to have faces to associate with the issue."

"That was fine for a while," said Marta, "but after we reached a certain level of visibility, it felt like there was a backlash against us. It was extremely painful," she added, "and to a certain extent, it still hurts me to this day."

While they were trying everything they could think of to help fix immigration problems for lesbian and gay binational couples, they met many elected officials. "We put together or participated in four or five meetings with Senator Dianne Feinstein's staff in order to try to get her to either introduce a Senate version of PPIA or to co-sponsor legislation that another legislator introduced," said Leslie.

"We also met with numerous other legislative staffers, for Senator Barbara Boxer and other, mostly California, legislators," added Marta. "We bugged Congresswoman Zoe Lofgren at every turn, and attended events where other legislators would be present in order to keep raising awareness," she remembered.

"We also met with staffers for Assemblymember Barbara Lee," said Leslie. "I also led a national effort to have Lesbian and Gay Immigration Rights Task Force (LGIRTF) chapter members contact members of Congress to ask them to co-sponsor PPIA, which resulted in the highest number of House co-sponsors for the bill in the 108th Congress in 2004, with 129 co-sponsors in the House and 12 in the Senate," she concluded. "The number of House co-sponsors has only recently exceeded that number in the 111th Congress in 2010," shared Marta.

When they were working on this issue, they contacted an impressive list of legislators, including Senators Dianne Feinstein and Barbara Boxer, Congressional Representatives Nancy Pelosi, Barbara Lee, Zoe Lofgren, Sheila Jackson Lee, and Ileana Ros-Lehtinen. They also visited the entire California Democratic Congressional delegation.

"During our Washington, D.C. visits," Marta added, "we would visit each Congressmember from California and give them a packet of information and/or thanks for their support. Leslie did most of this work."

"During one particular advocacy trip to Washington, when we were working with Nancy Buermeyer of the Raben Group [a Washington, D.C. lobbying organization that was assisting Immigration Equality with their PPIA efforts], we went to Senator Dianne Feinstein's constituent breakfast," said Leslie.

"At the end of the breakfast there was a question-and-answer period," Marta said, "and Leslie stood up and spoke about an issue that she, as a constituent, was facing. She introduced me and spoke about having a meeting with her staff later in the day, hoping that Senator Feinstein would eventually co-sponsor the legislation and asked for her support of PPIA, to which she replied that she was unaware of the legislation, even though we had previously met with her staff numerous times in San Francisco, Los Angeles and Washington, D.C to talk about it."

"To this day, as far as I'm aware, nobody associated with the LGBT immigration movement has ever personally met with Senator Feinstein, despite numerous requests made over the years," Leslie added.

Because they were working on this issue at a time that there wasn't much effort at a solution, Marta and Leslie knew and worked with other pioneers. "We worked closely alongside Immigration Equality, at the time known as the Lesbian and Gay Immigration Rights Task Force," said Marta, "and at one point we were the leaders of the San Francisco chapter."

"Out4Immigration was originally the San Francisco chapter of LGIRTF," said Leslie. "They split off from the national organization to do their own work, perhaps due to frustration that they felt that LGIRTF was doing too much work on things like asylum issues and not focusing exclusively on PPIA."

The other group working on this issue, Love Exiles, owes its existence to Leslie and Marta. "Martha and Lin have told us that we inspired them to start Love Exiles," shared Leslie. "We first met them at a pizza parlor in Oakland in Jack London Square after an event where Martha was talking about same-sex marriage, which had recently come to The Netherlands." Martha and Lin were one of the first lesbian couples to marry in The Netherlands.

Leslie and Marta have worked with other LGBT groups over the years and have asked for help from them. They worked with Human Rights Campaign (HRC) to try to get a Senate sponsor for a companion bill to PPIA. "We also pressured them to do it," said Leslie. "We pressured them to score the PPIA on their bi-annual Legislative Scorecard, which they had previously not done because adding it would lower the scores of many legislators who had 100 percent ratings."

Marta was able to attend a national strategy organized by HRC where she demanded, in no uncertain terms, that HRC push vigorously for PPIA, according to Leslie. She added "at the time, HRC was not making the legislation a top priority."

They worked with National Gay and Lesbian Task Force (NGLTF), where Marta was a panelist at an immigration workshop at their Creating Change conference.

They also worked with LGIRTF through their time of activism. Leslie presented at their first national conference in New York City, and later at a conference in Los Angeles. "We also worked with them to present together a national strategy group in order to help get a Senate sponsor of a companion bill to PPIA," shared Leslie.

The National Center for Lesbian Rights (NCLR) hired Marta after she got asylum and her green card. She was able to continue her work raising awareness of immigration issues as public education director for NCLR. They attended coalition meetings with Senator Feinstein's staff with Equality California (EQCA) and Marriage Equality California (MECA). They presented a workshop for Our Family Coalition.

"Under the leadership of Cathy Renna and the incredible work of Monica Taher, Gay and Lesbian Advocates Against Defamation (GLAAD) was the first organization to take us seriously," stressed Marta. "It was thanks to GLAAD that we were able to begin to get the word out," she added. GLAAD included information on their case and this issue to get the ball rolling.

Parents, Friends and Families of Lesbians and Gays (PFLAG) is another group with which Leslie and Marta worked. "We presented to local chapters and at a national conference held in Columbus, Ohio," Leslie shared. "We met with staff to ask them to help both support and raise awareness of PPIA."

They met with the leadership of the National Organization for Women (NOW) in Washington, D.C. and presented a workshop at NOW's national conference in Virginia. They also worked with the Mexican-American Legal Defense and Education Foundation (MALDEF), meeting with them in Washington, D.C. and asking them to support PPIA.

In addition, Marta and Leslie met with and asked for support from National Council of La Raza (NCLR) in Washington, D.C., as well as the Service Employees International Union (SEIU) and National Asian Pacific American Legal Consortium (NAPALC). The couple also joined a monthly meeting in Washington, D.C. of the

National Immigration Forum, where they asked for the Forum's support and that of the member organizations, and presented at a San Francisco chapter breakfast for Out and Equal and then made a presentation at their national conference in Minneapolis.

The ACLU of Northern California was another ally. The couple worked with the ACLU on Congressional visits. In San Francisco, they worked with the Log Cabin Republicans to present on immigration issues at a chapter meeting. And for a group called Affirmations and the Detroit-area LGBT community center, they collaborated on a Detroit-area immigration town hall meeting.

The International Gay and Lesbian Human Rights Campaign Commission (IGL-HRC), helped Marta gather information on the conditions in Brazil, which was key to the successful outcome of her asylum case.

"It is worth noting," shared Leslie, "that most of these trips were paid for with our own money." As a result, their finances dwindled. "When we first started Love Sees No Borders," she continued, "we thought we would have to leave for Canada." Since their goal at that time was to raise awareness, they didn't file for a 501c3 nonprofit organization. "All expenses of our work with Love Sees No Borders were financed by us," clarified Marta.

Today, the couple lives happily in Northern California. Besides their dog and bunny at home, Leslie has parents, cousins, aunts, and uncles in Michigan. Marta has a mother, brother and sister-in-law, nieces, and an aunt in Brazil, Ecuador and Panama.

Leslie is glad she didn't have to leave the United States. Her family, she feels, was in denial about the whole immigration issue. "My family had issues with me being a lesbian for a long time," she shared. "I think they were in denial about my immigration issues and didn't know how to deal with them." Her family attended the ACLU of Michigan/Affirmations/Love Sees No Borders immigration town hall the couple organized.

Marta's mother has been supportive, but she didn't know how to navigate the immigration issue at the time. In addition, she was abroad. "She offered to have us come over, but it would have reversed the problem, not solved it," said Marta. "On top of that, we would have had to move to Brazil, a very homophobic country."

Leslie is currently a senior field representative for California Assemblymember Paul Fong. Marta is unemployed, but trying to make ends meet by doing interpretation at asylum interviews and translating documents into English from Spanish and Portuguese and vice versa. She has also started a part-time travel agency, Sweetly Wild Adventures. She specializes in travel to Ecuador and South America, but can help people with their travel needs anywhere in the world.

Earlier, Leslie worked for SAP America and SAP Labs, doing technical software support. "It's worth mentioning that I was instrumental in pushing SAP to grant health insurance benefits to domestic partners," she said. "I then worked as a senior field representative for California Assemblymember Sally Lieber, who was also Speaker Pro Tem of the California State Assembly." It is important to note that Leslie joined Lieber's staff well after the assemblywoman successfully introduced and passed a statewide resolution in support of PPIA. She was on Lieber's District Office staff during the time that the statewide resolution in support of PPIA was introduced and passed.

Marta had worked for Ariba at the time of the layoffs, then she worked for a small computer hardware company, followed by her position as public education director for the National Center for Lesbian Rights. Because of the stress of the asylum case, and the whole process of the layoff and the possibility of deportation or moving to Canada, Marta took a year and a half off work because of health issues. When she had recuperated, she worked at The Health Trust, the Office of Assemblymember Sally Lieber, the AIDS Coalition of Silicon Valley and Coast Distribution Systems.

What happened to her and Marta served to direct Leslie's career path in a way. "After Marta got laid off, I became interested in issue advocacy and left my technical support job to try to find a job either in the nonprofit world or in the legislative field, because I wanted to make a difference," she shared.

Marta said: "Quite honestly, the overall health consequences of the stress from both the immigration issues and the ensuing activism left me with something like work-related PTSD. This didn't keep me from finding jobs in different areas, until a temporary position ended in 2008, immediately before the current economic slowdown."

"She has been officially unemployed since then," said Leslie. "She believes having NCLR and Love Sees No Borders on her resume has hurt many job prospects due to employers' biases."

Both of them have had support from their employers in their struggle to stay together in the United States. "My employer at the time understood the stresses of dealing with our immigration situation," shared Leslie, but couldn't provide a solution.

Marta said: "When this happened, I was hired at a software company that gave me all their support, and even a bit of latitude to do Love Sees No Borders work. "Naturally," she added, "the National Center for Lesbian Rights provided a wonderful platform for my work to continue. The hardware company I worked for wanted to sponsor my green card application," she went on, "and NCLR wanted to sponsor my work visa and my green card, so that I could leave the hardware company. Later, NCLR said they would sponsor my green card application. But since I received my request for asylum, they didn't need to do that."

The whole process took a toll on both their health.

"We are able to perform," Marta said. "We have to be very careful about how much we do, how we eat, and how much rest we get," Marta added, noting that "we can get sick and depleted very easily, and this can impact our job performance."

These women have learned a lot in the process and have a lot to say on gay and lesbian binational couples' immigration challenges. I want them to share with you as much as they shared with me, so here is more from each of them.

LESLIE: "I think one thing that is still stunning to me is that even with the increased visibility of this issue (often only brought up as it relates to marriage), so few people in our LGBT community know that immigration is an issue for LGBT people. I think people meet, fall in love, and then are stunned to find out they have no access to the immigration system straight binational couples take for granted once they, too, face the issue. Then the common reaction is for the American half of the couple to become active, irate that they, as American citizens in the land of the free, home of the brave, where all men are created equal, do not have the same 'rights' as others."

"Due to the dangers of coming out and identifying as a couple dealing with immigration issues, often the only person who feels able to speak out is the American, who is often not a person of color. Therefore, the most visible people in the LGBT immigrant rights movement are white, though the gay people mostly affected by immigration issues are often people of color, who face not only issues as members of binational same-gender couples but also issues related to obtaining visas, to being undocumented, to having faced abuse in their home countries, to having faced discrimination here due to their race or ethnicity."

"Those of us who are working on LGBT immigration issues need to embrace a more comprehensive understanding of what ALL the issues are that queer people face around immigration, not just issues related to being in a binational couple. I also believe that one of the greatest barriers to the movement to gain access to the immigration system is the fact that most Americans in binational same-sex couples do not feel that they are caught up in an immigration issue, but rather that they're excluded because they are a same-sex couple. That feeling leads to a disassociation from the broader immigrant rights movement and enables same-sex binational couples to feel that the issues other immigrants face are not their issues."

"Therefore," she continued, "couples generally only fight for their one issue, in a way that is oftentimes rightfully interpreted by the immigrant rights movement as elitist, and couples often feel that the issues undocumented immigrants face are not their own. Americans in this situation are often in denial that they're discriminated against in such a way, and as such are not able to associate their situation with that of other individuals or groups going through issues with immigration access."

"After spending years working on immigration issues, I can say that the worst thing couples can do is to only focus on their narrow issue, which in effect can negate the experience of the immigrant half of the couple, and prevents in a very real way the immigrant rights movement from advocating for our issues. The issue of same-gender immigration is at the intersection of two oppressions, the oppression of immigration and the oppression of being LGBT. In the past, the immigrant rights movement didn't want anything to do with the issues of queer people in the movement, and to this day, the vast majority of the gay rights movement has no clue how to address or even talk about issues related to the rights of immigrants and people of color."

She warns: "It is this chasm, more than any unwillingness of the immigrant rights movement to include us in immigration reform, that will hold us back."

MARTA: "This whole experience brought up many things regarding how our society treats people. We have to 'belong' to a country, a family, or a company. As individuals we don't count much. This is true regardless of who you are. In the case of LGBT people from other countries, you count in the LGBT movement ONLY IF you are in a relationship with an American."

"I've been told of people in binational couples criticizing Immigration Equality because they did too much work on asylum, and not enough for PPIA/UAFA in a 'me first' attitude that completely ignores the lives of people in danger. Thus, the fight for LGBT immigration equality is not really a fight for immigration reform, but a fight to give disenfranchised Americans their piece of the immigration benefits pie."

"In the immigrant rights community, on the other hand, the goal was to expand the definition of family as pertaining to same-sex couples. This is an important differentiator in my view because to the LGBT community I, as a foreigner, don't count unless I have an American by my side. Yet in the other, I do, but again, not as an individual but as someone who belongs within a group, aka 'family.'"

"Also, the same-sex marriage movement hijacked the issue of immigration as a talking point, while most of the large LGBT groups have done nothing to further advance UAFA. I still remember when the ACLU refused to support the bill because it didn't open a door for a lawsuit challenging DOMA."

"These experiences left me with a bitter taste in my mouth. I am very grateful to the committed group of people who continue to work for the passage of this legislation. I can no longer spend countless hours walking the halls of Congress wearing nice (read: uncomfortable) shoes. I hope that those who follow will do a much better job than we did and get this vital legislation passed."

"About the marriage movement, I would like to profusely thank Molly McKay and Davina Kotulski. Their leadership in the movement was always real, sincere, and tangible. They did not just use immigration as a talking point but did everything they could to promote the legislation, rather than asking us to wait for marriage, like most LGBT organizations do. The national organization's state-by-state strategy may be good for marriage, but it is not good for binational couples because it puts us on the back burner, which happens to be turned off. Immigration is a federal matter, not a state matter, so a state-by-state strategy does not benefit us."

"My last note is that I regret that the forming of an LGBT immigrant rights movement never came to be. At the time I was working on immigration issues, I spoke to many LGBT immigrants from various countries and backgrounds to start such a movement. Sadly, life got in our way, and it was not our turn to start it (although I still keep that door open). I still would like to see an organized LGBT immigrant rights movement that would advocate for ALL LGBT immigrants, not just the ones in a relationship with an American."

"I would like to thank Debanuj DasGupta for his unwavering commitment to the drafting of a unified LGBT immigrants platform. He lead this national effort which culminated in the distribution of the piece throughout the nation."

"Last, but certainly not least (quite the contrary), I would like to thank Kate Kendell and Shannon Minter. Their support of our work has been unabashedly strong. They enabled us to do important work. Kate, as my boss, empowered me to continue working on immigration justice and to participate in the Immigrant Workers Freedom Rides."

"Kate is the perfect example of the kind of leadership this country needs to advance the rights of ALL LGBT people, not just the ones facing ONE form of discrimination. She understands what justice IS, and it goes beyond equality for LGBT people who face only homophobia and not racism, sexism, discrimination based on immigration status and gender identity, etc."

"Shannon was involved in the writing of PPIA/UAFA. Although he did not draft the bill, he was instrumental in editing the legislation so that it is as perfect as it can be. This was a group effort, but somehow Shannon's and NCLR's involvement is often overlooked, and I would like to give them the props they deserve."

Karin and I thank Marta and Leslie for all their work and their support. We are lucky to know them and have them in our lives.

CHAPTER TWENTY-TWO

CARMEN AND ASTER: ONLY HIS WORK VISA KEEPS US TOGETHER IN AMERICA

Our trip to Washington, D.C., in June 2009 included meeting a won-
derful couple with our same challenge—sort of. We met Carmen at the
Senate Judiciary Committee hearing and his partner Aster at dinner that
evening. Carmen made us feel so welcome in a city we had never visited.
At a time when Karin and I were still feeling jangled from being sepa-
rated for so long, then together again but in Canada for several weeks,
it was very sweet to have Carmen call us and say, "Let's get together for
dinner tonight. We'll come and pick you up at your hotel." We will never
forget such friendliness.

Carmen and Aster's story has all the elements of gay or lesbian binational couples who are separated or have to leave America, except for their safety net: Aster's job. And because of that safety net, no full names are used, "obviously for fear of reprisal, for fear of losing the ability to be together," said Carmen.

"I met Aster in 1996," said Carmen. "He had come here from a South American country to work for its government as a procurement officer. We met when he had been here for about six months."

Karin and I remember them sharing this story at that dinner. Carmen and Aster both told it with mixed glee and a sort of embarrassment. The background details, which won't be shared here, were hysterical.

"We met on the street," Carmen continued. "That is, I saw him every day on my walk to work. He was always coming opposite me, and I saw him in many different places on my walk through the neighborhoods of D.C."

"After three months of passing each day and saying hi, we both stopped one day," said Aster. "Carmen asked me to dinner, and I handed him a postcard I had written asking him to coffee." Karin and I cracked up at that.

"His English was not very good," said Carmen with a smile. "He had someone he works with write the card for him." Aster also smiled at the memory.

Aster, left, and Carmen, right. Photo by Michael Du Bois.
From their private collection. Used by permission.

"We went to dinner that night and fell in love!" remembered Carmen. "We have been inseparable since. People hear our names and think we are a lesbian couple," he laughed. "Well, we might as well be, as we moved in together only a few weeks after we met," he said. Karin and I smile at that—the lesbian U-Haul on the second date joke has been around forever.

Because Aster is in the United States on a work visa, that doesn't make the couple completely safe, or their relationship in America guaranteed, as we have seen with other couples in several other stories.

"For 15 years, we have lived with the constant threat of his having to leave the country," said Carmen.

"My visa is renewed every two years," said Aster. "There are constant rumors coming out of my country that, for various reasons, my agency will close its doors here in D.C., either merging with other agencies or just going back there to do the work by internet that used to require that we be here in the U.S."

Sadly, Carmen and Aster say, "There is the constant fear that our lives will be torn apart." Aster says, "Every two years we wonder if this is the year."

"We are also kept from pursuing our dreams in life," adds Carmen, "because as long as Aster is here, he is required to keep his job and we are therefore required to live in D.C. We both would like to explore other options in our lives. We love the city, but we have so many dreams for places we want to live and businesses we want to have."

"We are not able to pursue them because of my work visa," said Aster. "We want to open a café in a resort town or a small coffee shop/gallery in a small progressive town," shared Carmen. "Dreams deferred," he added sadly. They'd like to live in California; Provincetown, Rhode Island; or Florida, for example.

While many would say that Carmen and Aster have it easy compared to so many other binational couples, not being in charge of your lives is a hard thing to deal with. It's location, it's opportunity, it's fluidity, it's many restrictions that other same-sex couples don't have to deal with in America. And it's also not being in charge of your own lives—the fear that one day something will change your lives forever.

Here's just one example of how their situation affects the life they want to share: "When we were first together and both in our early 30s," said Carmen, "we decided that we wanted to start a family. We undertook an in-depth investigation into how we might do it. We pursued many avenues that we thought would lead us to adoption."

"But it turned out that, because of my precarious situation in the United States, and because our relationship was not recognized by the federal government, that adopting and then providing legal security and safety for a family would be beyond our means," continued Aster.

"We also worried that, should Aster have to leave, our family would be torn apart," said Carmen. "We decided, after a long journey, that we should hold off having a family until the United States would recognize our relationship. At that time we were in the Clinton era," he continued. "We had foolish hopes that our country was moving swiftly toward the equal rights we would need and that we deserved."

"At the time, I was the local chapter chair for Immigration Equality (then called Lesbian and Gay Immigration Rights Task Force, or LGIRTF)," shared Carmen. "We had worked with Congress to introduce a bill, then called the Permanent Partners Immigration Act (PPIA). We felt that it would not be long before I would be able to sponsor Aster for a green card, just as so many of our heterosexual friends here had done."

But as you have read in this book and in the media, that bill (now called Uniting American Families Act, or UAFA) has inched along since 2000. It had still not reached the floor for a vote in Congress—much less passed—as I write these words in November 2010.

By late October 2010, UAFA had more co-sponsors than ever before in its history. Two other bills were introduced in Congress which included gay and lesbian binational couples in comprehensive immigration reform efforts. But comprehensive immigration reform had not been completed by the time I finished this book.

"The saying by Dr. Martin Luther King, Jr., is true," Carmen declared, "that rights delayed are rights denied. We now feel too old to have a family. We regret that we were essentially denied our ability to have a family by the prohibitive and expensive legal pathways we would have to pursue. At the time we wanted to be dads," he said sadly, "all of our friends and extended family were pursuing being parents."

Aster added, "We also sit here, stagnant, our dreams fading away, as year after year goes by."

"We are still denied the rights that everyone around us has," said Carmen, "to go where we want, pursue our dreams, and live free lives."

It's hard to exactly or completely describe how this long battle has taken its toll on this couple. "We have had to battle depression and hopelessness and even jealousy of others because of the freedoms we are denied," shared Carmen. "We have had hopes, only to have them dashed. I have also had to battle hatred for those who lead the charges against us. I can't stand the feelings of hurt and anger this has caused, and I don't like being a person who is hateful. It's a daily battle for me to overcome these things."

Aster added: "In life there are always disappointments and regrets for the things not chosen, or the paths that were not taken, for factors that are out of our control."

Carmen continued: "There is something insidious about the fact that all of our limits have been imposed on us by our fellow citizens, simply because we are gay. There is something very painful about the hatred that so many in this country spew each day at gay people, as they go forward living in freedom. We are lucky that we have been able to keep these hideous outside pressures from destroying our relationship. We have a strong love for each other that has stood the tests of these pressures, and we consider ourselves very fortunate to have each other. I could not imagine my life without Aster."

Carmen has tried to keep abreast of requirements and changes that affect them about their binational situation. "In the early years, I studied immigration law on my own," he shared. "We went to lawyer after lawyer based on recommendations, only to find that no one could help us. I routinely corrected these lawyers on immigration law, and after awhile we realized that not only were we not going to be able to get Aster a green card, we seemed to understand the law better than every lawyer we saw."

"At some point I found out about LGIRTF," he said, "and I found that there was a local chapter. I was so excited to hear about this group of activists who I was sure would be able to secure our rights. I joined and soon became chair of our group, holding the meetings in my condo building's meeting room."

"We made great headway in that time," Carmen remembered, "and as 2000 approached, Al Gore indicated that he would support immigration rights for same-sex couples. I was elated and naive. I thought it might only be a matter of a couple of years before Aster and I could have our freedom."

"When George Bush won," said Aster, "we saw the writing on the wall."

Carmen added: "I also became burned out by the work with LGIRTF. I was taking everything too personally, and the stress was taking a huge toll on me. When Bush won I went into a deep depression, and I turned over the reins of the local chapter to someone else and essentially gave up. I was unable to deal with how slow things were moving. I'm not a very good activist!"

But Carmen and Aster try to stay upbeat. They want to be together. They want to be in America together. They know they don't suffer nearly as much as those who are torn apart and cannot be together. "My heart is sick for all who suffer this horrifying indignity," Carmen said. Aster agreed.

"But my heart is also sick about the limitations that have been placed on our lives," said Carmen, "and by the constant struggle to be seen as equal."

It's hard for them to keep things on an even keel when even Carmen and Aster's gay friends throughout the years have not understood what they face. "People say 'you have good lives, why complain?' It's so hard to explain," Carmen said.

He elaborated: "I think that lots of people, maybe most people, accept their lives and don't steer the course as much as let life happen to them. I have always been very active about pursuing my dreams and by making things happen in my life. I always felt very empowered about the freedoms and the choices I had in life."

Carmen and Aster's reality is this: "Our choices have been taken from us. We have had to contend with the fact that our simple love for another person has meant the almost entire annihilation of our sense of direction and hope and our gusto for life. Everywhere we turn we find walls placed before us. So we have had a steady bitter decline in our dream lives as we sit waiting for our rights."

That's very powerful and very sad. Karin and I feel their pain. We wonder what it would be like to *have* to stay in one place, rather than *choose* to stay in one place.

Aster shared more on the problems they face—specifically regarding their flights out of the country to see his family: "Every time we return, we watch other families fill out their common forms and walk off the flights and go through the American lines for immigration," he said.

Carmen chimed in. "But Aster must go to his own line and must not let others know that he is with his husband, the love of his life. He goes in the long immigrants' line. I move through immigration and go forward to baggage claim and begin the long, fearful wait for my husband. Always, I wait in fear until he finally comes through those doors."

When Carmen sees Aster come through the doors, he said he feels a strange mix of relief and intense anger that they are put through this every single time, while other couples and families end their vacations with relaxed looks on their faces.

Carmen shared a horrible memory: "One time, in Miami, I found myself in baggage, and Aster did not appear. I began to panic, as time went by and he did not walk through those doors. I held his bags with mine and began to imagine what might be happening to him."

Carmen said he began to imagine that he might be losing Aster at that very minute. "I couldn't stop the tears from flowing, he said. "I sat down and tried to calm myself. More and more time went by, and I was a mess when he finally came through the doors."

Aster had had a minor delay, but Carmen had envisioned the end of his world as he knew it. "I hate to leave the country," Carmen stated, "as every return to my home ends with fear and anger."

Carmen, 46, has been active about this same-sex binational couples issue for years. Out since he was 27, he has written many letters to the editor, has worked with the organization Lesbian and Gay Immigration Rights Task Force for years, and has shared his and Aster's story with many people. "I get a sense sometimes that people are tired of hearing us talk about this, but I have to do what I can to let people know this is happening—not just our story but the stories of those families that have been torn apart by this," he said.

He cannot bring his story to his Congressional representatives, though, because "as DC residents," he explained, "we suffer the additional problem of not having a representative with any power in Congress." Foreign national Aster, 49, cannot advocate for his situation. He must keep his employment circumspect and be certain to comply with all requirements. And, he has to hope his work visa is renewed every two years.

The challenges and disappointments this couple faces may not appear that important to others, they think, "especially those who are torn apart and forced to live separately or who have had to leave their home because they cannot be together in America," said Carmen.

"But I think we represent the other face of this issue," said Aster. "We are the story of those who are able to remain together but who do it at the expense of freedom."

Carmen agreed, and added: "Yes, and who do it at the expense of freedom and then live with fear, anxiety, and a loss of our dreams and a slow destruction of our enthusiasm for living over many long years."

Carmen's extended family in Maryland has been active in helping through the years. "They understand and they support us," he shared. "Some have been active about writing to their representatives in Congress," he added. They have participated in marches, written letters, educated others via Facebook, and done local activism to help Carmen and Aster.

As an employee of a foreign government in the United States, Aster, who is openly gay at work, is not able to get assistance from his country or his family to obtain permanent U.S. residency.

Carmen works as a freelance graphic designer. He doesn't have to jump through the same hoops about work, so he is able to be more open and active about their situation and works to resolve the challenge.

A long life together has not turned out the way Carmen and Aster had hoped and planned, but they have not been torn apart by immigration laws that can destroy partnerships. So far, Aster's work visa keeps them in America together.

If his visa is not renewed, or when he chooses to retire, he must return to his country. "In essence, we will be going to a strange place," Aster says with a smile, "because I have lived here for 15 years. My life is here. My family is here. To go back and try to start a life, get a job at my age, it would be a terrifying prospect."

"But we would go," stresses Carmen. "I won't let my government tear us apart. Aster's country will welcome me with open arms. They are much more progressive about recognizing same-sex partners (or spouses in our case, since we got married in March 2010) for immigration."

"If I leave this country, Carmen is going with me, for sure," echoed Aster. "But this would also be terrible for him. He is so close to his family and he has built a life here—to tear him away from his life would be terribly unfair. It would not be a happy choice for either of us."

[A sad update about Carmen and Aster's story is this: Aster returned to his home country to be with his ailing mother. She died in late November. Because he is safely documented, travel is not an issue, but Carmen had to stay in the U.S. and the men could not be together at that sad time.]

MICKEY AND AMOS:
HIS GREEN CARD KEEPS US
TOGETHER IN AMERICA AND LETS
HIM TRAVEL WHEN NEEDED

Mickey and Amos Lim have been involved with each other since they started out as pen pals April 21, 1995, in the days before Yahoo groups and general internet social networking.

"There was the USENET," Mickey said, "and we were both reading and posting to a gay political list that had a thread that went something like 'Why are there no out gay role models'... " He laughed and remembered that "there was some bashing of Tom Cruise and others like him," but said "I responded that there were the body builders, Bob Paris and Rod Jackson."

Amos replied to him, asking "if it was indeed true," Mickey said. Because Amos was in Singapore and it was a very media-censored country, he didn't have access to much. "I sent him a copy of the book *Straight from the Heart, A Love Story*," shared Mickey.

"Our friendship grew from there," said Amos. "Over the course of the next two and a half years, we became close friends and confidants with each other."

"When I went to Singapore on vacation in November 1997," said Mickey, "I met him, and within minutes, we knew what others had long suspected—that we had indeed fallen in love."

"It took a few more days before we could admit it to each other," he shared, "and on my birthday, November 13, we shared a cup of tea and promised to try and make this work between us, completely unaware of the difficulty ahead," he said ruefully.

"In the next two years I visited the United States twice looking for a job," said Amos, "and Mickey came to Singapore to visit me." Finally, Amos was able to come to the United States on a student visa to get his MBA. After he completed it, he was able to stay for an additional year as optional practical training. "The company I worked for promised to sponsor me for a work visa and possibly a green card after that," shared Amos. "But halfway through the process, 9/11 happened and all bets were off."

Photo of Amos, left, and Mickey, right, Lim from their private collection.
Used by permission.

For the next several months, Mickey studied for and passed his pharmacy board exams in Vancouver, Canada. "We were preparing to emigrate to Canada," Mickey remembered. "A week after returning from the last of my exams," he said, "our San Francisco flat caught fire, and we had nothing of substance to move to Canada."

"As fate would have it," shared Mickey, "I had made a professional contact some months prior. They wanted a meeting to pick my brain and possibly offer me a job with a new, growing company."

"He told them he would meet with them," said Amos, "but as far as a job was concerned, he told them he was leaving the country because I had been unable to find a job that would sponsor my visa."

That's when the couple got lucky. "They asked for Amos' resumé," said Mickey, "because they were a growing company." Eventually the firm offered both Amos and Mickey jobs, a week before Amos' visa was to expire. A few years after that, Amos secured his green card.

"A few months after that," shared Mickey, "we started our adoption paperwork, and now we have a beautiful three-year-old little girl."

Amos, 40, and Mickey, 46, are together in the United States because Amos has his green card. That makes him a permanent resident alien. "Our relationship has endured so much," smiled Mickey, "that the little things that we argue about are… insignificant."

They are really together now, safe with Amos' status and able to have a family. "When we have to be apart," said Mickey, "we have constant phone calls and e-mails."

In the history of their journey to their current status, Amos and Mickey put in time with Lesbian and Gay Immigration (LGIRTF), today known as Immigration Equality. "I was chapter coordinator," said Mickey, "and then we started the nonprofit group Out4Immigration," he said.

"Only through action could I feel empowered while in a situation where I had essentially NO power," said Mickey. "Amos worked with these groups and with Chinese for Affirmative Action (CAA). He was also the project director for the San Francisco Immigrant Rights Summit.

Mickey arrived in San Francisco after living in Bakersfield. That's where he was when he started corresponding with Amos in 1995. "I had moved to San Francisco before we met in Singapore," Mickey said. "We've lived here together since Amos came to America in 1999." That's where the family wants to continue to live.

Mickey recalls that he was "rudely shocked to discover that I could not sponsor my partner for immigration, but a company could." He feels that his rights as an American have been denied him. For almost two years, and at considerable expense, Amos and Mickey were kept physically apart while trying to stay together. "Even when we were able to be together," said Mickey, "stability and certainty were denied us, and the threat always loomed that we could be ripped apart from our home, our work and our support network."

"The process to stay together was expensive and exhausting," agreed Amos. His permanent resident alien status has served him well, since he had to return to Singapore during the time I was interviewing them to deal with his father's health crisis and help his mother with paperwork and other things. "It is reassuring to know that I can fly without problems and can return home to San Francisco," he shared, relieved.

Amos and Mickey devote much of their time to working on the immigration problems same-sex binational couples face. They are basically safe from the problems, but they know the problems and they want to help others.

"No one should have to suffer the pain and fear that we endured," said Mickey.

Adds Amos: "As a matter of simple fairness, no one should be denied rights and privileges that are otherwise freely available to others, simply because they are gay or lesbian."

Though they have a good outcome, finally, they were separated by time and distance before they were finally united. And they have fought to remain together.

"We were lucky," recounted Amos. "But we've been tormented by the stories from so many people we've gotten to know where it has NOT worked out. It inspires us to continue to fight for those who have had to leave and for those who cannot speak for themselves."

Amos and Mickey want and need to stay in the United States.

"My professional life does not translate to Singapore," shared Mickey. "Canada was our plan B, but we didn't have to go through with that."

Their work on this issue involves speaking to groups and lobbying elected officials.

"We have been at many venues," said Mickey. "We have made trips to Washington, D.C. and Amos has traveled to Texas and Arizona." They do this to create greater public awareness for the issue. They have written letters to the newspaper, spoken to legislators, and been to meetings. "We've contacted all of the federal legislators," Mickey said.

"Senator Feinstein still has a deaf ear," said Mickey, "but I still have hope." He added that this year UAFA enjoys more co-sponsors than any other immigration proposal.

They have also contacted the main groups working on this issue: Immigration Equality, Love Exiles, and, of course, their own group, Out4Immigration. In addition, they have worked with or spoken to many other groups such as churches, unions, businesses, and employee groups.

Today Mickey works at Los Portales Pharmacy. He passed up many jobs that would have led to an upper-level management position because "I could not in good faith take a position when I could easily be forced to leave the country to stay with Amos with only 10 days' notice," he said. Amos does nonprofit work these days while he raises their daughter.

Employers have been mostly sympathetic, Mickey said. "Except for one, all have been unable to do anything about our situation, though," he shared. One employer hired both of them and made it possible for Amos to get his green card. "Amos actually worked for them years longer than I did," stated Mickey.

"As much as I didn't feel it would be professional to accept managerial employment, when my stability was in doubt, we didn't even feel that we could get a pet for fear of having to abandon it," Mickey recalled.

"To the extreme, we always knew that we wanted children, but without stability we didn't want to start a family until we could provide a stable home. As a result, we never had our daughter until I was in my mid-40s. To be 46 and the father of a three-year-old is exhausting," noted Mickey wryly.

Despite Mickey's concerns, Karin and I have seen their daughter. She is bright, articulate, and adorable—with two terrific fathers.

[A sad update to Amos and Mickey's story is the death of Amos' father as this book went to print. The Lim family flew to Singapore again, and once again Amos was glad to have his green card so he would not have entry problems returning to the United States.]

CHAPTER TWENTY-FOUR

MATT AND MICHAEL: HIS VISA KEEPS US TOGETHER IN AMERICA, BUT HE CAN'T TRAVEL HOME YET

Matt Hale and Michael Retter met online in June 2006. That's a pretty common beginning to many couples' lives these days. But for these men, it wasn't as simple as finding someone in the same town, or even the same state; they were in two different countries.

"We started talking online," recalled Michael, "and later met while I was on a business trip to England in August 2006." Over the next year, they visited one another three times, and when Matt finished his Ph.D., he got a job as a postdoctoral researcher at Purdue University, where he studies and teaches genetics.

"I was writing my Ph.D. thesis whilst in the United Kingdom," explained Matt. "I moved to the United States in September 2007 for work, and we moved in together the following month."

"We've been together ever since," Michael said with a smile.

Matt had been at Sheffield University for his doctoral work. He was employed at Purdue University when he shared his story with me. Michael relocated from Illinois to be in Indiana with Matt, where Matt is a postdoctoral researcher. He uses genetic techniques to answer questions about the ecology and evolution of fish, specifically steelhead and rainbow trout found in the Pacific Northwest. He's looking at the genetic basis of migration and trying to find the region of the genome that allows a steelhead trout to migrate into the Pacific for several years but does not induce the same behavior in resident rainbow trout. Matt has a ticking clock, but not the same one as Karin or others you have read about. He has a J-1 visa, which allows him to work temporarily in the United States. This non-immigrant visa is issued by the United States to exchange visitors participating in programs that promote cultural exchange, especially to those who obtain medical or business training. Matt's J-1 visa expires September 2012, "when my current employment contract is set to expire," he shared. That visa keeps the men together in the United States until it expires.

Matt Hale, left, and Michael Retter, right, from their private collection.
Used by permission.

Their immigration status has yet to be a problem, but it is possible, even probable, that it will be. Said Matt: "After 2012, I will have to go home to the United Kingdom for a period of time, before reapplying for a new visa if I get a job." By September 2012, Matt will have been in the United States for five years—the maximum time allowed on his visa.

The alphabet soup of Matt's visa is this: His extended DS-2019, or Certificate of Eligibility for Exchange Visitor (J-1 visa) Status, is valid until September 2012, but his actual J-1 visa, which allows him to enter the United States freely, expired in September 2008. He can't travel outside the U.S. except Canada and Mexico without a new visa.

Matt has family in the United Kingdom, including his parents, two siblings, a sister-in-law, three cousins, an aunt, and an uncle. But because of his J-1 visa restriction, he can't travel to visit family while he is in America at this job. "Family has come to see us twice," he said. "And we do lots of phone calls on Skype!"

But Matt worries that if an emergency comes up with his family back in England, he won't be able to be there with them. "This is troubling," he said. "Going back to the United Kingdom not only would cost the obvious air fees, which would have to be two one-way tickets as obtaining the visa could take a while, but it would cost an additional $500–$600. [Nonimmigrant visa application processing fees increased on June 4, 2010 and are tiered. Immigrant visa application processing fees and other immigrant visa services fees changed on July 13, 2010, and immigrant visa application processing fees are tiered. [For current details go to *http://travel.state.gov/visa/fees/fees_1341.html*]

"But the most scary scenario is that they could refuse me a new J-1 visa," stressed Matt. "So I could be in a situation where I have a good-paying job but cannot get back into the country."

Michael has the drill down on the visa and work permit world. He shared this about Matt's situation: "Visas (the right to enter the United States) and work permits (the right to remain in and work in the country) are handled by two different cabinet offices: visas by the State Department and work permits by the Office of Homeland Security.

"J-1 visas are only offered for a length of time equal to that which the university says it can guarantee funding," he went on. "In Matt's case, this was only one year at a time. While work permits can be easily renewed by mail from within the United States, visas cannot. To get a new visa, he would have to fly home, set up an appointment with the U.S. Embassy in London, apply for another visa—which costs about $600—and hope that it goes through.

"It may be rejected without cause," he added.

If Matt did this, it would cost more than $3,000 in lost wages, fees, lodging, and plane tickets. He added, "the new visa would be valid, at most, for 12 months."

Michael echoed Matt's take on the process: "We find that almost no one knows that one must leave the country to get a new visa. It's a ridiculous process, and now having learned about it, I see why no one would ever want to enter this country legally when he can just walk across the border from Mexico," he fumed.

"And of course, even if we did get married in Massachusetts or Iowa, the Defense of Marriage Act (DOMA) mandates that the federal government, who controls immigration, cannot recognize our marriage," Michael added. He summarized Matt's situation as this: "As a consequence of this, Matt has not been home to see his family and friends in more than three years. When he has been here for five years he must leave, and he cannot reenter the country on a J-1 visa for a couple years—I don't remember exactly how many."

We don't know what we'll do then," said Michael. "I'll probably have to move to the United Kingdom."

Matt was unaware of all this before he came to the United States, "but I don't think it would have changed my decision to come," he said. "Perhaps I would have been forthright in seeking a different visa status, such as an H1B," he shared. [H-1B work-authorization is strictly limited to employment by the sponsoring employer. This nonimmigrant visa allows U.S. employers to temporarily employ foreign workers in specialty occupations, including the sciences.] "Although I am happy living in the United States, I would like to go home, especially at Christmas, as I miss my friends and family immensely," he said, sadly.

Matt has a different perspective on the situation from some same-sex partners interviewed here, based on his expertise and country of origin. "Fortunately, being British, I am not subject to the two-year home residency condition," he said, "so starting in 2011 I will begin looking for a tenure track faculty position in the United States." [When an alien is on a J-1 visa, most countries require a two-year residency in the person's home country once the J-1 has expired. There are some countries that are exempt, including the UK.] "Although we have not had to deal with living apart," he continued, "I fear the time is coming. With jobs being tough to find, it is highly likely I'm going to have to spend some time in the United Kingdom."

At the time of our interview, Matt and Michael were living in West Lafayette, Indiana. "We would like to live on the West Coast or in Chicago," Matt confided.

Michael added: "Or Canada, where we have full and equal rights."

Matt and Michael (both 30) came out at an early age, Matt at 17 and Michael at 22. They were comfortable being out and didn't experience any issues in adult life until their same-sex binational couple status became a problem to deal with.

"Our story is important because, as a same-sex couple, there's nothing we can do to secure my presence in the United States," Matt declared. He stressed how important it is that UAFA or RFA or Comprehensive Immigration Act of 2010 or other legislation be passed, "so couples who love each other are not physically separated by immigration law."

Because they know that something will happen in the future, that they will likely be separated because of U.S. immigration law, "the fear that one day that will happen hangs over us almost all the time," said Matt, frowning. He also feels the pressure to find a job that will sponsor him to stay in the United States.

Both Matt and Michael want to be in the United States together. "Very much so!" stated Matt.

So have they given up on being together in the United States? I asked. "Absolutely not!" was Matt's answer.

Passing immigration law reform is "the only decent and humane thing to do," said Michael. "Love is love." He is frustrated at how discriminatory DOMA is and how ridiculous U.S. immigration law is. "We're gay and our relationship is not recognized by the U.S. State Department," he said.

"If Matt cannot get green card status in the United States, either through a permanent job or repeal of DOMA, I will have to move to the United Kingdom or to Canada to remain with him," said Michael. Michael has contacted his federal legislators, something Matt cannot do. "I have contacted Senators Richard Lugar (R-IN), Evan Bayh (D-IN), Richard J. Durbin (D-IL), and Roland W. Burris (D-IL)," shared Michael, but he said the outcome was "nothing." Michael leads birding tours in the Americas for Tropical Birding and is also self-employed as a writer. The portable nature of his jobs permitted him to continue his work after he relocated to Indiana, which helped the couple logistically. "My bosses at Tropical Birding have been very supportive," said Michael, "and have offered to help our situation if they can, but there's only so much an Ecuador-based company can do with regard to U.S. immigration status. And I'm not sure that flying me from the United Kingdom back to the Americas to lead tours is economically feasible." He has lots of family in Illinois, where he is from. He says they are very supportive of his relationship with Matt and help by "voting for Democrats" and have hope their situation will be resolved. Karin and I do, too. We may all four be in the United Kingdom before long.

■

CHAPTER TWENTY-FIVE

ERWIN AND JOHN:
RACE AGAINST TIME—LEGISLATION
OR NEW VISA

Erwin de Leon and John Beddingfield are living together in America on borrowed time, so to speak, since Erwin, a Filipino, is here on a student visa, which runs out in 2011. He can stay an additional year for optional practical training, policy research for a think tank in Washington, D.C., but by 2012 he will have to leave the United States—unless he chooses an illegal option or is able to qualify for a different visa.

He is faced with a race for time with big implications: Which will come first? UAFA or another proposed legislation, or the end of his student visa and year of optional practical training?

"Passage of UAFA before my visa runs out would make things less complicated," shared Erwin. "But considering the current political climate, I doubt that anything will pass soon. Moreover, I cannot help but think that even if an immigration bill were put forth, UAFA would be used as a bargaining chip, and once again we will be thrown under the bus."

A sad, but logical assessment, I think, based on history in the LGBT rights struggle. I hope both Erwin and I are proved wrong—and soon!

The couple, a 44-year old Ph.D. student in public and urban policy and the 46-year old rector of All Souls Episcopal Church in Washington, D.C., are married in their district—but not according to the U.S. government. The Defense of Marriage Act (DOMA) denies their union federally, which means, as we have seen, that John cannot sponsor Erwin for immigration after he gets his doctorate in urban and public policy and looks for employment.

John and Erwin have been together since 1998. They met in New York City and quickly knew that they wanted to be together. "I moved in with Erwin after we had known each other six weeks," said John with a smile.

"Throughout this time we have done our best to secure whatever protections are made available to us," continued Erwin. They registered as domestic partners in 2003, while living in New York City. In 2007, they did it again when they moved to Washington, D.C. "We immediately applied for a marriage license," said John, "when same-

John Beddingfield, left, and Erwin de Leon, right, from their private collection.
Used by permission.

sex marriage was legalized in the District. On April 5, 2010, we became a legally married couple," he said with a smile.

But that paperwork won't make it possible for Erwin to stay in America when his student visa runs out— thanks to DOMA. Even though Erwin plans on taking the additional year allowed in America for optional practical training, it still means that he will be required to leave the United States in 2012.

His mother, a permanent resident alien in the United States, has petitioned for him to stay as a legal permanent resident, "but due to the long processing time, it will not come soon enough, and I run the risk of being undocumented for a few years," he said.

Erwin pointed out the difference in how his case and his mother's case are handled by U.S. immigration. "The unfairness of it all is highlighted by the fact that my mother came much later than I did, but since she is a straight person, she was able to marry my stepfather, an American citizen, and get her green card in less than a year. Then she petitioned for me," he said.

Right now it takes about 10 years for Filipinos to sponsor their children for U.S. residency. To Erwin, that's a long time to wait for a right he says he should already have by virtue of his marriage to John. The couple, who want to stay in the United States, where all their family is, would like to continue to live in Washington, D.C.

"Fortunately, Erwin has options," John shared. "We have consulted with various immigration lawyers familiar with the plight of binational gay couples, and Erwin may have a viable option to pursue."

"I can apply for an EB-1 visa as an outstanding researcher," Erwin said, "since I have advanced degrees and have published research papers."

"As a gay and immigrant activist," said Erwin, "I have actively written and spoken about this and other issues that affect the LGBT and immigrant communities." Erwin and John willingly share their story "to shed light on the second-class status of LGBTs in the United States."

Like everyone else who has shared their story in these pages, John and Erwin know that they face immigration problems simply because they are gay. "If same-sex marriage had been allowed and recognized federally, I'd be a citizen by now," Erwin said.

"Our story is important because it is shared by thousands of other binational couples," added John. "Our reality challenges the notion that all are equal in the United States. The sad fact is that lesbians, gay men, bisexuals, and transgender persons are not treated equally and fairly."

As a rector, John is more familiar than some might be of the divisive nature of this issue among religious groups. But his view, shared by Erwin, is strong. "Families are the bedrock of all societies, and LGBT families are no different than others," he shared. "Passing Uniting American Families Act and ensuring LGBT rights allows America and its citizens to live up to the nation's founding principles of equality, freedom, and justice for all."

Karin and I appreciate their work on our issue and hope that Erwin is able to get his new visa and stay in Washington, D.C. with John and the congregation that is family to them.

CHAPTER TWENTY-SIX

DUAL CITIZENSHIP HURTS AND HELPS SAME-SEX BINATIONAL COUPLES

You would think that a partner with dual citizenship (meaning they carry passports from two different countries) would have an advantage in dealing with a gay or lesbian binational couple situation. But you would only be half right. I was shocked to find out that dual citizenship can also hurt a same-sex couple as is the case in this unique same-sex binational couple's story.

Andres Salazar works at the United Nations in Manhattan. On October 6, 2010, an op-ed piece he wrote on his personal situation was published in the *Los Angeles Times* with an intriguing headline that asked whether he should renounce his American citizenship so he could stay in the U.S. That caught my eye and his story made my eyes bug out.

The long and short of it is that Andres, a gay man in a same-sex binational partnership, is considering renouncing his U.S. citizenship and becoming solely a Spanish citizen. Why? Because even though he is an international civil servant working for the United Nations, he cannot get the proper visa for his partner, who he married legally in Spain in 2006.

Andres himself is a dual national. He was born in the United States to an American mother and a Spanish father. He grew up in Spain, but had frequent visits to America. In 1997, he came to the United States to work at the United Nations, where he is considered a Spaniard. That recognition made for an interesting wrinkle in his life: the United Nations recognized his same-sex marriage because his country, Spain, did.

The United States ordinarily issues visas to foreign nationals working for the United Nations that permits them to enter the United States freely and work legally. But because Andres has dual citizenship, he did not need a visa to enter the United States, so one was not issued. The problem arose because his same-sex marriage is recognized in Spain but not in the United States, so a separate visa could not be issued for his Spanish spouse José to enter the country and live with Andres. As a result, Andres is considering taking a stand and renouncing his U.S. citizenship so that he and his partner can get visas to stay in the United States while he works at the United Nations.

This couple suffers from the reach of DOMA. Even though a federal judge in Boston ruled parts of DOMA unconstitutional in 2010, the question of legality won't be solved soon, and this couple and others remain in visa limbo.

Andres and José have so far spent thousands of dollars for tuition so that his husband could qualify for a student visa to be able to legally live in the United States while Andres worked. They share the fear and frustration at airports that Jose won't be allowed into the United States. They have also had to pretend that they are not married so that Jose won't be seen as a visa overstay risk.

Andres grapples with a question I never thought I would hear: Should he renounce his U.S. citizenship so that he can be openly married to his husband and get the visas they need to be in the United States legally—or leave the United States and his job at the United Nations?

What would you do? I know what I would do. Karin and I will be watching the news to see how this turns out. We wish them well no matter how things turn out for them.

***

Dual citizenship had the opposite affect for another couple, who left the United States in order to be together. Dual citizenship was helpful to them when they relocated to Mexico because one partner is a dual citizen of America and Mexico and the other is a Mexican citizen.

Residents of San Angelo, Texas, lost their mayor because of the twofold same-sex marriage and same-sex binational couple immigration issue this book explores. Mayor J. W. Lown, reelected and ready to take office for his fourth term in May 2009, surprised the town when he resigned instead of swearing his oath and serving another term.

He told the press he had started a relationship with someone who did not have legal status in the United States. He could not take his oath of office and live in Texas any more, he felt, because he needed to make the right decision for his community, his partner, and himself.

J. W. made his abrupt resignation only 10 days after he received 89 percent of the mayoral vote in San Angelo. As reported by the *Abilene Reporter-News* on May 21, 2009, J. W. Lown said the following as part of his resignation letter: "While I know that the timing of this announcement is less than ideal, I have my own compelling reasons for making this decision. I have made thousands of decisions on behalf of our community, and I weighed this decision in the same manner that I approached other decisions."

Stories about J. W. Lown's decision appeared in local papers and made national media news. I have never run for office or held public office, but I know it shines a spotlight on everything people do. This brave man did the right thing. He followed his heart and upheld principles, though he should not have been put in that situation at all. America's laws need to change so that J.W. can continue to serve as mayor of San Angelo, Texas and even aspire to higher office if he wishes.

J. W. and his partner are living in Mexico easily with J. W.'s dual nationality but they want to live in the United States and are waiting for a visa so that his partner can come to America. In the same *Abilene Reporter-News* article, J. W. Lown was glad that "San Angelo responded with overwhelming support and will welcome us back. But the laws are particularly harsh. It will take a three- to 10-year process for my partner to qualify for a tourist visa to the United States." Because of that, the couple has no option but to make a life in Mexico in the meantime. They will be there for years before they can live together in America.

Karin and I wish them well in their new life and new location. We hope their dream of living together in America comes true.

CHAPTER TWENTY-SEVEN

NEAL AND FERNANDO: RISKY BEHAVIOR— HAVING A PARTNER WHO IS ILLEGAL OR UNDOCUMENTED

This important story carries a heavy responsibility and a heavy risk. Pay attention to what some people have to do/choose to do to stay together in a world that throws them nothing but hurdles, challenges, obstacles, and roadblocks. There are more binational couples like this—gay men and lesbian women—than we will ever know about because they live in the shadows of U.S. law and need to stay that way in order to be with their families in America—until the law changes.

I'm not going to share many details about this couple. Their story will unfold for you, and you can read their pain and gumption yourself. Just know that these two men, one aged 52 and one aged 42, have been together since 2000. They have done more than most couples I know to be together and stay together—where they want to be.

At a party, Neal (not his real name) met Fernando (not his real name), and their love story very nearly didn't happen. Laughing, Neal told me that he saw Fernando across the room and felt that magic feeling, so he approached him. Fernando was visiting friends in northern California at the time, and Neal, who lived there, was invited to the party. "I was the token white boy," he said with a laugh. Neal's now-partner spoke no English at the time. That made things a challenge, Neal joked.

He recalls calling Fernando three different times to ask him out for a date. The answer he got each time was "No." Just that one word, "No." Neal felt sad that he couldn't act on the strong feeling he had about this new man, but let it go.

One day he was at a bar on "gay night," when who should he see across the room but Fernando. "I had a few beers that night, which bolstered my courage," Neal recalled. "I walked across the room and put a firm lip lock on him—no English required—and I asked him out again. "I convinced him to go out with me, and he agreed," said Neal with a smile.

Their first date was at Capitola, a small beach community on the Pacific Ocean. "The romance started there," remembered Neal. Within two weeks, Fernando had left the small three-bedroom apartment he shared with many friends and moved in with Neal. Recalling how they got together, Neal laughed again and said that one of his bathrooms was being remodeled by a contractor, while he was fixing things in the other bathroom himself. "We had no shower to use for some time," Neal recalled. "So each day we would take dips in the pool until we got the shower back in use."

Neal worked in product marketing for a major high tech firm at the time, and Fernando had a part-time job in hospitality work for a major hotel chain. But the dotcom bust took Neal's job away, and he couldn't find other work in his field in northern California.

"I had always wanted to move to San Diego," Neal remembered. "So within a month, we had packed up our things and moved to San Diego. We had my cat, Kahlua, on a leash, so we could walk her at the rest stops along the way."

The other thing he remembered and laughed about was Fernando's shoes. "He has 79 pairs of shoes," said Neal, shocked. "It's a Latin thing," he said, smiling. "That, and name brands—he has to buy the major brands of things like underwear."

So the drive south with the cat among other things included two big garbage bags of shoes—which played into the story more as their journey together unfolded.

"I had rented an apartment in San Diego ahead of time," Neal related. "So we had somewhere to live when we got there."

They lived in the Hillcrest area, the gay and lesbian part of San Diego, which was something Neal had always wanted to do. "It was nice to be there," he shared. "I had never lived anywhere like that where you could walk right to the corner and shop or go to the coffee place across the street or be in the environment that it was."

Neal was raised in upstate New York, the Catskills, which he jokingly refers to as the Jewish Alps. Fernando is from South America. They enjoyed their time in San Diego for personal reasons, but professionally they both suffered. "There wasn't a lot of high-tech work there," remembered Neal, frowning. "So I couldn't get a job like I had up north." And Fernando, without his network of friends, could not find work on his own or with Neal's help.

The couple dealt with a new reality, and it was hard for them. "We were in each other's face 24/7," remembered Neal. "It was hard. We were stressed. We had some fights." After one such incident, Neal told Fernando he had to leave. He drove Fernando—and those two garbage bags of shoes—back to northern California.

Neal returned to San Diego, leaving Fernando in northern California, but later relented and called Fernando. The couple reconciled, and Neal once again drove back north and retrieved Fernando and those bags of shoes and brought them all back to San Diego.

This happened at least one more time. Besides the upsets and reconciliations, things were tough for the men as Fernando couldn't find work and Neal was on unemployment. "I was sending out resumes everywhere I could," said Neal. "Fernando could not work because he didn't have his support network and couldn't find a job in San Diego." So Neal went back to school and renewed his real estate license. It was not his first choice, but the situation demanded it.

He found a job with a major builder in San Diego, selling houses being built in new developments. His job entailed working at one location but representing 11 different sites in the San Diego area, a situation that gave him not only steady employment but earnings potential. The situation in the office he shared was far from ideal, though—Neal's co-workers, all interior sales people at one location, resented Neal's position, and friction developed. Eventually, Neal quit the job and looked for other work.

His next job ended up being stressful financially, because it didn't offer the earnings potential of the former job and Neal—recently off unemployment—was the sole financial support for the couple. "I had to start using my house in northern California, which was rented out, as an ATM," he said. "I was using line of credit money to support us, because I had a draw but sales were slow and I had to make ends meet for us."

Meanwhile, Fernando had become "out of compliance" with his visitor's visa, as ICE terms it. "I didn't know his visa had expired," remembered Neal. "I didn't know about the visa situation, that whole visa thing, and I found out what it meant."

Things continued to be slow financially for Neal for another two months in San Diego, and Fernando still wasn't working. Finally, Neal decided the best thing for them to do was to return to northern California. That way, Fernando could work and eventually they could move back into Neal's condo when his renters' lease ended.

So once again, they packed up their things in a U-Haul truck, put their car on a tow trailer behind it, leashed Kahlua for the journey, and headed back north. "We had scoped out the route ahead of time," Neal confided, "because there is a checkpoint on Highway 5 at San Onofre." They weren't overly concerned about the checkpoint, but they decided to take no chances and worked out an ingenious plan to make sure that Fernando would not be challenged. They drove to a Denny's restaurant just south of the checkpoint and parked the truck. They took the car off the tow trailer and drove north on Highway 5. When they got to the checkpoint, they went through the auto line and were waved through, no problem at all.

Neal drove to a restaurant a bit north of the checkpoint—he thinks it was a different chain—and left Fernando there to eat while he drove south alone in the car to the Denny's where they had left the truck and the cat and the tow trailer.

"I put the car back onto the tow trailer and got into the U-Haul with Kahlua and drove north by myself," he recalled. "When I got to the checkpoint and had to go in the truck line that time, I was by myself, and they waved me through no problem," he remembered with a smile. He retrieved Fernando and continued the drive back to northern California. Since Neal's condo was still rented out, they moved into a rental owned by a San Diego friend. "His place was vacant, so we could move right in," said Neal. "We lived there about a year, until my condo was available again."

Fernando got another hospitality position with his previous employer, and things were going well, so it seemed all would be bright for this couple's future.

But about six months into his new job, Fernando's employer, a major hotel chain, got a letter from the INS. Fernando brought it home and showed it to Neal. They were suddenly in the world of the immigration-challenged for good. The letter explained that the INS had discovered that the Social Security number Fernando had supplied didn't match his name and other identification. He was told he had to quit his job, if he couldn't prove otherwise.

So Fernando quit, and Neal resumed supporting them both on his salary, "At the time, I was working as a loan officer," Neal said. "My friend owned the company, and he thought I would like the work—I like math, and I have great people skills. But as it turned out, I didn't like that kind of work, and it didn't really match my interests, so after two years there I moved on to something else."

So once again, Fernando was unemployed and Neal had quit his job. "We were able to move out of the rental house and back into my condo," said Neal. When a FOR SALE BY OWNER sign went up on the condo next door to a friend, Neal and Fernando bought the unit, and in 2004 rented it out. "We're still in the same house," said Neal.

During this period, the sister of Fernando's brother-in-law came to the United States, leaving behind an abusive husband and her two daughters. She found employment, and through that job was able to get Fernando a job. She settled into her own apartment and brought her girls to live with her, and their life improved.

Both men are close to their families, but torn apart from visiting them together because of their situation with Fernando's status, something they cannot change the way immigration laws are today. Neal's family in upstate New York includes his parents, a brother and sister-in-law, his nephews, aunts and uncles, and cousins. Fernando's family in South America includes his sisters and brothers, parents, aunts and uncles, nephews and nieces and cousins.

In 2007, Neal was invited to a friend's birthday party in Chile. He went and had a great time, but Fernando couldn't travel with him because of his visa issues. While in South America, Neal visited Fernando's family and happened to be there at the right time to be named godfather to one of Fernando's nephews. "I visited Fernando's parents," said Neal. His parents are both law professors, and they live in the city, but they also have a farm." Although Fernando's family does well where they live, "he has a better life in America than he would at home," stated Neal.

The separation is tough on all of them. "Fernando's father, in his 80s, cried when I was there," said Neal. "He cries when he talks to Fernando on the phone. They talk every day," Neal said. "I feel guilty that he can't go home and visit his family."

Their particular situation is one of the worst same-sex binational sagas I have seen. "We have to be cautious of what we do," Neil related. "We can't register as domestic partners." He continued: "I had thought of moving to Canada, but I can't get a job there. I could send Fernando to Canada, but then we wouldn't be together."

Fernando has not seen his parents and other family members in his home country since 2000 due to his expired visa. He was able to renew his passport at his country's consulate in San Francisco, but it is of little use without a valid visa allowing him to reenter the United States. Neal's family on the other side of the country suffers, too. He is in unable to visit them, as Fernando could be in trouble taking a domestic flight and the distance means that driving is not a workable option. Neal's mother wants them to come and visit for the holidays, but "I have to tell her we can't and that's very sad," Neil said sadly.

Neal knows there are lots of fake marriages where a man or woman marries an American citizen of the opposite gender, but they have not considered that as an option. They actually know a couple who have done that in another state, but they are not willing to take that risk.

Their life continues to have employment and income challenges because of their immigration situation. Fernando hasn't been found out or caught, but they live with that possibility every day.

"I've signed Fernando up for the visa lottery several times. But then we found out he wouldn't have been eligible if he won," Neal related. "We talked with an immigration attorney once, who thought Fernando might be an asylum case, but since he was from a big city in his country, he would have to prove that his life was in danger for being gay, and he couldn't show that, so we couldn't proceed with that plan."

Fernando was working on his degree in psychology when he and Neal met. "Now he is reduced to working in a teashop," remarked Neal. "It's not what he planned for his life."

They have been together since 2000 in the United States. They plan to stay together. But they don't know now where their future will be geographically.

"This is my longest relationship ever, with a man or a woman," noted Neal. Fernando is his life, and he will do what he has to do to keep them together, as he has already for years. The only thing to change things is if Fernando were to get found out, then whatever happened would dictate their future. So far, they have dealt with challenges; fortunately, though, they have not yet been faced with separation.

Neal has not testified or written letters or spoken to groups about their situation. He is cautious about it because of Fernando's situation. And Fernando is naturally quiet and reluctant to talk to anyone but his friends and family. "He won't want to participate in this interview," Neal had shared with me before we met to create this chapter.

Reflecting on what might have been, Neal stated: "If I would redo my life I think I would be a lawyer, because I am really such an activist."

He has kept up on the same-sex binational couple immigration issue with newsletters and websites from the groups working on this issue: Out4Immigration, Immigration Equality, and Love Exiles. He also keeps track of the work of Equality California, but he has not contacted those groups or others to ask for help with his situation.

Neal does want a better life for his family, but he laughed at Fernando's plan to have Neal go to his family's country, marry his sister, and bring her and her children to America, so they could all be together and all have a better life. Marriage or not, any effort to reunite Fernando's family in California is on hold because of Neal's job and once again being the major breadwinner in the family.

Their plan now is to sell the house they live in and return to the condo Neal owned first, which has been rented for years, to make life simpler and less expensive and to regroup. "We live day by day with Fernando's situation," said Neal with a sigh. "We live job to job with my situation," he added.

Today, they live in a Silicon Valley town. Neal would love to return to San Diego, "but we will stay here for Fernando's network of friends and support group and his job," he said.

Fernando's perspective is simple: He let his visa expire to stay in America to be with Neal. This makes the situation very personal and tender for Neal. "He has lots of friends here and a great support network, and right now he is working," Neal related. They want to keep things that way so that Fernando has the best life he can.

Neal's personal story is an interesting one. He was in the U.S. Army from 1976 to 1980, in military intelligence. He is a trained linguist and studied at the Monterey Defense Language Institute Foreign Language Center. As a result, he said, his focus always was on teaching Fernando English, not learning Spanish to be able to converse with him in his native language.

As for coming out, Neal shared that it was always a gradual thing. He says he came out in his 30s, but it remains an unspoken issue with his parents. "My Catholic, upstate New York parents make it hard to talk about," he shared, "but I think my Mom has sort of always known." Meanwhile, because he is from a Latin culture, Fernando is not out to his family. "One sister knows, but his parents don't know," Neil said.

Immigration problems have profoundly affected this couple. Because Fernando is out of compliance with his visa—is now in the country illegally and is not a U.S. citizen—he can't work in the field he wants nor can he continue his university education. He can't get a driver's license, so he can't drive. He has no medical benefits and can't get them through Neal because they can't be domestic partners or get married. "He can't get insurance," continued Neal, "and he doesn't have a pension." And they can't fly together, or fly out of the country together, so that restricts where they go, who they see, and how they get there.

While Neal has been able to get different jobs to support them, their immigration situation has not affected his career per se, as it has Fernando's. But if they have to move to another country, Neal's career will be severely affected, and employment might be hard or impossible, depending on where they go.

"I can't do things with Fernando that I like to do," said Neal. "And Fernando can't do things with me he would like to do—or we would like to do together." Their friends and family are also restricted in what they can do with Neal and Fernando.

Their story is important to share, even at risk to themselves, "because we have to get it out," stressed Neal. "We have to let other people know about something they aren't aware of—the problems we have that need to be solved. They may think they know the issues, but they think it's one thing, and there are all these other things going on behind the scenes."

Neal shared an example that demonstrated the issue's importance, something he had heard radio personality Ronn Owens say. He recounted Owens's statement that the role of government is to issue licenses—hunting, fishing, marriage, whatever. If a church chooses to perform a ceremony, that's their option. But the role of government is not to choose who can marry or how, he recalled Owens saying.

It's very clear to Neal that UAFA, RFA, or some other comprehensive immigration reform bill that includes gay and lesbian families needs to pass. "We need it so Fernando and all the others can live here legally, and so they can get the benefits other spouses all get," he declared. "We need it so couples can travel freely and live a normal life."

He stressed the fact that he cannot use his real name or his partner's real name to share their important story. "We don't want to put out any unnecessary risks," he said, "even though sharing our story is a risk. Our story is another example of the various situations we have to live with that many other people don't have to live with. But many people do live with these and other problems. The majority of people don't have these problems, and we want to help solve the situation for everyone."

In the long run, Neal and Fernando may have to relocate in order to stay together, just like Karin and I may have to relocate, and others you have read about in other chapters have relocated, or will have to do so—just to stay together.

"We have not been separated yet," stressed Neal, "but if we become separated, then I will move to Fernando's country to be with him. I could get a job as an ESL [English as a Second Language] instructor, for example. I wouldn't be able to work in my field, but we would do what we have to do to stay together."

Their problem is not solved, their situation is ongoing and the solution is not here yet.

"How does our story turn out?" Neal repeated, when I asked him the standard question I have asked all interviewees, "Stay tuned!" he said with a laugh. "TBD."

Karin and I hope for the best solution for these men who have really stayed together through thick and thin, for better or for worse.

CHAPTER TWENTY-EIGHT

MARRIAGE TO SOMEONE OF THE OPPOSITE GENDER KEEPS US TOGETHER IN AMERICA

Many people have asked Karin why she doesn't marry a man so that she can stay in America. Her simple answer is that she won't, because it is illegal. We don't want to do anything like that, and we won't. But some people marry Americans to come to, or stay in, the United States and get residency—heterosexual couples as well as same-sex couples.

U.S. immigration law does not recognize same-sex relationships, so marriage fraud or a sham marriage is one option people may take. But it's very risky. And it's not legal. If you get found out, both the straight or gay or lesbian American citizen and the gay or lesbian non-citizen face stiff penalties. (Information on the process of fiancé/e visas for the legal way to proceed can be found at *www.uscis.gov/portal/site/uscis/menuitem.eb.*)

If a gay man or lesbian marries a person of the opposite sex to remain in the United States, he or she risks deportation and the possibility of being barred forever from returning to the United States. Additionally, the spouse he or she married may be fined and sent to jail for committing fraud.

In addition, men or women who pursue such a marriage need to be aware that when the American citizen spouse submits an application for a green card for the immigrant spouse, if they have been married for less than two years, the green card issued will be conditional.

After two years, the couple must return to the USCIS and demonstrate that the marriage is real and prove that they live together, own property together, and share their finances. In the verification process, USCIS may call employers and even visit the couple at home to investigate whether the marriage is valid.

Understandably, it was very hard to find a couple to interview for this chapter. I was excited when I finally got an anonymous couple to agree to share information, although names, locations, and other details would be omitted or changed to protect their identities. Someone who knew someone connected me. But then the interview couldn't happen. The couple felt that by changing all details to protect their identity, I might as well make up the story.

I understood but didn't want to make up a story, so I am just sharing the harsh reality of this option and including it to show what some couples might do to avoid the prospect of being Torn Apart.

So to that couple, and to the others out there, I share my heart and my love and my understanding and my hope. I am glad you found each other and you found a way to be together. May you escape the penalties that might come your way. Karin and I have a hard time staying together, but your situation is more than we are willing to risk.

CHAPTER TWENTY-NINE

Julia and Jo: We Couldn't Survive as a Couple—U.S. Laws Tore Us Apart

Sometimes people ask me why I got involved with Karin if she had a visa issue (or sometimes they say foreigner, or alien, or something similar). In the past, I didn't always know what to say to them. Some people were probably insensitive, but most people just seemed flustered or insatiably curious. They couldn't figure out why we have to leave the country to stay together, for example.

I don't want to be rude to them, but I don't go asking other people why they got involved with their partners. But some answers I could use next time might be:

You fall in love and you deal with things, or;

There was no question that we would not be together, or;

Visa-schmeeza!

Those are the nice answers I thought of… But if I or we had thought our different passports would be too big of an issue to deal with, our story would be in this chapter.

As sad as it is to report, some folks have had to abandon their dreams of being together. They actually do not get very far down the line with their relationship because of the problems associated with being a same-sex binational couple. Their stories are not stories of what was, but rather of what might have been. Karin and I are sad for them that they could not overcome the obstacles to be together.

Karin turned up this story, and it made both of us cry…

Jo (not her real name) met Julia (not her real name) in July 1998 when Jo was visiting friends in San Francisco. "We met at a welcome dinner party for Julia," said Jo, "and I liked her immediately. She was very English, and I loved listening to her speak. The way she said 'toe-mah-toe' and 'but-ter' was so sweet."

"I was 38 when I met Julia," she continued. "I had been out since I was in my early 20s, when I was working in a computer business in the San Francisco Bay Area."

She had been in a long-term relationship and had adopted a little boy, Billy, with her former partner. Billy was six at the time Jo met Julia. "My ex-partner and I had split up about a year earlier," she shared, "and we had joint custody of our son."

At that fateful dinner party, Julia shared that she was divorced, had been living on her own in London, and was a college instructor (what we call high school teacher in America).

"I offered to show Julia around the area, so we drove down to the coast, where she was surprised at the cold water of the Pacific Ocean," remembered Jo. (That makes me laugh because she sounds just like Karin did when she went to the Pacific and I explained about the Japan current and what it does to northern California beaches.)

"Julia was so enthusiastic about everything she saw, " Jo smiled. "It was her first time in the United States, and she loved the brash newness of everything over here."

Butch Jo struggled with her feelings. "I knew I was falling for Julia quite quickly," she shared. "I was very sensitive to the fact that she had been married to a man, and might not appreciate my advances."

But one day as they walked along the beach, "Julia took my hand, smiled that adorable smile at me, and said, 'I really like you, Jo.'" That was the magic moment for Jo and Julia!

"My heart was beating madly, and I turned to her and hugged her," remembered Jo with a smile. "I wanted to kiss her but was scared." She laughed at the memory of being scared. "This tough old butch who knew everything," she said with a grin. "But I didn't have to worry—she kissed me instead." Jo remembers it as the sweetest kiss she had ever experienced in her life. Julia felt the same, she said.

Their beginning was very romantic, "which made our subsequent life all the worse. Falling in love is easy; falling in love with an Englishwoman when you are American is not." Now, after it is all over, Jo said, frowning, "My problem was that at the time I had no idea what was going to happen and how heartbreaking it was all going to be."

Karin and I know that pain, too.

Julia returned home to England at the end of the summer, but promised Jo to return for the Christmas holidays. "Luckily, because she was a teacher, she had plenty of vacations," Jo said, "and we made the most of our time together."

Over Christmas, the couple really got to know each other and realized that they wanted to be together. "So we started making plans and inquiries about how we could do this," Jo said. "We soon realized that what we had hoped would be an easy decision— for Julia to move to America and live with me—was, in fact, a wish that was impossible to attain."

Jo and Julia talked to an immigration lawyer, who told them that because the United States did not have federally recognized same-sex marriage, Jo could not sponsor Julia to come to America. "We were shocked!" said Jo.

Trying another route, they thought perhaps Julia could work or study over here and explored those options. No luck there, either. "We even thought about finding a man who would be willing to marry Julia," Jo said. "We heard that this happens sometimes. But nothing worked for us," she said with a sigh.

By then it was summer 1999, and Julia was able to come over for six weeks. "At first we were ecstatic to be together, but as the summer continued we noticed there was a lot of stress between us," said Jo.

"I hadn't wanted to introduce Billy to Julia until she was able to live with us," Jo remarked, "but over such a long visit it was inevitable that they would meet sometime. Of course, they adored each other," she told me with a smile.

As Julia's day of departure arrived, Jo could tell something was very wrong. "Julia became very quiet," she remembered, "until I asked her what was wrong." She told me she couldn't do it anymore," said Jo. She said she couldn't bear the heartbreak of leaving again after a few weeks and being gone for months again. And after she had met Billy and adored him, she knew she could love him but didn't dare to hope for that whole experience. "We both cried and held each other, Jo said.

Something must be able to solve their problem, they thought, but they had tried everything they could think of.

"I couldn't leave the country because of Billy," said Jo, "and because of that and American laws, I couldn't have my darling Julia with me here." The fairytale love story had turned into a nightmare.

Jo kept working. And for a while Jo and Julia continued to be in contact. "We phoned and e-mailed," shared Jo. "I even went over to England for a short vacation."

They thought they might be able to stay together as a couple living in two countries, but the stress and separation and heartbreak were just too much. "So we decided to break off our relationship altogether," said Jo. "It was the hardest thing I have ever had to do. There was so much potential and love, but that had to be denied and broken off."

All this happened more than 10 years ago. Jo's life went on, and Billy grew up. "I now have a new partner," shared Jo, with a smile. "I love her very much, and luckily she is American like me."

Jo's new partner didn't want to be identified for this story, but she knows about Julia and Jo's failed same-sex binational relationship. "I will never forget the pain of our forced separation," she said. "Such a waste, so unnecessary."

Jo's question now is the same as mine, the same as Karin's, the same as so many others facing these obstacles: Will things ever change? If so, when?

"I know there are thousands of couples like Julia and me," Jo concluded, "I hope and pray that the laws in this country will make it possible for them to live together in peace and love."

Karin and I agree!

CHAPTER THIRTY

DAVID AND KARL: WE COULDN'T BECOME A COUPLE BECAUSE OF U.S. LAWS

The debate about gays and lesbians openly serving in the U.S. military has been in the news a lot in 2010. At the time this book went to print, it was still being batted back and forth in the courts and in Washington, D.C. Serving openly in the service is something many gays and lesbians want. It means that discrimination will be ended in enlistment processes, and gay men and lesbians can serve without fear of discharge and loss of employment and benefits.

But in the past, gay men and lesbians in the armed forces were not able to be open. They were there, but they were not acknowledged. They served in silence and hoped to not be the focus of witch hunts or hurtful discharge proceedings.

The following story involves that issue and the general issue of same-sex binational couples and their ability to make lives together in America.

David, serving in the military and posted overseas to Germany early in the 2000s, met Karl at a bar, where he was having a drink with some friends. "It wasn't a gay bar or anything like that," David recalled. "It was just an ordinary bar. I saw this man standing there, and we smiled at each other. I said in my best German, *'Guten Abend,'* ('Good Evening')."

He laughed when he remembered that most young Germans spoke English well and Karl spoke his second language much better than David did his. "We spent much of the evening talking," remembered David. "Karl told me about his job as a waiter in a local restaurant. I told him about my experiences in the Army."

David said that he had no idea at the time that Karl was also a gay man. "I just liked him, and he was easy to talk to," he shared. At the end of the evening, Karl asked David if he would meet him at the bar again another evening. He agreed, and they met the following week, when David again had free time.

David had been serving in Germany for six years without anyone knowing he was gay. At home in Detroit, "I was very carefully out to some close friends," he shared, "but not out to my family."

When he met Karl for the second time at the bar, Karl informed David that he was gay. "He told me he had guessed I was gay, too," confided David. "We felt an immediate connection—a strong attraction. And, of course, we wanted to see each other again."

This is when things got really difficult. "I could not tell anyone about my new relationship with Karl," shared David. "In order to see each other, Karl and I had to find places to meet that were far from the base," said David. "Luckily, Karl had his own flat near the edge of the town, and we could go there."

Over the ensuing weeks and months, David and Karl fell deeply in love.

"Of course, I told Karl about Don't Ask, Don't Tell, and what it meant to my career in the Army," said David. "It made everything more stressful and difficult because we wanted to become serious and be together. I actually thought about leaving the Army at one point, and asking Karl to move to the United States with me."

But that's when things got even more difficult. David made inquiries about how they could do that and learned there was absolutely no legal way to bring Karl to live with him in the United States. "I had no idea the law was like that," David exclaimed. "I was stunned!"

Not long after that, David learned he was to be transferred back to America. "Karl and I agonized about what to do," he said. "There seemed to be no way that we could both go to America and be together."

In the end, the day came when David had to leave, and say goodbye to Karl. "We tried to tell each other that it was not forever, that we would figure something out," David said, "but we couldn't." They said goodbye, and they were never together again.

"Leaving Karl in Germany was heartbreaking," David said sadly. "I knew he was the love of my life, and yet we never had the chance to live that life together. I'll never forget Karl. Sometimes I wish I could go back to Germany and be with him. It all seems so hopeless, though."

David is still in the Army, waiting for things to change so he can be more comfortable with his life and his future. He still is not out much, only to the close friends he shared his true self with when he was 20 years old. Now aged 34, he was willing to share his story with me for this book but not his full name or other identifying aspects, "because I am still in the Army, and there is still no end to DADT," he said.

The laws that affected this potential couple's life together still cause problems for gay men and lesbians today. Karin and I hope they change as soon as possible, so that all of us can live the life we want, with whoever we want and where we want.

PART III

BACKGROUND
AND RESOURCES

CHAPTER THIRTY-ONE

PROPOSED LEGISLATION FOR IMMIGRATION REFORM FOR US:

UNITING AMERICAN FAMILIES ACT (UAFA) SEEKS IMMIGRATION REFORM FOR SAME-SEX BINATIONAL COUPLES

Under current U.S. immigration law, if you want to live in the United States and you are not an American citizen, there are three ways to get permanent residence status, informally known as a green card:

- A relative living legally in the United States can sponsor you;
- You can qualify through employment status;
- Or you can meet the qualifications to become a refugee.

The standards for both employment visas and refugee status are extraordinarily high. Annually, the number of applications granted is small. There is no provision, for example, for granting green cards to untrained blue collar workers. Getting a green card in the category of skilled labor can take up to 10 years—or longer depending on your country of origin. There are no limits on visas granted to legal spouses: While these are carefully investigated to prove the authenticity of the relationship, approval for eligible partners is automatic.

That's what they say. But we know it's not that easy. And it's not automatic if your partner/spouse is of the same gender. Then, it's impossible.

The solution to the problem Karin and I and so many other same-sex binational couples face when trying to immigrate legally is immigration reform to include full spousal rights for same-sex binational couples. As it stands now, there are already lots of backlogs and quota problems and other things that impede the process and stall family unification. But beyond that, the law needs to be changed so that Karin and I and other families like ours receive equal rights under the law. Without that, comprehensive immigration reform is not worthy of the name because of one simple fact: If it doesn't include all of us, it isn't comprehensive.

There's been lots of talk about comprehensive immigration reformation. Arguments for and against it tend to focus specifically on the issue of Mexican illegal workers crossing into the United States in border states like Arizona. Copycat city and state movements to stop immigrants and control immigration and residency have sprung up elsewhere, too.

Almost no one mentions spouses/permanent partners of Americans who are gay or lesbian, though. Couples like mine need help to be together. We need the current law to change. That part of comprehensive immigration reform needs attention and action.

The best chance for immigration relief for same-sex binational couples is the passage of a stand-alone bill, Uniting American Families Act (UAFA), formerly called the Permanent Partners Immigration Act (PPIA).

UAFA seeks to amend the Immigration and Nationality Act to eliminate discrimination in immigration laws by permitting permanent partners of United States citizens and lawful permanent residents to obtain lawful permanent resident status in the same manner as spouses of citizens and lawful permanent residents and to protect the process by imposing the same penalties for immigration fraud in connection with permanent partnerships. Basically, it seeks to create a level playing field for gay and lesbian Americans who have permanent partners who were not born in America. Period. This needs to pass!

Senator Patrick Leahy (D-VT) and Congressman Jerrold Nadler (D-NY-8) first introduced the Permanent Partners Immigration Act in both houses of Congress in 2000. The bill went nowhere. It was reintroduced under its current name, Uniting American Families Act, on July 21, 2005 by Rep. Nadler, who reintroduced it each new Congressional term. On February 12, 2009, the bill was reintroduced in the House of Representatives for the 111th Congress by Rep. Nadler and it is currently pending. Thanks for your years of hard work on this bill, Congressman Nadler.

As of October 2010, H.R. 1024 had 134 cosponsors. For updates on progress and more information on this bill, go to http://thomas.loc.gov. For a graphic map of how a bill becomes a law, go to *http://www.mikewirthart.com/wp-content/uploads/2010/05/howlawsmadeWIRTH2.jpg*

Summary of Uniting American Families Act Legislation from the Library of Congress THOMAS Register H.R. 1024
Title: Uniting American Families Act of 2009
Sponsor: Rep Nadler, Jerrold [NY-8] (introduced 2/12/2009)
Cosponsors (124)
Related Bills: H.R. 2709, S. 424
Latest Major Action: 3/16/2009 Referred to House subcommittee.
Status: Referred to the Subcommittee on Immigration, Citizenship, Refugees, Border Security, and International Law.

Summary As Of: 2/12/2009 — Introduced.
- Uniting American Families Act of 2009 - Amends the Immigration and Nationality Act to include a "permanent partner" within the scope of such Act. Defines a "permanent partner" as an individual 18 or older who: (1) is in a committed, intimate relationship with another individual 18 or older in which both individuals intend a lifelong commitment; (2) is financially interdependent with the other individual; (3) is not married to, or in a permanent partnership with, any other individual other than the individual; (4) is unable to contract with the other individual a marriage cognizable under this Act; and (5) is not a first, second, or third degree blood relation of the other individual. Defines a "permanent partnership" as the relationship existing between two permanent partners.

Uniting American Families Act legislation was reintroduced into the Senate on February 12, 2009, by Senator Patrick Leahy (D-VT). As Rep. Nadler has done in the House, Senator Leahy reintroduced the bill every term of Congress, including the 111th where it moved forward. Thanks for your years of hard work on this bill, Senator Leahy.

In 2009 the Senate bill gained traction, and a Senate Judiciary Committee hearing was held on June 3, 2009. Karin and I were there in the room as the committee heard testimony. It was a thrill to witness action on the bill—a sign that there is hope for us. And we were proud to see Senator Leahy conducting the meeting and hearing testimony from partners in two couples affected by the current immigration law, Gordon Stewart and Shirley Tan, both of whom are profiled in this book. Also testifying in support of the bill were Julian Bond from the National Association of Colored People (NAACP), Christopher Nugent from the American Bar Association, and Jessica Vaughn of the Center for Immigration Studies (CIS). As of October 2010, S. 424 had 25 co-sponsors. For updates on progress and more information on this bill, go to http://thomas.loc.gov. For a graphic map of how a bill becomes a law, go to *http://www.mikewirthart.com/wp-content/uploads/2010/05/howlawsmadeWIRTH2.jpg*

Summary of Uniting American Families Act Legislation from the Library of Congress THOMAS Register S. 424
Title: Uniting American Families Act of 2009
Sponsor: Sen Leahy, Patrick J. [VT] (introduced 2/12/2009)
Cosponsors (23)
Related Bills: H.R. 1024, H.R. 2709
Latest Major Action: 2/12/2009 Referred to Senate committee.

Status: Read twice and referred to the
Committee on the Judiciary.

Summary As Of: 2/12/2009 — Introduced.

- Uniting American Families Act of 2009 - Amends the Immigration and
  Nationality Act to include a "permanent partner" within the scope of such
  Act. Defines a "permanent partner" as an individual 18 or older who: (1) is
  in a committed, intimate relationship with another individual 18 or older
  in which both individuals intend a lifelong commitment; (2) is financially
  interdependent with the other individual; (3) is not married to, or in a
  permanent partnership with, any other individual other than the individual;
  (4) is unable to contract with the other individual a marriage cognizable
  under this Act; and (5) is not a first, second, or third degree blood relation
  of the other individual. Defines a "permanent partnership" as the relationship existing between two permanent partners.

CHAPTER THIRTY-TWO

PROPOSED LEGISLATION FOR IMMIGRATION REFORM THAT INCLUDES UAFA:

REUNITING FAMILIES ACT (RFA)

Another way for couples like Karin and me to get immigration relief is if UAFA, or similar language, is included in a comprehensive immigration reform bill such as the June 4, 2009, Reuniting Families Act (RFA) bill that was introduced by Congressman Michael Honda (D-CA-15), my congressional representative. This legislation was an effort to correct the problems with immigration processes—and a way to achieve comprehensive immigration reform without having a stand-alone bill for gay men and lesbians and their partners.

I shared my story with Congressman Honda in February 2009, and he got it! He added language pertaining to same sex binational couples to his bill-in-progress in order to cover an aspect of immigration reform that had not been in his proposed legislation. Karin and I thank him for that. Thanks for your understanding of what needed to be added to the bill, Congressman Honda.

Karin and I were proud to be at the June 4, 2009, press conference in Washington, D.C. when Congressman Honda introduced his Reuniting Families Act legislation. What a thrill! It made us proud to see the collection of legislators and civil rights leaders assembled there to support the effort to include same-sex binational couples in comprehensive immigration reform. As of October, 2010, H. R. 2709 had 81 co-sponsors. For updates on progress and more information on this bill, go to http://thomas.loc.gov.

For a graphic map of how a bill becomes a law, go to *http://www.mikewirthart.com/wp-content/uploads/2010/05/howlawsmadeWIRTH2.jpg*

Summary of Reuniting Families Act Legislation from the Library of Congress THOMAS Register H.R. 2709
Title: Reuniting Families Act
Sponsor: Rep Honda, Michael M. [CA-15] (introduced 6/4/2009)
Cosponsors (81)

Related Bills: H.R. 1024, S. 424, S. 1085, S. 1247

Latest Major Action: 8/19/2009 Referred to House subcommittee. Status: Referred to the Subcommittee on Immigration, Citizenship, Refugees, Border Security, and International Law.

Summary As Of: 6/4/2009 — Introduced.

- Reuniting Families Act - Amends the Immigration and Nationality Act (INA) to establish the fiscal year worldwide level of employment-based immigrants at 140,000 plus: (1) the previous year's unused visas; and (2) the number of unused visas from FY1992-FY2007.
- Establishes the fiscal year worldwide level of family-sponsored immigrants at 480,000 plus: (1) the previous year's unused visas; and (2) the number of unused visas from FY1992-FY2007.
- Revises the definition of "immediate relative" to: (1) mean a child, spouse, or parent of a U.S. citizen or lawful permanent resident (and for each family member of a citizen or resident, such individual's accompanying spouse or child), except that in the case of parents such citizens shall be at least 21 years old; (2) permit a widow or widower of a U.S. citizen or resident to seek permanent resident status if married at least two years at the time of the citizen's or resident's death or, if married less than two years, by showing through a preponderance of the evidence that the marriage was entered into in good faith and not solely to obtain an immigration benefit; and (3) include an alien who was the child or parent of a U.S. citizen or resident at the time of the citizen's or resident's death if the alien files a petition within two years after such date or prior to reaching 21 years old.
- Increases immigration visas for: (1) unmarried sons and daughters of U.S. citizens; and (2) brothers and sisters of U.S. citizens.
- Provides a 60,000 visa allocation for the unmarried sons and daughters of permanent resident aliens.
- Increases annual per country (10% of annual total) and dependent area (5% of annual total) limits for employment-based and family-sponsored immigrant visas.
- Expands specified family-unity exceptions to unlawful presence-based inadmissibility.
- Provides specified relief for orphans and spouses regarding: (1) petitions for immediate relative status; (2) parole eligibility; (3) permanent resident status adjustment; and (4) processing of immigrant visas.
- Filipino Veterans Family Reunification Act - Exempts children of naturalized

Filipino World War II veterans from worldwide or numerical immigrant limitations.

- Makes a minor child of an alien fiancee/fiance or of an alien spouse of a U.S. citizen eligible for derivative K-visa status provided that the child's age is determined using such child's age at the date that the petition to classify such child's parent as a K-visa alien is filed with the Secretary of Homeland Security.
- Authorizes the Secretary or the Attorney General to adjust the status of a fiancee/fiance or alien spouse and any minor children (K-visa) to conditional permanent resident status if such alien marries the petitioner within three months after U.S. admission.
- Redefines "child" for purposes of titles I and II of the Act to include a stepchild under 21 years old. (Current law includes a stepchild who has not reached 18 years old at the time the marriage creating the status of stepchild occurred.)
- Uniting American Families Act of 2009 - Amends INA to include a "permanent partner" within the scope of such Act.
- Defines "permanent partner" as an individual 18 or older who: (1) is in a committed, intimate relationship with another individual 18 or older in which both individuals intend a lifelong commitment; (2) is financially interdependent with the other individual; (3) is not married to, or in a permanent partnership with, anyone other than the individual; (4) is unable to contract with the other individual a marriage cognizable under this Act; and (5) is not a first, second, or third degree blood relation of the other individual.
- Defines "permanent partnership" as the relationship existing between two permanent partners.
- Defines "alien permanent partner" as the individual in a permanent partnership who is being sponsored for a visa.

CHAPTER THIRTY-THREE

PROPOSED LEGISLATION FOR IMMIGRATION REFORM THAT INCLUDES UAFA:

COMPREHENSIVE IMMIGRATION REFORM (CIR) ACT OF 2010

To bring our story up to date, the Comprehensive Immigration Reform Act of 2010 was introduced by Senator Robert Menendez (D-NJ) and Senator Patrick Leahy (D-VT) on September 29, 2010. It seeks to reduce waiting times for separated families to be reunited, protect both U.S.-born and immigrant workers, provide a pathway by which undocumented immigrants could earn their legal status and eventual citizenship, admit refugees as lawful permanent residents, improve immigration detention conditions, and increase the quality of border enforcement by working with local border communities.

Most pertinent for us, it includes UAFA in its language.

This bill was introduced right before the 111th Congress took its midterm election recess. While some thought it was an odd time to introduce such a measure, some immigrant rights activists thought there would be a chance to pass it during the lame duck session between the November 2010 elections and the start of the new Congressional term in January 2011. It had no co-sponsors at introduction; as of October 2010, S. 3932 had one co-sponsor. Any progress on it was happening while this book was in production. For updates on progress and more information on this bill, go to http://thomas.loc.gov. For a graphic map of how a bill becomes a law, go to *http:// www.mikewirthart.com/wp-content/uploads/2010/05/howlawsmadeWIRTH2.jpg*

Analysis by the Immigration Policy Center, reported in *Peoples World,* October 11, 2010, showed these key points about S. 3932:

> The approximately 11 million undocumented immigrants thought to be in the U.S. will be given a chance to legalize themselves and become legal permanent residents after six years, eligible for eventual U.S. citizenship. Legal immigration categories will be reconfigured to allow more immigration for family

unity and for work. A bipartisan commission will be created to determine legal immigration quotas for the future. A new guest worker program, H-2C, for areas of the U.S. economy with a shortage of labor, will be created. This is likely to be opposed by organized labor. New initiatives on border and internal enforcement are included. After five years, all U.S. employers will be required to electronically verify employees' authorization to work in America. A new electronic Social Security card will be phased in. Programs will be in place to assure immigrants detained by the government are not abused or separated from minor children, have health care and attorney services. DREAM and AgJobs Acts are included in their entirety. UAFA is included in its entirety.

Here is a summary of the bill before it was included in the online THOMAS Register:

The Comprehensive Immigration Reform Act Of 2010
Introduced by Senator Robert Menendez (D-NJ) and Senator Patrick Leahy (D-VT)

Title I Border Enforcement
- Establishes border enforcement triggers that must be met before any unauthorized immigrants can apply for permanent residency.
- Requires DHS to review assets and staffing needed for border security and enforcement.
- Funds port of entry improvements and tools and technology, in line with this review.
- Expands Customs and Border Protection (CBP) and Immigration and Customs Enforcement (ICE) staffing, in line with this review.
- Improves training and accountability for Department of Homeland Security (DHS) border and immigration officers.
- Enhances cooperation with Canada and Mexico, as well as local law enforcement agencies, to improve border security and coordinate crime fighting.
- Clarifies that the power to regulate immigration resides with the federal government, not states and localities, and that state and local police do not have the inherent authority to enforce federal immigration laws (outside of 287(g) agreements).
- Involves border communities in enforcement policy through creation of a U.S. Mexico Border Enforcement Commission and a Border Communities Liaison Office.

Title II   Interior Enforcement

- Requires DHS to track the departure of non-citizens to ensure that individuals do not overstay their visas.
- Denies visa waiver privileges to countries whose citizens attempt to overstay visas.
- Refines existing law on illegal entry, illegal reentry and voluntary departure of non-citizens to ensure enforcement of those provisions and heighten penalties for those who commit serious offenses.
- Funds and expands the State Criminal Alien Assistance Program to cover additional criminal justice costs borne by state and local governments.
- Enhances efforts to ensure that DHS does not mistakenly deport U.S. citizens and residents.
- Expands penalties for passport, visa, and immigration fraud; unlawful flight from immigration or customs controls; and gang activity.
- Expands other civil penalties and grounds of inadmissibility for certain criminals.
- Provides common sense rules governing the detention of families, elderly or ill immigrants, crime victims, and other vulnerable populations like torture survivors, as well as enforcement actions that involve children.
- Improves detention conditions to meet basic standards; expands secure alternatives to detention.
- Ends the waiting period for refugees and asylees to obtain green cards.

Title III   Worksite Enforcement

- Mandates the use of an employment verification system for all employers within five years.
- Creates a new fraud resistant, tamper resistant Social Security card; requires workers to use fraud and tamper resistant documents to prove authorization to work in the United States.
- Requires the Social Security Administration to create a reliable and secure way of verifying Social Security numbers and work authorization.
- Adds criminal penalties for fraud and misuse of Social Security numbers.
- Provides protections for workers to prevent fraudulent use of social security numbers, correct government database errors, and combat employment discrimination.
- Creates a voluntary pilot program using biometric identifiers to demonstrate work authorization.

Title IV Reforming America's Legal Immigration System

- Creates a Standing Commission on Immigration, Labor Markets, and the National interest to evaluate labor market and economic conditions and recommend quotas for employment based visa programs that Congress and the President would act on. The Commission will be made up of the Secretaries of DHS, State, Labor, Health and Human Services, and Agriculture, as well as the Attorney General, Social Security Commissioner, and seven non -governmental members appointed by the President.
- Creates the structure for a new nonimmigrant visa program (H 2C) to address gaps in existing worker programs that have lead to undocumented migration. The number of H 2C workers admitted to the program is completely dependent upon the Commission's recommendations regarding the impact on the labor market and economy. Workers must have a job offer and meet various application requirements. Once in the U.S., H 2C visa holders are able to change jobs, provided their new employer is authorized to hire H 2C workers.
- The H 2C program has various features to protect U.S. workers, such as: bars to use of the program in high unemployment areas; requirements for employers to recruit and hire American workers first; employer paid program fees; employer banishment from the program for improper use or misrepresentation; etc.
- H 2C workers are eligible to apply for green cards after having worked in the U.S. for four years, or immediately if they are sponsored by their employer.
- Significantly expands labor protections in current H 2A, H 2B, H 1B, and L 1 visa programs.
- Ensures that the number of family and employment green cards authorized by Congress do not expire because of processing delays; expands the share of visas that each country can access within existing quotas that limit overall immigration.
- Exempts certain immigrants from counting against the annual green card quotas so that they can immediately reunite with loved ones in the U.S., including spouses and minor children of green card holders.
- Revises unlawful presence bars to immigration so that individuals with family ties are not permanently banished from the U.S.
- Incorporates the AgJOBS bill, which provides a path to permanent residency for farm workers and revises agricultural employer sponsorship requirements.

- Incorporates the Uniting American Families Act, which allows permanent partners to access the family-based immigration system.

Title V Legalization of Undocumented Individuals

- Creates Lawful Prospective Immigrant (LPI) status for non criminal undocumented immigrants living in the U.S. since 9/30/10. Requires applicants to submit biometric and biographical data, undergo security and law enforcement checks, and pay a $500 fine plus application fees. LPI status lasts four years and can be extended. It includes work authorization and permission to travel abroad; immediate family members are also eligible for status under the program.
- Immigrants may apply for LPI status even if they are in deportation proceedings at the time of application or have an outstanding removal order. In order to transition from LPI status to Legal Permanent Residency (i.e. a green card), applicants are required to wait at least six years; pay taxes and a $1000 fine; learn English and U.S. civics; and undergo additional background checks. They will not obtain green cards before those who were waiting in line to immigrate as of date of enactment.
- The LPI program includes a level of administrative and judicial review, confidentiality protections for applicants and their employers, and fraud prevention measures.
- Incorporates the DREAM Act, which creates a path to legal status for individuals who were brought to the U.S. illegally as children, provided they meet age and other criteria and enroll in college or the U.S. military.

Title VI Immigrant Integration and Other Reforms

- Enhances programs and policies to help immigrants learn English and U.S. civics, such as: tax credits for teachers of English language learners and businesses who provide such training for their employees; a revamped DHS Office of Citizenship and New Americans to assist with immigrant integration; and grants for states who work to successfully integrate newcomers.
- Provides humanitarian immigration visas for Haitian children orphaned by the 2010 earthquake; Liberian nationals who fled civil strife and received Temporary Protected Status in the U.S.; and the immediate relatives of September 11th terrorism victims.
- Establishes a Commission on Wartime Treatment of European Americans and a Commission on Wartime Treatment of Jewish Refugees to review

the country's immigration and foreign policies during World War II.

-   Improves access to interpreters in state courts.
-   Evaluates the factors that drive undocumented migration from key send-ing countries and requires the State Department to develop a strategy to reduce migration pressures.

CHAPTER THIRTY-FOUR

WHAT YOU CAN DO
TO HELP

Share Your Story

A post on the LGBT issues website *10,000 Couples* (*www.10thousandcouples.com/*) states: "Poll after poll shows the most powerful thing we can do to change hearts and minds about gay issues is to come out."

Karin and I agree: If you are part of a same-sex binational couple, the most powerful thing you can do is share your story.

There are many ways to explain the challenges you face in keeping your family together. Make sure your family and friends know that sharing your story is important, and get them to help, too. If you are family or friends of a same-sex binational couple, you can do the same. This can be scary, but the more people who know about this situation—especially those in the LGBT community—the better, for all of us.

I am embarrassed to admit that I didn't know much about a problem that affects the lives and livelihoods of so many until it became my daily life. Don't assume that you can't do anything to help. Be counted. Add your voice. Get your story moving—the power of it helps all of us. One voice, one story, can truly make a difference. Photographs help, too.

The other important and powerful thing you can do is share stories about people facing this issue. Really listen when people tell you their story. Take it to heart. Share it with others. It helps the larger community understand the challenges same-sex binational couples face and helps work to the solution we need.

Make sure that others who are facing different immigration obstacles understand that there are gay men and lesbians with an immigration issue that is also unsolved and hard to live with. When other immigration reform groups and the LGBT community combine forces it leverages power for all. Working together, we can speed up truly comprehensive immigration reform for everyone.

Write letters. Write e-mails. Use social media like Facebook and Twitter to network and share resources. Make phone calls. Send faxes. Go to *Friendfactor.org* and join their network.

You can quickly write a letter to your local newspaper about your story. If you are afraid to self-identify you can talk about the subject in general, or have someone else write the letter and share that they know someone who is having this problem. That way you can share the details of the problem without outing yourself or creating risk for someone who is not able to come out.

Tell your local community through your newspaper why it is important that comprehensive immigration reform includes same-sex binational couples and that Congress needs to pass the Uniting American Families Act, or the Reuniting Families Act, or the Comprehensive Immigration Reform Act of 2010, or another truly inclusive comprehensive immigration reform bill soon, so that Americans can sponsor their same-sex partners for immigration. Get help with writing a letter from Immigration Equality at *http://www.immigrationequality.org/template.php?pageid=20*

Contact your three federal elected officials: your member of Congress and your two Senators. To find out who your Senators and Members of Congress are, look in your local phonebook under the Federal Offices listing section, or by going online to *www.contactingthecongress.org* or to *www.congressmerge.com*. At their websites, you can find out how to contact them on their site or get their phone, e-mail, U.S. Mail and fax listings. You can phone, write, fax, or e-mail them in their district offices in your state or at their Washington, D.C. office, or via their website pages. It's not hard.

Visit Your Elected Federal Representatives

If you can, make a personal visit to your two senators and member of Congress. It's not impossible to see him or her, especially during their recess periods, but it may seem impossible to get an appointment. Try getting an appointment with a staff person, especially the staff person assigned to LGBT or immigration issues. Talk to that person about your story and why UAFA and RFA and CIR Act of 2010 are crucial for same-sex binational couples.

Out4Immigration has a link that shows you how to assemble a booklet to share your plight. Log on to *http://tinyurl.com/o4i-toolkit1* and prepare your best presentation to show your federal officials what you face with current U.S. immigration laws—the laws that need to change.

Immigration Equality also has information and online contact forms to help you do this and get involved in other ways to help in the fight. Log on to *http://www.immigrationequality.org/template.php?pageid=20*

Gather up your courage. Take a parent or sibling or friend along, if your partner is out of the country. Put a face on the issue: it helps you, and it helps all of us.

Volunteer

Find a group you know that is working on this issue, or check the Resource Groups and Websites chapter. See how you can help them with their project. An easy way to make an impact is to join the online letter-writing campaign conducted each week by Out4Immigration. Go to *www.out4immigration.org* and find out how to help. If you have a new idea that will help, suggest it to a group and get people to help implement it.

Whether or not this is your personal issue, you can make a difference in the lives of same-sex binational couples and their families. We will all appreciate the help and support.

Donate

Money always helps move things along. Even if it is a small amount, all donations help the cause. If you already know a group working on this issue, send them what you can. If you need to find a group to assist financially, look in the Resource Groups and Websites chapter and write a check or go online to their donation site and help. We all appreciate every penny.

Organize A Fundraiser With This Book

If your school, church, meeting, synagogue, mosque, temple, LGBT center, LGBT club, political club, women's group, PFLAG chapter, ACLU chapter, NAACP chapter, labor union, immigration group, or other organization wants to hold a fundraiser by selling *Torn Apart*, it's easy. Earn money to help your efforts at LGBT rights, civil rights, immigration reform, education, and advocacy.

Go to the back of the book and find out how to do it. All you have to do is make a flyer (or publicize it in your newsletter or on your website) and have people buy directly from Findhorn Press. Just arrange with the publisher (*tornapart@findhornpress. com*) to get a unique ordering code for your organization.

You then put your organization code name on the flyer you make or in your newsletter or on your website. People buy the book directly from the publisher and your group earns money for every book sold. The money you earn will be sent to you directly each year after royalties are computed.

Another way you can do it is to buy books in bulk at the reduced price (you must pay shipping and handling costs) and sell them for the retail price at any events you hold. If you take this route, the money you get for selling *Torn Apart* is yours to keep.

You can organize a meeting about same-sex binational couples' immigration problems and sell books there. Or advertise them in your newsletter or in flyers or on your website and sell them directly to your members and their contacts.

If you want to arrange a book signing with the author, inquire about that with Findhorn Press (*tornapart@findhornpress.com*). They will discuss the details with you.

CHAPTER THIRTY-FIVE

RESOURCE GROUPS AND WEBSITES

This chapter includes listings of groups and social media websites, and anything else I located that is devoted to the issue at hand and/or related issues. Read it carefully. It could be very helpful to you and your situation.

I've divided the chapter into three parts.

The first section focuses on the three groups who work on same-sex binational couples' immigration issues solely or primarily. These three groups are also the major beneficiaries of the proceeds from sales of this book. They are: Immigration Equality, Love Exiles, and Out4Immigration. Thanks for all the work you do.

The second section includes many groups, including those who work on marriage equality and/or same-sex binational couples' immigration issues as part of a larger LGBT/civil rights or immigration reform agenda. While they are not the major recipients of proceeds from the sale of this book, they will benefit from some of the proceeds as more books are sold. Thanks for all the work you do. Karin and I hope donations will also go their way when readers find out about their work. So thanks in advance for all of your donations to help groups fight for LGBT rights and immigration reform and the overall cause of civil rights and equality.

Section three includes organizations or sources of information that deal with the law, legislative process, or legal issues in general or with political parties.

These listings are what I have been able to find in printed and online sources. Please note: even though I am providing contact information on a variety of resources here, I specifically do not endorse any particular plan of action or advise anyone on who to see or what to do in your situation. See what these resource groups and sites may offer you and your family and friends in your struggle for immigration equality or your support for those of us in the struggle. Get complete and current information about groups at their websites.

A. Resource Groups Who Work on Same-Sex
Binational Couples' Immigration Issues Solely or Primarily

These three groups have been in the trenches for years, seeking solutions to the immigration discrimination faced by Americans with same-sex partners from outside the United States—discrimination that tears apart families and destroys lives, careers, and livelihoods. These groups work hard to keep families together and fight to allow Americans the right to sponsor their permanent partners for immigration to America.

1. Immigration Equality

Immigration Equality (*www.immigrationequality.org*) was founded in 1994 as the Lesbian and Gay Immigration Rights Task Force and is a national organization that works to end immigration discrimination against lesbian, gay, bisexual, transgender, and HIV-positive people. It is leading the fight for fair immigration laws for LGBT families, including the Uniting American Families Act and the more recent bills that include it. Immigration Equality provides LGBT immigrants and their loved ones with timely, accurate, and legal information and access to qualified attorneys. Persons needing help with immigration, asylum, and related issues for same-sex binational couples can access informational materials, trainings, and personal help by email and telephone inquiries.

The organization provides legal services, information, and support to immigrants, activists, attorneys, and legislators. It also has a pro bono asylum project to assist LGBT and HIV-positive asylum seekers find free or low-cost representation.

Immigration Equality helps win asylum in the United States for those persecuted in their home country because of their sexual orientation, transgender identity, or HIV-status. The organization also maintains a list of LGBT/HIV-friendly private immigration attorneys who provide legal representation to people who need it.

With help from the nation's leading law firms, Immigration Equality has won freedom and safety in America for hundreds of LGBT and HIV-positive asylum-seekers. Immigration Equality's work with precedent-setting cases has helped shape sexual orientation-based asylum law.

Through education, outreach, advocacy, and the maintenance of a nationwide network of resources, Immigration Equality fights for those who are threatened by persecution or the discriminatory impact of immigration law.

Immigration Equality's new Action Fund advocates on Capitol Hill for equality for lesbian, gay, bisexual, transgender, and HIV-positive immigrants and their families.

To end discrimination in U.S. immigration law, Immigration Equality Action Fund works to pass the Uniting American Families Act and LGBT- inclusive Comprehensive Immigration Reform. The Action Fund lobbies legislators and other policy makers, builds coalitions, and empowers LGBT immigrant families around the country to fight for change.

You can support Immigration Equality by buying this book (use online ordering code IEAF15 at *www.findhornpress.com*) or donate directly by contacting them at:

Immigration Equality, Inc.
40 Exchange Place, 17th Floor
New York, NY 10005
Phone: 212-714-2904
Fax: 212-714-2973
E-mail: *info@immigrationequality.org*
Blog: *http://www.immigrationequality.org/blog/*
Facebook: *http://www.facebook.com/immigrationequality*
Twitter: *http://www.twitter.com/IEquality*
YouTube: *http://www.youtube.com/immigrationequality*
Website: *www.immigrationequality.org*

2. Love Exiles Foundation

The Love Exiles Foundation (*www.loveexiles.org*) is a resource that helps binational couples navigate the legal, social, emotional and geographical hurdles they face every day. Love Exiles was born out of real-life experiences of men and women from all walks of life, from countries around the world with a common goal: to love and live and build a life together with their partners legally and securely. These first-hand experiences are a tremendous source of practical and logistical knowledge. Love Exiles has an extensive network of individuals, couples, families, professionals, colleagues, and organizations around the world.

Love Exiles encourages and supports same-sex couples to powerfully advocate for change by sharing their stories with the media, friends, colleagues, family, strangers. Love Exiles has been empowering people to speak out and connecting binational couples to information, resources, and networks to assist them navigate their future together since 2002. There are Love Exiles online communities in Germany, the Netherlands, Spain, the United Kingdom, Canada and Australia. If you'd like more information, to join a group, or to volunteer, visit *www.loveexiles.org*. Find Love Exiles Foundation on Facebook at Love Exiles.

You can support Love Exiles Foundation by buying this book (use online ordering code LOEX17 at www.findhornpress.com) or donate directly by contacting them at:

Love Exiles Foundation
Phone: +31 6 2150 4249
E-mail: exiles@xs4all.nl
YouTube: (in process)
Website: *http://www.loveexiles.org/*

3. Out4Immigration

Out4immigration (*www.out4immigration.org*) began as the San Francisco chapter of the Lesbian and Gay Immigration Rights Task Force and became Out4Immigration in 2006. Out4Immigration is an all-volunteer grassroots organization that addresses the widespread discriminatory impact of U.S. immigration laws on the lives of lesbian, gay, bisexual, transgender and HIV+ people and their families through education, outreach, advocacy, and the maintenance of a resource and support network.

The organization was started in 2006 by a group of grassroots same-sex binational couples from San Francisco and Los Angeles who were members of Lesbian and Gay Immigration Rights Task Force.

Out4Immigration's website says: NO U.S. citizen should be forced to choose between country and partner! If YOU believe, as we do, that it is outrageous that gay/lesbian U.S. citizens are forced to choose between country and partner if they happen to have a partner from another country, please join us and help us raise awareness of this issue. You can support Out4Immigration by buying this book (use online ordering code OUT416 at *www.findhornpress.com*) or donate directly by contacting them at:

Out4Immigration
P.O. Box 14073
San Francisco, CA 94114
Voicemail: (347)-Out4Imm, 347-688-4466
E-mail: info@out4immigration.org
Facebook: *http://www.facebook.com/out4immigration*
Twitter: *http://www.twitter.com/out4immigration*
YouTube: *http://www.youtube.com/out4immigration*
Blog: *http://out4immigration.blogspot.com*
Action: *http://www.change.org/actions/search?search=lgbt+immigration+rights*
Website: *http://www.out4immigration.org*

B. Resource Groups or Websites Who Work on Marriage Equality and/or Same-Sex Binational Couples' Immigration Issues as Part of a Larger LGBT/Civil Rights or Immigration Reform Agenda and Groups Who Have Endorsed UAFA

This section includes those organizations who work on marriage equality and/or immigration equality as part of a larger LGBT or civil rights or immigration reform agenda. The groups are not limited to same-sex binational couples or LGBT issues but, nevertheless, work on issues that affect couples like Karin and me.

This section also includes employee groups that have signed on to support the Uniting American Families Act (UAFA). If your particular marriage equality/civil rights/LGBT/immigration reform group is not listed here, then I missed it in my search and I apologize. If you do not find your particular employer group listed here, urge them to sign up to support the Uniting American Families Act (UAFA).

If you are really starting from scratch or need a support group, the place to begin your search is to find the LGBT center nearest you by logging on to the national online website CenterLink (*www.lgbtcenters.org*). I'm glad technology has advanced so much since I was a suddenly-single lesbian in the 1980s and needed to know where to find my tribe.

A Day in Hand: *www.adayinhand.com/*
About.com - Immigration Issues: *http://immigration.about.com/?nl=1*
Advocates for Youth: *www.advocatesforyouth.org/*
Al-Fatiha Foundation: *www.al-fatiha.org/*
All Out: *www.allout.org*
Alternatives to Marriage Project, Inc. (AIMP): *www.unmarried.org/*
American Civil Liberties Union (ACLU): *www.aclu.org*
American Families United (AFU): *www.americanfamiliesunited.org/*
American Foundation for Equal Rights (AFER): *www.equalrightsfoundation.org/*
American Immigration Council: *www.americanimmigrationcouncil.org/*
American Immigration Lawyers Association (AILA): *www.aila.org/*
American Jewish Committee (AJC): *www.ajc.org/*
American Veterans for Equal Rights (AVER) (formerly Gay, Lesbian, and Bisexual Veterans of America): *http://aver.us/aver/*
American-Arab Anti-Discrimination Committee (ADC): *www.adc.org/*
Americans for Democratic Action (ADA): *www.adaction.org/*
Americans United for Separation of Church and State (AU): *www.au.org/*
Amnesty International (AI): *www.amnesty.org/*
Anti-Defamation League (ADL): *www.adl.org/*
ARC International: *www.arc-international.net*
Asian American Institute (AAI): *www.aaichicago.org/*
Asian American Justice Center (AAJC): *www.napalc.org/*

Asian Americans for Community Involvement (AACI): *www.aaci.org/*
Asian & Pacific Island Family Pride (API Pride): *www.apifamilypride.org/*
Asian Law Alliance (ALA): *www.asianlawalliance.org/*
Asian Law Caucus: *www.asianlawcaucus.org/*
Asian Pacific American Labor Alliance (APALA): *http://www.apalanet.org/*
Asian Pacific American Legal Center (APALC): *www.apalc.org/*
Asian-Pacific Islander Legal Outreach (APILO): *www.apilegaloutreach.org/*
Asian Pacific Islander Lesbian Bisexual Queer Women and Transgender Coalition
    (APIQWTC): *www.apiqwtc.org/*
Asian and Pacific Islander Wellness Center: *www.apiwellness.org/history.html*
Association of Flight Attendants – CWA: *www.afanet.org/*
Association of Unity Churches: *www.unity.org/*
Association of Welcoming and Affirming Baptists: *www.wabaptists.org/*
Audre Lorde Project: *www.alp.org*
Axios (Eastern and Orthodox Gay and Lesbian Christians):
    www.eskimo.com/~nickz/axios.html

Basic Rights Oregon: *www.basicrights.org*
Bay Area Immigrant Rights Coalition: *www.immigrantrights.org/resources.asp*
Bay Area Municipal Elections Committee (BAYMEC): *www.baymec.net*
BIENESTAR: *www.bienestar.org/*
Billy De Frank LGBT Community Center: *www.defrankcenter.org/*
BiNet USA: *www.binetusa.org/*
Bullying Info: *www.BullyingInfo.org*

California Faith for Equality: *www.cafaithforequality.org/*
Call to Action: *www.cta-usa.org/*
Catholics for Equality: *www.catholicsforequality.org*
Center for American Progress (CAP): *www.americanprogress.org/*
Center for Community Change : *www.communitychange.org/*
Center for Immigration Studies (CIS): *www.cis.org*
Center for Lesbian and Gay Studies in Religion and Ministry: *www.clgs.org*
CenterLink: The Community of LGBT Centers:
    E-mail: *CenterLink@lgbtcenters.org*
    Website: *http://resources.lgbtcenters.org/Directory/Find-A-Center.aspx*
Change.org: *www.change.org*
Christian Church (Disciples of Christ) in the United States and Canada:
    www.disciples.org/
Christians for Comprehensive Immigration Reform:
    http://www.faithandimmigration.org/
Church World Service, Immigration and Refugee Program:
    www.churchworldservice.org/refugees
Civil Rights Fast: *civilrightsfast.com*
Clergy United, Inc.: *http://www.clergyunited.org/*
Coalition for Humane Immigrant Rights of Los Angeles (CHIRLA): *www.chirla.org/*
COLAGE - People with a Lesbian, Gay, Bisexual, Transgender or Queer Parent:
    www.colage.org
Common Cause: *www.commoncause.org*

Community Relations Council of the Jewish Federation of Silicon Valley: *jvalley.org/*
ctEQUALITY: *www.ctequality.com*
Council of Churches of Santa Clara County: *www.councilofchurches-scc.org/*
Council for Global Equality: *www.GlobalEquality.org*
Courage Campaign: *www.couragecampaign.org/*
Covenant Network: *www.covnetpres.org/*

DignityUSA: *www.dignityusa.org/*
Disciples Home Missions: *http://www.discipleshomemissions.org/*
Dolores Huerta Foundation: *http://www.doloreshuerta.org/*

Episcopal Church: *www.episcopalchurch.org/*
Equal Rights Washington: *www.equalrightswashington.org*
Equality Across America: *www.equalityacrossamerica.org/*
Equality America: *www.facebook.com/pages/Equality-America/114055221948808*
Equality California (EQCA): *www.eqca.org*
Equality Illinois (EQIL): *www.equalityillinois.org/*
Equality Maine (EQME): *www.equalitymaine.org/*
Equality North Carolina: *www.equalitync.org/*
Equality Ohio: *www.equalityohio.org/*
Evangelicals Concerned: *www.ecwr.org/*
Every Student Deserves a Safe Space!: *www.SafeSpaceKit.com*

Fair Immigration Reform Movement (FIRM): *www.communitychange.org*
Faith in America: *www.faithinamerica.org*
Family Equality Council (FEC): *www.familyequality.org/*
Family Pride Coalition: (formerly Gay and Lesbian Parents Coalition International)
   www.familypride.org
Feetin2Worlds: *http://news.feetintwoworlds.org*
Fellowship of Reconciling Pentecostals International (RPI):
   http://www.religioustolerance.org/hom_upci.htm
Feministing – Young Feminists Blogging, Organizing, Kicking Ass: *www.feministing.com/*
Fight Back New York: *fightbackpac.com/*
Freedom to Marry: *www.freedomtomarry.org*
Frente Unido Pro Inmigrantes/United Front for Immigrants: *www.casaaztlan.org*
Friendfactor: *www.friendfactor.org*
Friends Committee on National Legislation (FCNL): *www.fcnl.org/*
Friends General Conference: *www.fgcquaker.org/*

Gay and Lesbian Activists Alliance of Washington, D.C. (GLAA): *www.glaa.org/*
Gay and Lesbian Advocates and Defenders (GLAD): *www.glad.org*
Gay and Lesbian Alliance Against Defamation (GLAAD): *www.glaad.org*
(GLAAD has an Immigration Inequality Kit for media available at:
   www.glaad.org/immigrationinequalitykit)
Gay and Lesbian Vaishnava Association: *www.galva108.org/*
Gay and Lesbian Victory Fund (also called Victory Fund): *www.victoryfund.org/*
Gay Asian Pacific Alliance (GAPA): *www.gapa.org/*
Gay, Lesbian, and Straight Education Network (GLSEN): *www.glsen.org*
Gay Men's Health Crisis (GMHC): *www.gmhc.org/*

Gay Liberation Network (GLN): *www.gayliberation.net/home.html*
Gay Rights Media: *www.gayrightsmedia.org/*
GetEQUAL.org: *www.getequal.org/*
GetEQUAL NOW!: *www.getequalnow.org/*
Give a Damn! Campaign: *www.wegiveadamn.org/*
Global Alliance of Affirming Apostolic Pentecostals (GAAAP):
  www.affirmingapostolic.com/
GOProud: *www.goproud.org/*

Harvey Milk Festival: *www.harveymilkfestival.com*
Harvey Milk Foundation: *www.milkfoundation.org*
Hebrew Immigrant Aid Society (HIAS): *www.hias.org/*
Horizons Foundation: *www.horizonsfoundation.org*
Hotel Employees & Restaurant Employees International Union (HERE):
  www.unitehere.org/
Hudson Valley LGBTQ Center: *www.lgbtqcenter.org/*
Human Rights Campaign (HRC): *www.hrc.org*
Human Rights First: *www.humanrightsfirst.org*
Human Rights Watch: *www.hrw.org*

Immigrant Connect: *www.immigrantconnect.org/*
Immigrant Legal Resource Center: *www.ilrc.org/*
Immigrant Rights: *http://immigration.change.org/*
Immigrants List PAC: *http://www.immigrantslist.org*
ImmigrationDirect.com: *http://www.immigrationdirect.com/visas/visitor/Get-a-US-Tourist-Business-Visa-Visitors-Visa-B1-B2-Visa.jsp*
Immigration Impact: *http://immigrationimpact.com/*
Immigration Policy Center: *www.immigrationpolicy.org/*
Institute for Welcoming Resources: *http://www.welcomingresources.org/marriage.xml*
Integrity USA: *http://www.integrityusa.org/*
Interagency Working Group on Youth Programs (IWGYP): *www.findyouthinfo.gov/about.shtml, www.findyouthinfo.org, www.solutionsdesk.ou.edu/*
International Gay and Lesbian Human Rights Commission (IGLHRC):
  www.iglhrc.org
International Lesbian, Gay, Bisexual, Trans and Intersex Association (ILGA):
  www.ilga.org/
International Lesbian and Gay Association (ILGA): *old.ilga.org/*
Interfaith Council on Economics and Justice:
  www.wpusa.org/Interfaith-Council/index.htm
InterPride – International Association of Gay Pride Coordinators: *www.interpride.org/*
It Gets Better Project: *www.ItGetsBetterProject.com*

Japanese American Citizens League (JACL): *www.jacl.org/*
Join the Impact: National Grassroots: *jointheimpact.com/about-us/*
Keshet: *www.keshetonline.org/*

Labor Council for Latin American Advancement: *www.lclaa.org/*
Lambda Legal: *www.lambdalegal.org*
Lambda Literary Foundation: *http://www.lambdaliterary.org/*

League of United Latin American Citizens (LULAC): *www.lulac.org/*
Legal Momentum: *www.legalmomentum.org/*
LGBT Aging Project: *www.lgbtagingproject.org/*
LGBT Immigration Equality Rights: *http://imeq.us/*
LGBTQ Youth Space: *http://events.mercurynews.com/san-jose-ca/venues/show/*
  2691805-lgbtq-youth-space
Lesbian and Gay Lawyers Association of Los Angeles (LGLA): *www.lgla.net*
Log Cabin Republicans: *www.logcabin.org*
Lord's New Church Which is Nova Hierosolyma: *www.thelordsnewchurch.com/*
Lutherans Concerned/North America: *www.lcna.org/*

Make It Better Project: *www.makeitbetterproject.org*
Marriage Equality Rhode Island (MERI): *www.marriageequalityri.org*
Marriage Equality Silicon Valley: *http://marriageequalitysiliconvalley.org*
Marriage Equality USA: *www.marriageequality.org*
Marriage Project - Hawaii: *http://members.tripod.com/~MPHAWAII/*
Mass Equality: *www.massequality.org*
Matthew Shepard Foundation: *www.matthewshepard.org/*
Men Who Have Sex with Men (MSM): *www.caps.ucsf.edu/pubs/FS/MSMrev.php*
Metropolitan Community Churches: *www.ufmcc.com/*
Mexican-American Legal Defense Education Fund (MALDEF): *www.maldef.org/*

National Asian Pacific American Women's Forum (NAPAWF): *www.napawf.org/*
National Association for the Advancement of Colored People (NAACP):
  www.naacp.org/
National Association of Latino Elected and Appointed Officials (NALEO):
  www.naleo.org
National Asylum Partnership on Sexual Minorities at the National Immigrant Justice
  Center in Chicago: *www.immigrantjustice.org/news/napso/*
National Black Justice Coalition: *www.nbjc.org/*
National Center for Lesbian Rights (NCLR): *www.nclrights.org*
National Center for Transgender Equality (NCTE): *http://transequality.org/*
National Coalition for LGBT Health: *http://lgbthealth.webolutionary.com/*
National Council of Churches of Christ in the USA: *http://www.ncccusa.org/*
National Council of Churches of Christ in the USA Immigration Ministries:
  www.ncccusa.org/immigration/immigmain.html
National Council of La Raza (NCLR): *www.nclr.org*
National Equality March: *www.en.wikipedia.org/wiki/National_Equality_March,*
  www.equalityacrossamerica.org/blog/?page_id=19
National Gay and Lesbian Chamber of Commerce (NGLCC): *www.nglcc.org/*
National Gay and Lesbian Task Force (NGLTF): *www.ngltf.org*
National Immigrant Justice Center (NIJC): *www.immigrantjustice.org/*
National Immigration Forum (NIF): *www.immigrationforum.org/*
National Immigration Law Center (NILC): *www.nilc.org/*
National Latina Institute for Immigrant Women's Rights (NCWIR):
  www.latinainstitute.org/issues/immigrant-rights
National Lesbian and Gay Bar Association: *www.lavenderlaw.org/*
National Lesbian Political Action Committee (US): *www.lesbian.org/nlpac*

National LGBT Bar Association: *www.lgbtbar.org*
National Lesbian and Gay Journalists Association: *www.nlgjany.org/*
National Organization for Women/Lesbian Rights: *www.now.org/issues/lgbi*
National Queer Asian Pacific Islander Alliance: *www.nqapia.org/*
National Transgender Advocacy Coalition: *www.ntac.org*
National Youth Advocacy Coalition (NYAC): *www.nyacyouth.org/*
New York Civil Liberties Union: *www.nyclu.org/immigrationreform*
NOLO Lawyer Directory: *www.nolo.com/ldir/find/lawyer.do*
NOW Legal Defense League: *www.nowldef.org*

Office & Professional Employees International Union (OPEIU): *www.opeiu.org/*
One Nation Working Together: *www.onenationworkingtogether.org*
Organization of Chinese Americans (OCA): *www.ocanational.org/*
Out and Equal Workplace Advocates (Out and Equal): *www.outandequal.org/*
!OutProud!: *www.outproud.org*
Outfront, Amnesty International: Lesbian, Gay Men, Bisexual and Transgender
    People's Human Rights Program: *www.amnestyusa.org/group/outfront*
Outlet: *www.projectoutlet.org/*
Outserve: *www.outserve.org/*

Parents, Families and Friends of Lesbians and Gays (PFLAG): *www.pflag.org*
Partners Task Force for Gay and Lesbian Couples: *http://buddybuddy.com/partners.html*
Personal PAC: *www.personalpac.org/*
People for the American Way: *www.pfaw.org/*
Presbyterian Church (USA): *www.pcusa.org/*
Presente.org: *http://presente.org*
Pride Agenda: *www.prideagenda.org/*
Pride at Work (AFL-CIO): *www.igc.org/prideatwork*
ProLatino: *http://www.prolatino.org/*
Proud Parenting: *www.proudparenting.com*
Proyecto Orgullo (Project Pride): *www.bienestar.org/eng/page/59/Proyecto-Orgullo.html*

Queer Immigrant Rights Project: *www.idealist.org/en/org/150520-102*
Queer or Ally at Cal: *http://queer.berkeley.edu/*

"REEL Images of Immigration: A Movie Guide to Discussing Faith and
    Immigration": *http://www.faithandimmigration.org/action/download-reel-images-immigration-movie-guide-discussing-faith-and-immigration*
Reform Immigration for America: *www.reformimmigrationforamerica.org/*
Religion Dispatches: *www.religiondispatches.org/*
Restore Fairness: *www.restorefairness.org*
RU12? Community Center: *http://www.ru12.org/*

Safe Schools Coalition (SSC): *www.safeschoolscoalition.org/*
Service Employees International Union (SEIU): *www.seiu.org/*
Service Members Legal Defense Network (SLDN): *www.sldn.org/*
Services and Advocacy for Gay, Lesbian, Bisexual and Transgender Elders (SAGE):
    www.sageusa.org
Services, Immigrant Rights, and Education Network (SIREN): *www.siren-bayarea.org/*
Seventh-day Adventist Kinship: *www.sdakinship.org/*

Sexual Minority Youth Assistance League (SMYAL): *www.smyal.org*
Shades of Yellow (SOY): *www.myspace.com/shadesofyellow_hmong*
Silicon Valley FACES: *www.svccj.org/*
Sojourners: *www.sojo.net*
Sojourner's Christians for Comprehensive Immigration Reform Campaign:
    www.faithandimmigration.org
South Asian Americans Leading Together (SAALT): *http://www.saalt.org/*
South Bay AFL-CIO Labor Council: *www.atwork.org/*
Southern Poverty Law Center (SPLC): *www.splcenter.org/*
Standing on the Side of Love (SSL): *www.standingonthesideoflove.org/*
Stonewall Democrats: *www.stonewalldemocrats.org/*
Straight for Equality: *http://straightforequality.org/*
Swedenborgian Church of North America: *www.swedenborg.org/*

TAGALA (Your key to connecting the Gay, Lesian, Bisexual, Transgender and Ally
    community of Northwest Ohio and Southeast Michigan): *www.tagalaonline.org*
Take Back Pride: *www. TakeBackPride.org*
The Center for Community Change: *www.communitychange.org/*
The Center for Lesbian and Gay Civil Rights: *www.center4civilrights.org*
The Coming Out Project (HRC): *http://www.hrc.org/issues/coming_out.asp*
The Council for Global Equality: *www.globalequality.org*
The Jewish Federations of North America: *www.ujc.org/*
The Leadership Conference on Civil and Human Rights (LCCR):
    http://www.civilrights.org
The Point Foundation - LGBT Scholars: *www.thepointfoundation.org/*
The Task Force 2010 Action Center: *ActionFund@theTaskForceActionFund.org*
The Trevor Project - 24-hour hotline 1-866-4-U-TREVOR (1-866-488-7386):
    www.thetrevorproject.org/
Torn Apart: United by Love, Divided by Law: *http://tornapart.findhornpress.com*
Transgender Law Center: *www.transgenderlawcenter.org/*
True Colors Fund: *http://www.truecolorsfund.org/*
Truth Wins Out (TWO): *www.truthwinsout.org/*

Unid@s: *www.unidoslgbt.org/*
Union for Reform Judaism: *www.urj.org/*
Unitarian Universalist Association of Congregations: *www.uua.org/*
UNITE HERE!: *www.unitehere.org/*
United Church of Christ (UCC): *www.ucc.org/*
United Church of Christ Coalition for Lesbian, Gay, Bisexual, and Transgender
    Concerns: *www.ucccoalition.org/*
United Front for Immigrants/Frente Unido Pro Inmigrantes:
    http://www.casaaztlan.org/united_front
United Methodist Church: *www.umc.org/*
United Nations Gay and Lesbian Organization (UN GLOBE): *www.unglobe.org/*
United States Hispanic Leadership Institute (USHLI): *www.ushli.org/*

Vermont Freedom to Marry: *www.vtfreetomarry.org*
Vermont Freedom to Marry Task Force: *www.vtfreetomarrytaskforce.org*

Vermont Fund for Families: *www.vermontfundforfamilies.org*
Victory Fund (also called Gay and Lesbian Victory Fund): *www.victoryfund.org/*
Voto Latino: *www.votolatino.org/*

We the People: *www.gaysonoma.com/*
Welcoming Schools: *http://www.welcomingschools.org/*
Williams Project: *www.law.ucla.edu/williamsinstitute/home.html*
We Are America Stories: *www.weareamericastories.org*
Working Partnerships USA: *www.wpusa.org/*

C. Organizations or Sources of Information Dealing with the Law, Legislative Process, Legal Issues in General or Political Parties

ACT On Principles: *http://www.actonprinciples.org/*
ACT on Principles: Turning Principles into Equality (American Equality Bill in House): *http://www.actonprinciples.org/aeb-house/*
ACT on Principles: Turning Principles into Equality (American Equality Bill in Senate): *http://www.actonprinciples.org/aeb-senate/*
ACT on Principles: Turning Principles into Equality (How the Public Whip Count Works): *http://www.actonprinciples.org/public-whip-count/*
ACT on Principles: Turning Principles into Equality (Uniting American Families Act (UAFA) in the House): *http://www.actonprinciples.org/uafa-house/*
ACT on Principles: Turning Principles into Equality (Uniting American Families Act (UAFA) in the Senate): *http://www.actonprinciples.org/uafa-senate/*
American Bar Association (ABA): *www.abanet.org/*
American Independent Party: *http://www.aipca.org/*
America's Independent Party: *http://www.selfgovernment.us/*

Common Cause: *www.commoncause.org*
Communist Party USA: *http://www.cpusa.org/*

Democratic National Committee: *www.democrats.org/*
Democrats Abroad: *www.democratsabroad.org/*

GovTrack.us: (Tracking the U.S. Congress) *www.govtrack.us/*
Green Party of the United States: *www.gp.org/index.php*

How to Find Your Senators and Congressional Representative:
www.contactingthecongress.org
www.congressmerge.com

Libertarian Party: *http://www.lp.org/*
Library of Congress THOMAS: *http://thomas.loc.gov/*

National LGBT Bar Association: *www.lgbtbar.org/*
Project Vote Smart: *www.votesmart.org/index.htm*
Raise Your Vote: *https://www.raiseyourvote.com*
Republican National Committee: *www.gop.com/*
Republicans Abroad: *www.republicansabroad.org*
Rock the Vote!: *http://rockthevote.org/*

RESOURCE GROUPS AND WEBSITES

Socialist Party USA: *http://www.sp-usa.org/*

United States Census: *http://2010.census.gov/2010census/*
United States Citizenship and Immigration Services: *www.uscis.gov/portal/site/uscis*
USA.Gov: *http://www.usa.gov/*

VoteEquality.com: *http://www.VoteEquality.com/*
Vote from Abroad: *www.VotefromAbroad.org*
Voting Information Project: *www.votinginfoproject.org*

Call or Write the President

The White House
1600 Pennsylvania Avenue NW
Washington, DC 20500
Please include your e-mail address

PHONE NUMBERS
Comments: 202-456-1111
Switchboard: 202-456-1414
FAX: 202-456-2461
TTY/TDD
Comments: 202-456-6213
Visitors Office: 202-456-2121

E-MAIL the President - individuals
http://www.whitehouse.gov/contact

E-MAIL the President - organizations
http://www.whitehouse.gov/contact/
organizations

CHAPTER THIRTY-SIX

MEDIA, WEBSITES,
AND SOURCES

Articles

- "A Call to Action on Comprehensive Immigration Reform," *National Council of Churches USA*, NCCUSA's Immigration Task Force, *http://www.ncccusa.org/NCCpolicies/immigrationreform092110.pdf*

- "A Final Request," *Advocate*, September 8, 2010, Andrew Harmon, *http://www.advocate.com/News/Daily_News/2010/09/08/A_Final_Request/*

- "A Hero for Our Time," *Uniting American Families*, October 20, 2009 *http://www.unitingamericanfamilies.net/true-stories-of-bad-law/a-hero-for-our-time/*

- "A Right to Marry: Same-Sex Marriage and Constitutional Law," *Dissent*, June 29, 2009, Martha Nussbaum, *http://www.dissentmagazine.org/online.php?id=266 on Gay*

- "A Risky Proposal: Is It Too Soon to Petition the Supreme Court on Gay Marriage?" *New Yorker*, January 18, 2010, Margaret Talbot, *http://www.newyorker.com/reporting/2010/01/18/100118fa_fact_talbot*

- "Activists Press for Homosexual 'Rights' to Be Included in Comprehensive Immigration Reform," *CNS News*, October 26, 2009, Penny Starr, *http://www.cnsnews.com/news/article/56102*

- "Administration Deporting Legally Married Gay Spouses Because of DOMA, The Law Obama Is Defending in Court," *Gay America Blog*, November 1, 2010, John Aravosis (DC) *http://gay.americablog.com/2010/11/administration-deporting-legally.html*

- "An American Dream," *Give a Damn Campaign*, July 13, 2010, Joern, *http://www.wegiveadamn.org/category/immigration/*

- "American Tourist Visas for LGBT Bi-national Couples," *World Info Finance*, October 3, 2010, *http://worldinfofinance.com/legal/lawyer/american-tourist-visas-for-lgbt-bi-national-couples/*

- "An American Marriage: Legislation Would Erase the Choice Between Love and Country for Same-Sex Couples, *mndaily.com*, November 8, 2010, Ian J Byrne, *http://www.mndaily.com/2010/11/08/american-marriage*

- "Anonymous (Britain) and Anonymous (US)," *LGBT Immigration Stories*, October 20, 2010, *http://wp.me/pGRFk-5X and http://loveexiles.org/UK_US_story.htm*

- "Another Gay Couple Kept Apart by Immigration Law," *change.org*, November 3, 2010, Dana Rudolph *http://gayrights.change.org/blog/view/another_gay_couple_kept_ apart_by_immigration_law*

- "Anti-UAFA Ads Planned: Petition Asks USCCB (United States Congress of Catholic Bishops) and NAE (National Association of Evangelicals) to Stop Fighting LGBT Issues," Uniting American Families, June 4, 2010 *http://www.unitingamerican families.net/making-our-case/anti-uafa-ads-planned-petition-asks-usccb-and-nae-to-stop-fighting-lgbt-issues/*

- "As Gay Issues Arise, Obama Is Pressed to Engage," *New York Times*, May 6, 2009, Sheryl Gay Stolberg, *http://www.nytimes.com/2009/05/07/us/politics/07obama.html*

- Audio: the challenges for binational American gay couples, *LGBT Asylum News*, November 1, 2010 *http://madikazemi.blogspot.com/2010/11/audio-challenges-for-binational.html*

- "Baca Hopes Budget, Immigration Come Up Before GOP Takeover," *San Bernardino Sun*, www.sbsun.com, November 6, 2010, James Rufus Koren, *http://www.sbsun.com/ news/ci_16543933*

- "Betty White for Marriage Equality," *Advocate*, October 29, 2010, Julie Bolcer, *http://www.advocate.com/Arts_and_Entertainment/Entertainment_News/Betty_ White_for_Marriage_Equality//*

- "Bill Proposes Immigration Rights for Gay Couples," *New York Times*, June 3, 2009, Julia Preston, *http://www.nytimes.com/2009/06/03/us/politics/03immig.html*

- "Binational Couple," *About.com*, Ramon Johnson, *http://gaylife.about.com/od/ gayslang/g/binational.htm*

- "Binational Couples and Same-Sex Immigration," *10,000 Couples*, January 1, 2010, *http://10thousandcouples.com/issue/april-2010/article/binational-couples-and-same-sex-immigration*

- "Binational Gay Couple to Reunite, Others Not So Lucky," *Feministing*, November 15, 2010, Miriam, *http://feministing.com/2010/11/15/binational-gay-couple-to-reunite-others-not-so-lucky/*

- "Bipartisanship—With a Twist," *Political Animal*, November 14, 2010, Steve Benen *http://www.washingtonmonthly.com/archives/individual/2010_11/026627.php*

- "California Couples Tell of Gay Marriage Ban's Toll: Prop 8 Trial Begins," *MSNBC*, January 11, 2010, Associated Press, *http://www.msnbc.msn.com/id/34801259/*

- "CA Weighs Support for Same-Sex Immigrant Partner Bill: Call for Congress to Act to Unite Gay Couples Across National Boundaries," *Bay Citizen*, June 17, 2010, Jude Joffe-Block, *http://www.baycitizen.org/government/story/ca-weighs-support-same-sex-immigrant/*

- "Carla and Britta, Living in Fear," *LGBT Immigration Equality Rights*, April 15, 2009, *http://imeq.us/our_stories/files/category-living-in-fear.html*

- "Can a Non-American Lesbian Marry a Gay Man to Stay in the United States?" *About.com*, Kathy Belge, *http://lesbianlife.about.com/od/lesbianactivism/f/Marrya Friend.htm*

- "Civil Partners Will Be Included In Immigration Bill," *Gay Community News* (GCN), November 11, 2010, *http://www.gcn.ie/feature.aspx?sectionid=14&articleid=3025*
- "Closing The Loop On Legislator's Homophobia," *Equality North Carolina*, October 14, 2010, *http://equalitync.org/news1/closing-the-loop-on-legislators-homophobia*
- "Coming Out To My Teenager," *The New Gay*, November 2, 2010, Ann, *http://thenewgay.net/2010/11/coming-out-to-my-teenager.html*
- "Comprehensive Immigration Reform Act of 2010," *h1bvisalawyerblog.com*, October 27, 2010, Kellie N. Lego, *http://www.h1bvisalawyerblog.com/2010/10/comprehensive_immigration_refo.html*
- "Comprehensive Immigration Reform: Quiet, Not Dead," *About.com*, October 21, 2009, Jennifer McFadyen, *http://immigration.about.com/b/2009/10/21/comprehensive-immigration-reform-quiet-not-dead.htm*
- "Congressman's Office Reaches Out to Gay Couple Separated by Immigration Law," *Dallas Voice*, September 7, 2010, Tammye Nash, *http://www.dallasvoice.com/progress-roi-aurelio-congressmans-office-reaches-gay-couple-separated-immigration-law-1042827.html*
- "Congressmen Offer Support for Same-Sex Immigrant Couples," *Immigration Chronicles*, May 24, 2010, Susan Carroll, *http://blogs.chron.com/immigration/archives/2010/05/congressmen_off_1.html*
- "Constant Fear Because of Inequality," *Give a Damn Campaign*, April 27, 2010, Badger, *http://www.wegiveadamn.org/category/immigration/page/3/*
- "Cornell Law Professors Discuss How the New Congress Will Handle Immigration," *Newswise,* November 8, 2010, Cornell University, *http://www.newswise.com/articles/cornell-law-professors-discuss-how-the-new-congress-will-handle-immigration-on-nov-15-in-washington*
- "Dart Strikes Map: An Interview with Tony and Thomas," *Travel Blogs*, August, 2010, *http://www.travelblogs.com/interviews/dart-strikes-map-an-interview-with-tony-and-thomas*
- "Definition of Family Becoming Broader," *National Catholic Reporter*, September 29, 2010, Religion News Service and NCR Staff, *http://ncronline.org/news/faith-parish/definition-family-becoming-broader*
- "Divided by Law: An American Takes On Immigration to Reunite with the Person He Loves," *Huffington Post*, October 10, 2010, Steve Ralls, *http://www.huffingtonpost.com/steve-ralls/divided-by-law-an-america_b_708677.html*
- "Doctor in Exile," *Give a Damn Campaign*, July 13, 2010, Lisa, *http://www.wegiveadamn.org/category/immigration/page/2/*
- "Dodging Accountability on Gay Marriage," *Reform NY*, June 2, 2009, Lawrence Norden, *http://reformny.blogspot.com/2009/06/dodging-accountability-on-gay-marriage.html*
- "Dodging Marriage: View from Washington," *Advocate,* August 20, 2010, Kerry Eleveld, *http://www.advocate.com/Politics/Washington_D_C_/View_from_Washington_Dodging_Marriage/*

- "Does the White House Get It?" *Religion Dispatches*, October 14, 2010, Sarah Posner, *http://www.religiondispatches.org/dispatches/sarahposner/3544/does_the_white_house_get_it*

- "DOMA Repeal Bill Could Give Same-Sex Couples Equal Protection Under Immigration Laws," *About.com*, September 15, 2009, Jennifer McFadyen, *http://immigration.about.com/b/2009/09/15/doma-repeal-bill-could-give-same-sex-couples-equal-protection-under-immigration-laws.htm*

- "Don't Deport Henry: Repeal DOMA Now," *Change.org*, October 27, 2010, *http://www.change.org/freedomtomarry/petitions/view/dont_deport_henry_repeal_doma_now*

- "Don't Leave LGBT Families Out of Immigration Reform," *California Progress Report*, August 2, 2010, Amos Lim, *http://www.californiaprogressreport.com/site?q=node/8016*

- "Eat, Pray... Lobby?" *Politico*, August 20, 2010, Patrick Gavin, *http://www.politico.com/click/stories/1008/eat_pray_lobby.html*

- "81-Year-Old Woman Sues Feds For Not Recognizing Her Gay Marriage," *DNAInfo-beta*, www.dnainfo.com, November 9, 2010, Tara Kyle, *http://www.dnainfo.com/20101109/greenwich-village-soho/81yearold-woman-sues-feds-for-not-recognizing-her-gay-marriage*

- "Elections Show Growing Support for LGBT from People of Faith," *Religion Dispatches*, November 3, 2010, Candace Chellew-Hodge, *http://www.religiondispatches.org/dispatches/candacechellew-hodge/3681/elections_show_growing_support_for_lgbt_from_people_of_faith*

- "Eric and Neto: Living in Fear," *LGBT Immigration Equality Rights*, March 19, 2010, *http://imeq.us/our_stories/files/3b781bf509c9fc764857a94c8630d092-83.html*

- "Exiled for Love is Exiled From Love," *Saiofrelief*, *http://saiofrelief.com/?p=230*

- "Fighting For Equality," *About.com*, March 23, 2009, Jennifer McFadyen, *http://immigration.about.com/b/2009/03/23/fighting-for-equality.htm*

- "For Same-Sex Binational Couples, Is the Time Right to Start Focusing on Repealing DOMA?" *KazzaDrask New Media*, October 26, 2010, *http://kazzadraskmedia.blogspot.com/2010/10/for-same-sex-binational-couples-is-time.html*

- "For Same-Sex Couples, A Patchwork of Marriage Laws," *ABC News*, May 10, 2010, David Crary, Associated Press, *http://abcnews.go.com/US/wireStory?id=10600418*

- "For the Second Time, Rafiq Salleh Sits in Singapore Waiting for a Visa Renewal as His Business, His Spouse in Dallas Suffer from the Separation," *Dallas Voice*, October 28, 2010, David Taffet, *http://www.dallasvoice.com/tag/chill*

- "Former San Angelo Mayor Joseph W. Lown," *US Immigration Woes*, June 5, 2009, Matt Phinney, *http://www.usimmigrationwoes.com/2009/06/05/former-san-angelo-mayor-joseph-w-lown/*

- "4 Reasons Why Unions Are Important for LGBT Rights," *Alternet*, October 29, 2010, Lauren Kelley, *http://blogs.alternet.org/speakeasy/2010/10/29/4-reasons-why-unions-are-important-for-lgbt-rights/*

- "Gallagher, Wolfson Debate Gay Marriage," *Yale Daily News*, October 7, 2010, Zoe Gorman, *http://www.yaledailynews.com/news/2010/oct/07/gallagher-wolfson-debate-gay-marriage/*

- "Gay Black Church: Radically Inclusive and Spirit-Filled: An interview with Bishop Yvette Flunder," *Religion Dispatches*, October 1, 2010, Lisa Webster, *http://www.religiondispatches.org/archive/sexandgender/3435/gay_black_church%3A_radically_inclusive_and_spirit-filled*

- "Gay Brazilian May Be Deported from U.S.," *Advocate*, November 9, 2010, Julie Bolcer, *http://www.advocate.com/News/Daily_News/2010/11/09/Gay_Brazilian_May_Be_Deported_from_US/?utm_source=feedburner&utm_medium=feed&utm_campaign=Feed%3A+AdvocatecomDailyNews+%28Advocate.com+Daily+News%29&utm_content=FaceBook*

- "Gay Cancer Patient Struggles to Bring Partner to U.S.," *Washington Blade*, September 17, 2010, Lou Chibbaro, Jr., *http://www.washingtonblade.com/2010/09/17/gay-cancer-patient-struggles-to-bring-partner-to-u-s/*

- "Gay Couples Are Fighting for Their Immigration Rights," *Digital Journal*, June 4, 2009, Kera Ellingson, *http://www.digitaljournal.com/print/article/273591*

- "Gay Couples Seeking Immigration Rights," *Anglicans United*, September 14, 2010, Cherie, *http://www.anglicansunited.com/?p=8491*

- "Gay Couples Seeking Immigration Rights," *Washington Post*, September 13, 2010, Shankar Vedantam, *http://www.washingtonpost.com/wp-dyn/content/article/2010/09/12/AR2010091204159_pf.html*

- "Gay Couples to Sue Over U.S. Marriage Law," *New York Times*, November 8, 2010, John Schwartz, *http://www.nytimes.com/2010/11/09/us/09marriage.html?_r=2&hpw*

- "Gay Couples Take on an Immigration Divide," *Boston.com*, October 16, 2010, Maria Sacchetti, *http://www.boston.com/news/local/massachusetts/articles/2010/10/16/gay_couples_take_on_an_immigrant_divide/*

- "Gay Families Score Lower Than Dogs," *Religion Dispatches*, October 4, 2010, Candace Chellew-Hodge, *http://www.religiondispatches.org/dispatches/candacechellew-hodge/3457/gay_families_score_lower_than_dogs*

- "Gay-Inclusive Uniting American Families Act Included in Senate Immigration Reform Bill," *Miami Herald,* Steve Rothaus' Gay South Florida, September 30, 2010, *http://miamiherald.typepad.com/gaysouthflorida/2010/09/gay-inclusive-uniting-american-families-act-included-in-senate-immigration-reform-bill.html*

- "Gay Partners Seeking Immigration Changes," *Pittsburgh Post Gazette,* October 23, 2009, Mackenzie Carpenter, *http://www.post-gazette.com/pg/09296/1007756-84.stm*

- "Gay and Lesbian Immigration Policies," *About.com*, February 13, 2009, Ramon Johnson, *http://gaylife.about.com/od/gayimmigration/i/gayimmigration_1.htm*

- "Gay Marriage: California Prop 8 Trial Rests and a Key Ruling Awaits," *Time* magazine, January 29, 2010, Michael A. Lindenberger, *http://www.time.com/time/nation/article/0,8599,1957505,00.html*

- "Gay Mayor's Illicit Love Shakes a Texas Town." *Buzzle*, May 30, 2009, *http://www.buzzle.com/articles/273074.html*

- "Gays Excluded From Immigration Bill," *Advocate*, December 21, 2009, Andrew Harmon, *http://www.advocate.com/printArticle.aspx?id=104564*

- "Gays: Voting 'Straight' Republican," *The Bilerico Project*, November 8, 2010, Bil Browning, *http://www.bilerico.com/2010/11/gays_voting_straight_republican.php? utm_source=feedburner&utm_medium=email&utm_campaign=Feed%3A+Bilerico Project+%28The+Bilerico+Project%29*

- "Global Gaze: Caught Between Love and Country, Part II," *The New Gay*, August 19, 2009, Jolly, *http://thenewgay.net/2009/08/caught-between-love-and-country-part-ii.html*

- "Governments Remove Sexual Orientation from UN Resolution Condemning Extrajudicial, Summary or Arbitrary Executions," ARC International and IGLHRC press release, November 17, 2010, John Fisher and Sara Perle, *http://www.iglhrc.org/ cgi-bin/iowa/article/pressroom/pressrelease/1257.html*

- "Green Card Victory for Same-Sex Binational Couple Takes 30 Years," *KazzaDrask New Media*, May 14, 2010, Kathy Drasky, *http://kazzadraskmedia.blogspot.com/ 2010/05/green-card-victory-for-same-sex.html*

- "Greene: U.S. Policy and Same-Sex Love are Ocean Apart," *Denver Post*, November 18, 2010, Susan Greene, *http://www.denverpost.com/news/ci_16643687?source=rss*

- "Growing Calls for Immigration Reform That Leaves No Family Behind," October 21, 2009, *Huffington Post*, Steve Ralls, *http://www.huffingtonpost.com/steve-ralls/ growing-calls-for-immigra_b_328359.html*

- "Gutierrez and Honda Push for Gay Rights in Immigration Law," *Washington Independent*, July 15, 2010, Elise Foley, *http://washingtonindependent.com/91592/ gutierrez-and-honda-push-for-gay-rights-in-immigration-law*

- "Gutierrez: Gays Are in Immigration Bill," *Windy City Times*, May 26, 2010, John Fenoglio, *http://www.windycitymediagroup.com/gay/lesbian/news/ARTICLE.php? AID=26660*

- "Gutierrez, Quigley Call for Immigration Reforms to Cover Gay Couples," *chicago. gopride*, May 24, 2010, Kevin Wayne, *http://chicago.gopride.com/news/article.cfm/ articleid/10848400*

- "Gutierrez Wants Same-Sex Partner Rights in Immigration Reform Bill," *Chicago Tribune*, May 20, 2010, Rex W. Huppke, *http://articles.chicagotribune.com/ 2010-05-20/news/ct-met-binational-gay-couples-20100520_1_immigration-reform-comprehensive-immigration-same-sex-couples*

- "Half a World Away," *Give a Damn Campaign*, May 28, 2010, Dean, *http://www.we giveadamn.org/category/immigration/page/2/*

- "Hart2Hart A Fight for Gay Rights! *Give a Damn Campaign*, July 13, 2010, Laurie, *http://www.wegiveadamn.org/category/immigration/page/2/*

- *"Heartbreak For Binational Same-Sex Couples: A First-Person Story," SheWired.com*, October 8, 2010, Philippa Judd, *http://www.shewired.com/Article.cfm?ID=25890*

- "Helpless," *Give a Damn Campaign*, April 29, 2010, Trevor, *http://www.wegiveadamn.org/category/immigration/page/3/*

- "Henry Velandia, Legally Married Gay Man, Faces US Deportation," *AOL News,* October 27, 2010, Mara Gay, *http://www.aolnews.com/nation/article/legally-married-gay-man-faces-us-deportation/19691601*

- "Homeland Insecurity," *wglb-tv.blogspot*, November 6, 2010, Hannah Clay Wareham, *http://wglb-tv.blogspot.com/2010/11/homeland-insecurity.html*

- "Honda Promises to Push for Visa Reform with Gay Rights in the Next Congress," *The Washington Independent*, November 5, 2010, Elise Foley, *http://washingtonindependent.com/102806/honda-promises-to-push-for-visa-reform-with-gay-rights-in-the-next-congress*

- "How Many of Us Are There: Showing the Math," *Uniting American Families,* November 26, 2009, *http://www.unitingamericanfamilies.net/making-our-case/how-many-of-us-are-there-showing-the-math/*

- "How Discrimination Against Gays Affects My Family," *Give a Damn Campaign,* July 13, 2010, Andy, *http://www.wegiveadamn.org/category/immigration/page/2/*

- "How the Defense of Marriage Act Destroys Marriage," *One More Lesbian, www.onemorelesbian.com/blog*, November 2, 2010, *http://www.onemorelesbian.com/blog/how-the-defense-of-marriage-act-destroys-marriage.html*

- "How the Dems' Attempt at Immigration Reform Led to Major Expansion of Deportations: How a Political Strategy Can Lead to the Exact Opposite of its Intentions," *AlterNet*, Seth Freed Wessler, *http://www.alternet.org/story/148453/how_the_dems%27_attempt_at_immigration_reform_led_to_major_expansion_of_deportations*

- "How to Choose a Country," *Give a Damn Campaign*, October 3, 2010, Trish, *http://www.wegiveadamn.org/2010/10/how-to-choose-a-country/*

- "How Two Gay Men Used Skype To Have A Legal Wedding In Texas," *GIZMODO, www.gizmodo.com.au*, November 12, 2010, Kyle VanHemert, *http://www.gizmodo.com.au/2010/11/how-two-gay-men-used-skype-to-have-a-legal-wedding-in-texas/*

- "Immigration Bill to Include LGBTs," *Advocate,* September 29, 2010, Kerry Eleveld, *http://www.advocate.com/News/Daily_News/2010/09/29/Immigration_Bill_To_Include_LGBT_Families*

- "Immigration Change Could Hurt Gay Marriage," U.S. News, UPI.com, September 13, 2010, *http://www.upi.com/Top_News/US/2010/09/13/Immigration-change-could-hurt-gay-marriage/UPI-56061284383439/*

- "Immigration Equality Action Fund Calls for Comprehensive Immigration Reform in 'Lame-Duck' Congressional Session," *Cherrygrrl,* November 18, 2010, *http://cherrygrrl.com/immigration-equality-action-fund-calls-for-comprehensive-immigration-reform-in-lame-duck-congressional-session/*

- "Immigration Equality's Tiven: 'Very Difficult to Move Immigration Reform' in 2011," *Metro Weekly*, November 4, 2010, Chris Geidner, *http://www.metroweekly.com/poliglot/2010/11/immigration-equalitys-tiven-ve.html*

- "Immigration Fairness for Gays," *Jewish Daily Forward*, October 29, 2010, Rachel B. Tiven, *http://www.forward.com/articles/132287/#ixzz12vFsU6HQ*

- "Immigration Laws Tearing Couples Apart," *Change.org*, September 9, 2010, Dana Rudolph, *http://gayrights.change.org/blog/view/immigration_laws_tearing_couples_apart*

- "Immigration Lawyer Sees New Immigration Reform Bill as Step in the Right Direction," *Law Firm Wire,* October 20, 2010, *http://www.lawfirmnewswire. com/2010/10/immigration-lawyer-sees-new-immigration-reform-bill-as-step-in-the-right-direction/*

- "Immigration Officials Allow Gay Couple to Reunite," *Advocate,* June 4, 2010, *http://www.advocate.com/News/Daily_News/2010/06/04/Immigration_Officials_Allow_Gay_Couple_to_Reunite/*

- "Immigration Overhaul Could Leave Gay Couples Out," *Washington Post*, September 13, 2010, Shankar Vedantam, *http://www.washingtonpost.com/wp-dyn/content/article/2010/09/12/AR2010091204157.html*

- "Immigration Plan Includes LGBT Families," *Advocate*, April 29, 2010, Kerry Eleveld, *http://www.advocate.com/News/Daily_News/2010/04/29/Immigration_Outline_Includes_Gay_Partners/*

- "Immigration Reform, According to Obama," Yahoo News, yahoonews.com, November 15, 2010, Sylvia Cochran, *http://news.yahoo.com/s/ac/20101115/us_ac/7196144_immigration_reform_according_to_obama*

- "Immigration Reform Advocates Head to Washington," *ABC News*, September 13, 2010, *http://abclocal.go.com/kgo/story?section=news/local&id=7665489*

- "Immigration Reform: Binational Gay Couples Fear They'll Be Left Out," *Worldwide Faith News*, October 13, 2010, Pat McCaughan, *http://www.wfn.org/2010/10/msg00065.html*

- "Immigration Reform Highly Unlikely," *Newsdesk International's Blog*, November 6, 2010, *http://newsdeskinternational.wordpress.com/2010/11/06/immigration-reform-highly-unlikely/*

- "Immigration Rights for Same-Sex Couples Possible?" *Cross Currrents from KALW*, June 14, 2010, Heather Gilligan, *http://kalwnews.org/blogs/heathergilligan/2010/06/14/immigration-rights-same-sex-couples-possible_415891.html*

- "In Congress: Many Bills, But No Timetable for Progress," *Washington Blade, www.washingtonblade.com,* June 10, 2010, Chris Johnson, *http://www.washingtonblade.com/2010/06/10/in-congress-many-bills-but-no-timetable-for-progress/*

- "In the USA, Binational Couples May Be Left Out of Immigration Reform," *LGBT Asylum News,* September 22, 2010, Paul Canning, *http://madikazemi.blogspot.com/2010/09/in-usa-binational-couples-may-be-left.html*

- "In The Wake of DREAM Act, Senators Introduce Comprehensive Immigration Reform Bill: Will Obstructionists in Congress Keep Using Immigration as a Political Pinata in the Name of Election Politics, Or Put Partisanship Aside and Fix Our Broken System?" *AlterNet,* October 4, 2010, Seth Hoy, *http://www.alternet.org/immigration/148405/in_the_wake_of_dream_act,_senators_introduce_comprehensive_immigration_reform_bill*

- "Inhumane Impact of DOMA," *Salon.com*, Glenn Greenwald, October 26, 2010, *http://www.salon.com/news/opinion/glenn_greenwald/2010/10/26/doma/index.html*
- "Is There Justice For All?" *Standing on the Side of Love*, Allison Woolbert, *http://www.standingonthesideoflove.org/blog/is-there-justice-for-all/*
- "Josh's Story: A Binational Couple Separated by Unjust Immigration Laws," We Are America Stories, *http://www.weareamericastories.org/written/joshs-story-a-binational-couple-separated-by-unjust-immigration-laws/*
- "Just One Voice," *Give a Damn Campaign*, July 12, 2010, Brian, *http://www.wegiveadamn.org/category/immigration/page/2/*
- "Keep Our Families Together: Reform Immigration Laws," *DREAM Act Portal*, October 19, 2009, Rep. Mike Honda, *http://dreamact.info/node/36283*
- "Keep Our Families Together: Reform Immigration Laws," *Roll Call*, October 19, 2009, Rep. Mike Honda, *http://www.rollcall.com/issues/55_42/guest/39576-1.html*
- "Knowledge Changes Everything," *Give a Damn Campaign*, July 23, 2010, Sara, *http://www.wegiveadamn.org/category/immigration/*
- "Lame-Duck Congress Will Face Immigration Issue," *Human Events*, October 22, 2010, Virgil Goode, October 22, 2010, *http://www.humanevents.com/article.php?id=39525*
- "Lawmakers Push Immigration/UAFA," *Advocate*, July 15, 2010, Kerry Eleveld, *http://www.advocate.com/News/Daily_News/2010/07/15/Lawmakers_Push_Immigration_UAFA*
- "Lawmakers: Reform LGBT Immigration Rules," *Redeye, Chicago Now*, May 25, 2010, Georgia Garvey, *http://www.chicagonow.com/blogs/redeye/2010/05/lawmakers-reform-lgbt-immigration-rules.html*
- "Legislation Watch: A Nation of Immigrants," *The Nation*, November 10, 2009, Greg Kaufmann, *http://www.thenation.com/article/legislation-watch-nation-immigrants*
- "Lesbian Couple Credited with Federal Law Leaves US," *Bay Area Reporter, www.ebar.com*, November 4, 2009, Matthew S. Bajko, *http://ebar.com/blogs/?p=259*
- "LGBT Rights Activists Discuss Strategies to Achieve Same Sex Immigration Legislation," *Integrity Legal Blog*, November 5, 2010, *http://integrity-legal.com/legal-blog/lgbt-immigration/lgbt-rights-advocates-discuss-strategies-to-achieve-same-sex-immigration-legislation/*
- "LGBT Rights and Immigration Reforms Intersect on Capitol Hill," *Bay Area Reporter*, September 23, 2010, Matthew S. Bajko, *http://ebar.com/news/article.php?sec=news&article=5078*
- "LGBTs Face Immigration Hurdles in United States," *Bay Area Reporter Online*, September 9, 2010, Matthew Bajko, *www.ebar.com/news/article.php?sec=news&article=5049*
- "Living in Exile," *Give a Damn Campaign*, July 13, 2010, Shannon, *http://www.wegiveadamn.org/category/immigration/*

- "Log Cabin's R. Clarke Cooper: The LGBT Community's New Inside Man," *Bilerico Project,* November 8, 2010, Karen Ocamb, *http://www.bilerico.com/2010/11/log_cabins_r_clarke_cooper_the_lgbt_communitys_new.php#more*

- "Love Without Borders," *Give a Damn Campaign,* July 13, 2010, Nicolas, *http://www.wegiveadamn.org/category/immigration/page/2/*

- "Loving for All: Prepared for Delivery on June 12, 2007, the 40th Anniversary of the *Loving v. Virginia* Announcement," Mildred Loving, *www.freedomtomarry.org/page/-/files/pdfs/mildred_loving-statement.pdf*

- "Making Sure Immigration Reform Keeps LGBT Families Together," *Change.org,* May 24, 2010, Michael A. Jones, *http://gayrights.change.org/blog/view/making_sure_immigration_reform_keeps_lgbt_families_together*

- "Marriage Equality: Connecticut Does Well by Doing Good," *Hartford Courant (www.courant.com),* posted on *Freedom To Marry,* October 15, 2010, *www.freedomtomarry.org/blog/entry/marriage-equality-connecticut-does-well-by-doing-good*

- "Marriage Equality USA, Out4Immigration, and Love Exiles Report: Shirley Tan Given Reprieve," *California Chronicle,* April 2, 2009, California Desk, *http://www.californiachronicle.com/articles/view/97093*

- "May Day March Urges Support for UAFA," *Bay Area Reporter,* May 7, 2009, Seth Hemmelgarn, *http://www.ebar.com/news/article.php?sec=news&article=3902*

- "Mayor Quits Job for Gay Illegal Immigrant He Loves," *Houston Chronicle,* May 21, 2009, Rick Casey, *http://www.chron.com/disp/story.mpl/metropolitan/casey/6436282.html*

- "Meet Roi and Aurelio: A Story of Enduring Love, Illness and Discrimination," *The Seminal,* September 8, 2010, posted by glownz, *http://seminal.firedoglake.com/diary/tag/roi-whaley-and-aurelio-tolentino*

- "Megachurch Pastor Comes Out ," *The Advocate,* October 29, 2010, *http://www.advocate.com/News/Daily_News/2010/10/29/Megachurch_Pastor_Jim_Swilley_Comes_Out/*

- "Menendez Introduces LGBT Inclusive Immigration Bill," *Washington Blade,* September 30, 2010, Chris Johnson, *http://www.washingtonblade.com/2010/09/30/menendez-introduces-lgbt-inclusive-immigration-bill/*

- "Menendez Offers Comprehensive Immigration Bill, Unlikely to Move This Year," *SENATEUS,* senateus.wordpress.com, October 1, 2010, Josh, *http://senatus.wordpress.com/2010/10/01/menendez-offers-comprehensive-immigration-bill-unlikely-to-move-this-year/*

- "MetroWeekly's Analysis of LGBT Movement: Evolution and Failure," *Bilerico Project,* October 7, 2010, Dr. Jillian T. Weiss, *http://www.bilerico.com/2010/10/metroweeklys_analysis_of_lgbt_movement_evolution.php*

- "Mississippi Man Fights to Block Deportation of HIV-Positive Partner," *EDGE, Boston, Massachusetts,* September 21, 2010, Conswella Bennett, *http://www.edgeboston.com/index.php?ch=news&sc=&sc2=news&sc3=&id=110553*

- "My Brazilian Fiance," *Give a Damn Campaign,* July 29, 2010, Sandra, *http://www.wegiveadamn.org/category/immigration/*

- "Potential Split in Immigration Coalition: Gay Rights Issue Resurfaces in Debate for Overhaul," *Congress.org*, May 24, 2010, Ambreen Ali, *http://www.congress.org/news/2010/05/24/potential_split_in_immigration_coalition*
- "NALEO Educational Fund Welcomes Comprehensive Immigration Legislation," *Business Wire*, September 30, 2010, *http://www.businesswire.com/news/home/20100930006732/en/NALEO-Educational-Fund-Welcomes-Comprehensive-Immigration-Legislation*
- "NCC Governing Board Presses Immigration Reform," *Worldwide Faith News*, September 23, 2010, Philip Jenks, *http://www.wfn.org/2010/09/msg00145.html*
- "NCLR Applauds Senate Inclusion of Same-Sex Couples and Relief for Youth in Comprehensive Immigration Reform Bill," *NCLR Blog: Out for Justice*, September 30, 2010, *http://nclrights.wordpress.com/2010/09/30/nclr-applauds-senate-inclusion-of-same-sex-couples-and-relief-for-youth-in-comprehensive-immigration-reform-bill/*
- "New Catholic LGBT Organization Launches," *Washington Blade*, September 23, 2010, Chris Johnson, *http://www.washingtonblade.com/2010/09/23/new-catholic-lgbt-organization-launches/*
- "New Jersey Sen. Robert Menendez Introduces Immigration Reform Bill That Features Clear Path to Residency and Would Reunite Families Separated by Outdated Laws," *NJ.com*, October 2, 2010, Karina L. Arrue, *http://www.nj.com/news/jjournal/index.ssf?/base/news-5/1286000733305410.xml&coll=3*
- "New Immigration Bill Introduced in Senate," *People's World*, October 11, 2010, Emile Schepers, *http://peoplesworld.org/new-immigration-bill-introduced-in-senate/*
- "New US Immigration Bill to Include Gay/Lesbian Binational Couples," *Gayopolis News*, September 30, 2010, *http://www.gayapolis.com/news/artdisplay.php?artid=4919*
- "No Marriage, No Greencard," *We Give a Damn Campaign*, July 13, Amanda, *http://www.wegiveadamn.org/category/immigration/page/2/*
- "No Way Out: Bi-national, Same-Sex Couples—People are NOT Created Equally," *Real Immigration Stories*, November 3, 2009, Sivan J. Fraser, *http://realimmigrationstories.blogspot.com/*
- "Nomads in My Own Country," *We Give a Damn Campaign*, March 30, 2010, Christopher, *http://www.wegiveadamn.org/category/immigration/page/3/*
- "Obama: Fate of Immigration Reform Hinges on Election," *The Hill*, October 25, 2010, Michael O'Brien, *http://thehill.com/blogs/blog-briefing-room/news/125677-obama-fate-of-immigration-reform-hinges-on-election*
- "Obama's Gay Childhood Nanny," *The Advocate*, November 9, 2010, *http://advocate.com/News/Daily_News/2010/11/09/Obamas_Gay_Childhood_Nanny/*
- "Obama's Message at the March 2010 Immigration Rally – March for America: Change Takes Courage," *About.com*, Jennifer McFadyen, *http://immigration.about.com/od/usimmigrationhistory/a/March2010_ImmigrationRally.htm*
- "Obama on Marriage: 'Attitudes Evolve, Including Mine'," *The Advocate*, October 27, 2010, Kerry Eleveld, *http://www.advocate.com/News/Daily_News/2010/10/27/Obama_on_Marriage_Times_Are_Changing/*

{3}

- "Obama Once Supported Same-Sex Marriage 'Unequivocally'," *Huffington Post*, January 13, 2009, Jason Linkins, *http://www.huffingtonpost.com/2009/01/13/obama-once-supported-same_n_157656.html*

- "Obama Opposes Proposed Ban on Gay Marriage," *San Francisco Chronicle*, July 2, 2008, John Wildermuth, *http://articles.sfgate.com/2008-07-02/news/17171328_1_same-sex-marriage-civil-unions-ban-on-gay-marriage*

- "Obama Says He Has 'Worked to Improve' the Uniting American Families Act (UAFA), *San Francisco Bay Area Independent Media Center*, February 29, 2008, Kathy Drasky, *http://www.indybay.org/newsitems/2008/02/29/18482630.php*

- "Obama Still Committed to 'Comprehensive Immigration Reform'," *The Oval, USA Today*, September 17, 2010, David Jackson, *http://content.usatoday.com/communities/theoval/post/2010/09/obama-still-committed-to-comprehensive-immigration-reform/1*

- "One Couple's Fight to Stay Together: Lesbian and Gay Immigration Rights Task Force," *About.com*, Gina Daggett, *http://lesbianlife.about.com/cs/wedding/a/immigration.htm*

- "Online Extra: Political Notes: LGBT Rights and Immigration Reforms Intersect on Capitol Hill," *Bay Area Reporter*, September 23, 2010, Matthew S. Bajko, *http://www.ebar.com/news/article.php?sec=news&article=5078*

- "Our Love Matters," *Give a Damn Campaign*, May 28th, 2010, Gavern, *http://www.wegiveadamn.org/category/immigration/page/2/*

- "Our Story: A Gay Couple, Torn Apart by DOMA," *Gay Online News*, April 19, 2010, *http://gayonlinenews.com/2010/04/our-story-a-gay-couple-torn-apart-by-doma/*

- "Our Story," *Give a Damn Campaign*, Jun 30, 2010, Janice, *http://www.wegiveadamn.org/category/immigration/page/2/*

- "People are People," *Give a Damn Campaign*, April 4, 2010, Melissa, *http://www.wegiveadamn.org/category/immigration/page/3/*

- "Polis Statement on New Senate Immigration Reform Bill," *Inside Colorado News*, October 1, 2010, Congressman Jared Polis, (D-CO-2), *http://insidecoloradonews.com/?p=818*

- "Politicians Pushing for 'Comprehensive Immigration Reform'," *News Blaze*, October 27, 2010, Michael Cutler, *http://newsblaze.com/story/20101027221908mcut.nb/topstory.html*

- "Poll: Protestant Support for Gay Marriage Rises," *Christian Post*, October 8, 2010, Audrey Barrick, *http://www.christianpost.com/article/20101008/poll-protestant-support-for-gay-marriage-rises/*

- "Poll: What Kind of Federal Recognition Is Most Important for Same-Sex Couples?" *10,000 Couples*, August 12, 2010 Delena Wilkerson, *http://10thousandcouples.com/issue/september-2010/article/poll-what-kind-of-federal-recognition-is-most-important-for-same-sex-couples*

- "Potential Split in Immigration Coalition: Gay Rights Issue Resurfaces in Debate for Overhaul," Congress.org, May 24, 2010, Ambreen Ali, *http://www.congress.org/news/2010/05/24/potential_split_in_immigration_coalition*

- "Proud to Support the Rule of Law and Immigration, Too (Rep. Luis Gutierrez), *The Hill*, October 28, 2010, Rep. Luis Gutierrez, *http://thehill.com/blogs/congress-blog/judicial/126417-proud-to-support-the-rule-of-law-and-immigration-too-rep-luis-gutierrez*
- "Record Number of Congressional Co-Sponsors Support Uniting American Families Act: Bill Would End Discrimination Against LGBT Binational Families," *Windy City News*, September 23, 2010, *http://www.windycitymediagroup.com/gay/lesbian/news/ARTICLE.php?AID=28703*
- "Rep. Gutierrez Won't Run for Mayor," *UPI.com*, October 15, 2010, John Chase, *http://www.upi.com/Top_News/US/2010/10/15/Rep-Gutierrez-wont-run-for-Chicago-mayor/UPI-79961287185291/*
- "Republican Resurgence Likely to Derail 'Immigration Reform'," *Fox News*, November 6, 2010, *http://www.foxnews.com/politics/2010/11/06/republican-resurgence-likely-derail-immigration-reform/*
- "Republicans Block Move on Gays, Immigration," *Washington Times*, September 21, 2010, Stephen Dinan, *http://www.washingtontimes.com/news/2010/sep/21/gop-blocks-moves-on-gays-immigration/*
- "Rift Grows Between Immigration Allies: Religious Leaders, Gay Rights Activists Disagree on Same-Sex Issue," *Congress.org*, May 26, 2010, Ambreen Ali, *http://www.congress.org/news/2010/05/26/rift_grows_between_immigration_allies*
- "Ron and Charles, Living in Separation," *LGBT Immigration Equality Rights*, September 4, 2010, *http://imeq.us/our_stories/files/5cff5a172979e4fabd227e6e34f04754-85.html*
- "Ruling Against Prop. 8 Could Lead to Federal Precedent on Gay Marriage," *Los Angeles Times*, August 5, 2010, Maura Dolan and Carol J. Williams, *http://www.infowars.com/ruling-against-prop-8-could-lead-to-federal-precedent-on-gay-marriage*
- "Same-Sex Bi-National Couples Gain More Support from House Reps.," *examiner.com*, September 15, 2010, Gina Caprio, *http://www.examiner.com/civil-rights-in-sacramento/same-sex-bi-national-couples-gain-more-support-from-house-reps*
- "Same-Sex Couples Seek Immigration Benefit: Gay-Rights Groups Hopeful for Inclusion, Which Might Threaten Bills' Passage," July 18, 2009, *MSNBC*, Kevin Freking, Associated Press, *http://www.msnbc.msn.com/id/31982718/ns/politics-more_politics/*
- "Same-Sex Couples Seek Immigration Benefit," *MSNBC* PolitiFi, Associated Press, July 18, 2009, *http://www.msnbc.msn.com/id/31982718/*
- "San Angelo Mayor Resigns to be with Gay Partner," *365 Gay*, June 5, 2009, *http://www.365gay.com/news/san-angelo-mayor-resigns-to-be-with-gay-partner/*
- "Save Our Marriage: Stop the Deportation of Henry Velandia," published by Henry Velandia on Oct 25, 2010, *http://www.gopetition.com/petitions/saveourmarriage.html*
- "'Say No to Hate' Notable Gay and Lesbian Books," *Kirkus Reviews*, *http://www.kirkusreviews.com/lists/say-no-hate-notable-gay-lesbian-books/*

- "Secret Lovers: Same-Sex Marriage and Immigration Reform," *News Real Blog*, August 18, 2010, Paul Cooper, *http://www.newsrealblog.com/2010/08/18/secret-lovers-same-sex-marriage-and-immigration-reform/*

- "Sen. Menendez Aims for Lame Duck, Urges Advocates to Focus on Policy of CIR 2010," *Immigration Impact*, October 4, 2010, Mary Giovagnoli, *http://immigration impact.com/2010/10/04/sen-menendez-aims-for-lame-duck-urges-advocates-to-focus-on-policy-of-cir-2010/*

- "Senator Menendez (Finally) Unveils Immigration Reform Bill," *change.org*, October 1, 2010, Prerna Lal, *http://immigration.change.org/blog/view/senator_menendez_finally_unveils_immigration_reform_bill*

- "Senators Attempt to Revive Immigration Reform Debate," *Medill Reports*, October 5, 2010, Kelsey Sheehy, *http://news.medill.northwestern.edu/chicago/news.aspx?id=169908*

- "Senators Menendez and Leahy Introduce the Comprehensive Immigration Reform Act of 2010," *LA Progressive*, October 2, 2010, Seth Hoy, *http://www.laprogressive.com/immigration-reform/comprehensive-immigration-reform/*

- "Senators Menendez and Leahy Introduce Comprehensive Immigration Reform Bill," *Global Immigration Counsel*, October 6, 2010, *http://www.globalimmigrationcounsel.com/2010/10/articles/us-immigration/federal-legislation/senators-menendez-and-leahy-introduce-comprehensive-immigration-reform-bill/index.html*

- "Separation Anxiety: Gay Couples Should Be Allowed to Stay Together in the United States," *Washington Post*, March 16, 2009, *http://www.washingtonpost.com/wp-dyn/content/article/2009/03/15/AR2009031501669.html*

- "She Knows How to Eat, How to Pray and How to Love, But Can She Lobby?" *POLITICO*, August 20, 2010, Patrick Gavin, *http://www.politico.com/click/stories/1008/eat_pray_lobby.html*

- "Steve Ralls: Growing Calls for Immigration Reform That Leaves No Family Behind," *Huffington Post*, October 21, 2009, *http://www.huffingtonpost.com/steve-ralls/growing-calls-for-immigra_b_328359.html*

- "Straight People Are Hurt by Homophobia Too," *Bilerico Project*, October 6, 2010, Alex Blaze, *http://www.bilerico.com/2010/10/straight_people_are_hurt_by_homophobia_too.php*

- "Texas Mayor Resigns For The Man He Loves." *Box Turtle Bulletin*, May 20, 2009, Jim Burroway, *http://www.boxturtlebulletin.com/2009/05/20/11522*

- "The Anatomy of Hate: A Dialogue for Hope," *Current Online*, August 28, 2009, *http://www.cnn.com/2009/LIVING/08/27/anatomy.of.hate/index.html?eref=igoogle_cnn*, *http://current.com/entertainment/movies/90808179_the-anatomy-of-hate-a-dialogue-for-hope.htm*

- "The Comprehensive Immigration Reform Act of 2010," *Immigration Inform*, October 11, 2010, *http://immigrationinform.wordpress.com/2010/10/11/the-comprehensive-immigration-reform-act-of-2010/*

- "The Conservative Case for Gay Marriage: Why Same-Sex Marriage is an American Value," *Newsweek*, January 9, 2010, *http://www.newsweek.com/2010/01/08/the-conservative-case-for-gay-marriage.html*

- "The End of the Rainbow," *Give a Damn Campaign*, October 1, 2010, Benjamin, *http://www.wegiveadamn.org/category/immigration/*

- "The Homophobia Epidemic and How to Avoid It," *The Daily Barometer*, October 11, Sara Gwin, *http://media.barometer.orst.edu/media/storage/paper854/news/2010/ 10/11/Forum/The-Homophobia.Epidemic.And.How.To.Avoid.It-3943283.shtml*

- "The Tipping Point on LGBT Equality Has Arrived," *Huffington Post*, June 9, 2010, Wayne Besen, *http://www.huffingtonpost.com/wayne-besen/the-tipping-point-on-lgbt_b_604868.html*

- "Time's Up: Immigration Inequality Forces Local Man's Husband Out of the Country," *Metro Weekly*, October 29, 2009, Will O'Bryan, *http://www.metroweekly.com/news/?ak=4605*

- "Together But Apart: The Challenging World of Same-Sex Binational Couples," *365 Gay*, June 3, 2009, Jennifer Vanasco, *www.365gay.com/living/together-but-apart-the-challenging-world-of-same-sex-binational-couples/*

- "Torn by Two Countries," *Give a Damn Campaign*, July 13, 2010, Esperanza, *http://www.wegiveadamn.org/category/immigration/*

- "Two Broads Abroad," *Give a Damn Campaign,* March 30, 2010, Judy and Karin, *http://www.wegiveadamn.org/category/immigration/page/3/*

- "Two Countries, One Heart," *Give a Damn Campaign*, September 21, 2010, Luis, *http://www.wegiveadamn.org/category/immigration/*

- "2010 Elections: Implications for Immigration Reform," *Americas Quarterly*, November 3, 2010, Jason Marczak, *http://www.americasquarterly.org/node/1975*

- "Understanding the Flip Flop – Congressman Gutierrez and UAFA in Immigration Reform," *Lez Get Real*, May 25, 2010, Melanie Nathan, *http://lezgetreal.com/2010/05/ understanding-the-flip-flop-congressman-gutierrez-and-uafa-in-immigration-reform/*

- "United by Love, Exiled by Law," *Give a Damn Campaign*, Jun 23, 2010, Robert, *http://www.wegiveadamn.org/category/immigration/page/2/*

- "Uniting American Love: Binational Couples Press for End to Deportations," *Chelsea Now*, October 27, 2010 Paul Schindler, *http://www.chelseanow.com/articles/2010/10/ 27/gay_city_news/news/doc4cc864960dd0e614278662.txt*

- "US Bi-National Couple Win Fight to Stay Together," *LGBT Asylum News*, June 8, 2010, *http://friendfeed.com/gayrightsmedia/f433e023/us-bi-national-couple-win-fight-to-stay-together*

- "US Immigration's Gay Rights Divide," *Guardian*, April 18, 2010, Stuart J. Lawrence, *http://www.guardian.co.uk/commentisfree/cifamerica/2010/apr/16/us-immigration-gay-rights*

- "US Tourist Visas for LGBT Couples," *SubmitYourArticle.com*, Ben Hart, *http://www. submityourarticle.com/articles/Ben-Hart-5829/LGBT-Immigration-121273.php*

- "Uniting American Families Act," *About.com,* Jennifer McFadyen, *http://immigration.about.com/od/glossary/g/UAFA_Glossary.htm*

- "Uniting American Families Act," *About.com*, February 13, 2009, Ramon Johnson, *http://gaylife.about.com/od/gayimmigration/p/unitedfamilies.htm*

- "UAFA Senate Hearing Set For June 3rd," *About.com*, May 22, 2009, Jennifer McFadyen, *http://immigration.about.com/b/2009/05/22/uafa-senate-hearing-set-for-june-3rd.htm*
- "US Churches Call for Comprehensive Immigration Reform," *Ekklesia*, September 26, 2010, agency reporter, *www.ekklesia.co.uk/node/13188*
- "US Immigration Reform Off the Agenda," *Global Visas*, November 4, 2010, Mario Hannah, *http://www.globalvisas.com/news/us_immigration_reform_off_the_agenda2725.html*
- "US Tourist Visas for LGBT Couples," *Ezinearticles,* Ben Hart, *http://ezinearticles.com/?US-Tourist-Visas-for-LGBT-Couples&id=5123280*
- "Unrequited Love," *Give a Damn Campaign*, September 28, 2010, Erin, *http://www.wegiveadamn.org/category/immigration/*
- "Waleska and Fabienne, Living in Exile," *LGBT Immigration Equality Rights*, June 10, 2010, *http://imeq.us/our_stories/files/ed3cef6d1db35f31af5681cb201b2460-86.html*
- "Warning for Same-Sex Binational Couples: Binational Couples Immigration Warning," *Free Download Books*, *http://freedownloadbooks.net/binational-pdf-2.html*
- "We're Sorry, That's Not Official Unless We Say It Is," *BlogHer*, October 26, 2010, Lucretia, *http://www.blogher.com/were-sorry-thats-not-official-unless-we-say-it*
- "What is the Uniting American Families Act?" *About.com*, Kathy Blege, *http://lesbianlife.about.com/od/lesbianactivism/f/UnitingFamiliesAct.htm*
- "What Next for Immigration Equality – Binationals Are Concerned," *Lez Get Real*, November 4, 2010, Melanie Nathan, *http://lezgetreal.com/2010/11/what-next-for-immigration-equality-binationals-are-concerned/*
- "When The Government Deports Your Spouse," *The Atlantic: The Daily Dish*, October 27, 2010, Andrew Sullivan, *http://andrewsullivan.theatlantic.com/the_daily_dish/2010/10/when-the-government-deports-your-spouse.html*
- "Where Are Gay Partner Immigration Benefits Granted?" *About.com*, February 13, 2009, Ramon Johnson, *http://gaylife.about.com/od/gayimmigration/qt/visasponsorship.htm*
- "White House Continues Push for Immigration Reform," *Xinhua News Agency*, September 29, 2010, Matthew Rusling, *http://news.xinhuanet.com/english2010/world/2010-09/29/c_13535350.htm*
- "White House Statement on Prop. 8," *Advocate,* August 4, 2010, Kerry Eleveld, *http://www.advocate.com/News/Daily_News/2010/08/04/White_House_Statement_Prop_8/*
- "White House to Continue with US Visa and Immigration Reform," *American Visa Bureau*, September 30, 2010, *http://www.visabureau.com/america/news/30-09-2010/white-house-to-continue-with-us-visa-and-immigration-reform.aspx*
- "Why Gay Marriage and Not Civil Unions?" *About.com,* Ramon Johnson, *http://gaylife.about.com/od/samesexmarriage/f/civilmarriage.htm*
- "Why Obama Sticks with Civil Unions," *The Economist*, August 24, 2010, posted by M.S., *http://www.economist.com/blogs/democracyinamerica/2010/08/gay_marriage_2*

- "Why Push an Immigration Reform Bill That Won't Pass?" *Washington Independent*, September 29, 2010, Elise Foley, *http://washingtonindependent.com/98988/why-push-an-immigration-reform-bill-that-wont-pass*
- "Will Immigration Reform Include Provisions for Gay Couples?" *Washington Independent, http://washingtonindependent.com, September 13, 2010, Elise Foley, http://washingtonindependent.com/97225/will-immigration-reform-include-provisions-for-gay-couples*
- "Windsor v. United States: Frequently Asked Questions (FAQ)," ACLU, *www.aclu.org*, November 11, 2010, *http://www.aclu.org/lgbt-rights/windsor-v-united-states-frequently-asked-questions-faq*

Blogs/Online Magazines/Online Newspapers/ Online Radio and TV

After Ellen: *www.afterellen.com*
After Elton: *www.afterelton.com*
Allvoices.com: *www.allvoices.com*
AMERICAblog: *www.americablog.com*

Bay Area Reporter: *www.ebar.com*
Big Queer: *www.bigqueer.com*
Breakthrough: *www.breakthrough.tv*
BuggBlog: *www.seanbugg.typepad.com/buggblog/2008/.../my-personal-bi.html*

Cherry Grrl: *www.cherrygrrl.com*
Citizen Crain: *www.citizenchris.typepad.com*
Community Marketing: *www.communitymarketinginc.com*
Crooks and Liars: *www.crooksandliars.com/*
Culture Kitchen: *www.culturekitchen.com*
Curve Magazine: *www.curvemag.com*
Cybersocket Web Magazine: *www.magazinecity.com/cybersocket-web-magazine.html*

Daily Kos: State of the Nation: *www.dailykos.com*
DIVA Magazine : *www.divamag.co.uk/diva*
DiversityInc: *www.diversityinc.com*

Echelon Magazine: *www.echelonmagazine.com*
Equally Wed: *www.equallywed.com/equally-wed-press.html*
Escape OKC Magazine: *www.escapeokc.com/*
Eschaton Blog: *www.eschatonblog.com/*
eurOut: *http://eurOut.org*
Exit.co.za - Home: *www.exit.co.za*

Faith in America: *www.faithinamerica.com*
Feetin2Worlds: *http://news.feetintwoworlds.org/*
FlawLes: *www.flawles.com/pages/flawles_culture.php*
Focus On The Rainbow: *www.focusontherainbowopine.outloudblogs.com*

Friendfactor: *www.friendfactor.org*
Fuse: *www.fusemagazine.com.au/index.php/fuse/view-fuse-online*
Fyne Times Gay and Lesbian Magazine, UK: *www.fyne.co.uk/index.php?item=95*

Gay Albany Online: *www.gayalbanyonline.com*
Gay.AmericaBlog.com: *www.gay.americablog.com/*
GayBlade.com: *www.gayblade.com*
Gaybloger.com: *http://gaybloger.com*
Gay Chicago Magazine: *www.gaychicagomag.com*
Gay Christian Online: *www.gaychristianonline.org*
Gay.com: *www.gay.com*
Gay City News: *http://www.gaycitynews.com*
Gay Married Californian: *www.gaymarriedcalifornian.blogspot.com*
Gay Parent: *www.gayparentmag.com*
Gay Rights Online: *www.gaysuperiority.com*
Gay Times: *www.gaytimes.co.uk*
Gay & Lesbian Convention & Visitors Bureau: *www.glcvb.org*
Gay and Lesbian Humanist: *http://www.gayandlesbianhumanist.org*
Gay & Lesbian Relocation & Real Estate National Online Magazine:
www.rainbowrelocation.com
Gay & Lesbian Review Magazine: *www.glreview.com*
GLT: Gay & Lesbian Times: *www.gaylesbiantimes.com*
Gay and Lesbian Toronto: *www.gaycrawler.com/search/V2/uk/index.asp?category=*
721000
GAY e-magazine: *www.gay-e-magazine.com*
Gay Politics Report/Smart Brief: *www.smartbrief.com*
Get Equal: *www.getequal.org*
Get Equal NOW!: *www.getequalnow.org*
GLAAD: *www.glaadblog.org*
GLAAD Religion, Faith and Values News Summary: *www.faith@glaad.org*
Good as You (G-A-Y): *www.goodasyou.org*
GRITtv: *http://www.grittv.org*
Gscene Magazine: *www.gscene.com*

here! Gay, Lesbian, Bisexual and Transgender Television: *www.heretv.com*

HIVPlus Mag.com: *www.hivplusmag.com*
HotSpots! Magazine: *www.hotspotsmagazine.com*

Immigration Equality: *www.immigrationequality.org/blog/*
Instinct Magazine: *www.ccgdata.com/7269-10.html*
In the Life: *www.inthelifetv.org*
I Want the World to Know: *www.iwanttheworldtoknow.org*

Jesus in Love Blog: American Academy of Religion hosts LGBT programs:
www.jesusinlove.blogspot.com
Joe. My. God.: *www.joemygod.blogspot.com*

Kate Clinton: *www.kateclinton.com*

Las Vegas' Gay and Lesbian Voice: *www.epinions.com*

Lavender Magazine: *www.lavendermagazine.com*
Lesbian News: *www.lesbiannews.com*
LGBT ASYLUM NEWS (formerly Save Mehdi Kazemi): *http://madikazemi.blogspot.com/2010/10/video-binational-lgbt-couples-join-new.html*
LGBT Immigration Stories: *http://lgbtculture.wordpress.com*
LGBTQ Nation: *www.lgbtqnation.com/*
LGBT POV: *www.lgbtpov.com*
Lez Get Real: *www.lezgetreal.com*
Little Rainbow Comics: *www.littlerainbowcomics.blogspot.com*
Live From Hell's Kitchen: *www.davidmixner.com*
Logo: Fierce TV: *www.logotv.com*

Magatopia.com - Free Online Gay & Lesbian Magazines: *www.magatopia.com/gay-lesbian-magazines-01.html*
Metroline Online: *www.metroline-online.com*
Metro Weekly: *www.metroweekly.com*
Mombian: *www.mombian.com*

Next Magazine: *www.nextmagazine.com/*

Oasis Magazine: *www.oasisjournals.com*
oneGoodLove.com: *www.onegoodlove.com*
One More Lesbian: *www.onemorelesbian.com*
Open Left: *www.openleft.com*
Our Lives Magazine: *www.ourlivesmadison.com*
Our World Magazine: *www.qrd.org/qrd/media/magazines*
Out4Immigration: *http://out4immigration.blogspot.com/*
Out Front Blog: *www.outfrontblog.com*
Out in America: *www.outinamerica.com*
Out in Jersey: *www.outinjersey.net*
Out Magazine: *www.out.com*
Outbeat.Now!: *www.kcrb.org*
Outbeat Radio: *http://www.outbeatradio.org*
Outbeat Youth: *www.outbeatyouth.com*
OutSmart Magazine Online: *www.outsmartmagazine.com*
Outsports: *www.outsports.com*
OutTraveler.com: *www.outtraveler.com*

PM Magazine: *www.pmentertainmentonline.com*
PageOneQ: *www.pageoneq.com*
Pam's House Blend: *www.pamshouseblend.com*
Pink News: *www.pinknews.co.uk*
Pink Play Mags: *www.pinkplaymags.com*
PNN Pride Nation: *www.pridenation.com*
POLITICO.com: *www.politico.com*
Politics1: *www.politics1.com*
PopCulture Shack: *www.popcultureshack.com/gay1.html*
PRIDE & Equality : *www.myprideonline.com*

qPDX.co: *www.qpdx.com*

Queer Magazine Online: *www.queermagazineonline.com*
Queercents: *www.queercents.com*
QSaltLake: *www.qsaltlake.com/about*
Queers United: *www.queersunited.blogspot.com*
Queerscape.co.uk : *www.gaysurrey.org/links.htm*
Queerty: *www.queerty.com*

Rage Monthly: *www.ragemonthly.com*
Rational Review: *www.rationalreview.com*
RE:ACT, the NLGJA Blog: *www.nlgjareact.wordpress.com*
RealClearPolitics: *http://www.realclearpolitics.com*
Religion Dispatches: *www.religiondispatches.org*
Religious Action Center : RACBlog: *http://blogs.rj.org/rac/*
Restore Fairness: *www.restorefairness@breakthrough.tv*

SDGLN: San Diego Gay and Lesbian News: *www.sdgln.com*
San Francisco Spectrum Magazine: *www.thecompletebear.com/GayLGBTMedia.php*
See Hear Speak: Ending All Silence: to view: *http://www.seehearspeak.us/*
    to submit your story: *submissions@seehearspeak.us*
She Wired: *www.shewired.com*
Slog: The Stranger: *www.slog.thestranger.com*
Steve Rothaus' Gay South Florida: *www.miamiherald.typepad.com/gaysouthflorida*
Stonewall Democrats: *www.stonewalldemocrats.org/blog*
Stop the Deportations: The DOMA Project: *http://stopthedeportations.blogspot.com*
Straight for Equality: *www.community.pflag.org/Page.aspx?pid=565*
Street Prophets: *www.streetprophets.com*

10,000 Couples: *http://www.10thousandcouples.com*
The Advocate: *www.advocate.com*
The Bilerico Project: *www.bilerico.com*
The Daily Dish: *www.andrewsullivan.theatlantic.com*
The Fix: *www.blog.washingtonpost.com/thefix*
The Gist: Michelangelo Signorile: *www.signorile.com*
The Huffington Post: *www.huffingtonpost.com*
The Lesbian Lifestyle: *www.helesbianlifestyle.com*
The New Civil Rights Movement: A Journal of News & Opinion on Gay Rights &
Marriage Equality: *www.thenewcivilrightsmovement.com*
The Trevor Project – 24 Hour Help Line 866-4-U-TREVOR (866-488-7386):
    www.thetrevorproject.org
"The White House Blog – President Obama: It Gets Better," October 21, 2010,
    posted by Brian Bond, *http://www.whitehouse.gov/ItGetsBetter?utm_source=*
    email81&utm_medium=text&utm_campaign=itgetsbetter
Thought Theater: *www.thoughttheater.com*
365 Gay: *www.365gay.com*
Time Out London: *www.timeout.com/london/gay*
Torn Apart: United by Love, Divided by Law: *http://tornapart.findhornpress.com*
Towleroad: *www.towleroad.com*
Trevorade: Freshly Squeezed Gay Analysis: *www.trevorhoppe.com*

2015place.com: *http://www.2015place.com*
TV Gawker.com: *http://tv.gawker.com*
Voices for Equality: *www.immigrationequality.org/blog/*
Waking Up Now: *www.wakingupnow.com*
Washington Blade - LGBTQ News: *www.washingtonblade.com*
Watermark Online: *www.watermarkonline.com*
Wayne Besen: *www.waynebesen.com*
We Are America Stories: *www.weareamericastories.org/*
We Are Many: *www.wearemany.org*
WGLB News Magazine: *www.wglb-tv.blogspot.com/*
What Will You Lose?: *www.whatwillyoulose.org*
Whosoever: *http://whosoever.org*
Youth Today: *www.youthtoday.org*

Books

A More Perfect Union: Why Straight America Must Stand Up for Gay Rights, Richard D. Mohr, Boston, MA: Beacon Press, 1994.

Always My Child: A Parent's Guide to Understanding Your Gay, Lesbian, Bisexual, Transgendered or Questioning Son or Daughter, Kevin Jennings and Pat Shapiro, New York, NY: Fireside Books, 2003.

America's Struggle for Same-Sex Marriage, Daniel R. Pinello, Cambridge, MA and New York, NY: Cambridge University Press, 2006.

Anti-Gay Rights: Assessing Voter Initiatives, Stephanie L. Witt and Suzanne McCorkle, editors, Westport, CT: Praeger Publishers, 1997.

Beloved Daughter: Letters From Parents to Their Lesbian Daughters, Chinese and English editions, order from info@apifamilypride.org for $5, including shipping in the United States.

Beyond (Straight and Gay) Marriage: Valuing All Families Under the Law, Nancy D. Polikoff, Boston, MA: Beacon Press, 2008.

Brave Journeys: Profiles in Gay and Lesbian Courage, David Mixner and Dennis Bailey, New York, NY: Bantam, 2001.

Bulletproof Faith: A Spiritual Survival Guide for Gay and Lesbian Christians, Candace Chellew-Hodge, Hoboken, NJ: Jossey-Bass, John Wiley & Sons, Inc., 2008.

Committed: A Skeptic Makes Peace with Marriage, Elizabeth Gilbert, New York, NY: Viking Penguin Group, 2010.

Counted Out: Same-Sex Relations and Americans' Definition of Family (The American Sociological Association's Rose Series in Sociology), Brian Powell, Catherine Bolzendahl, Claudia Geist, Lala Carr Steelman, New York, NY: Russell Sage Foundation, 2010.

Courting Equality: A Documentary History of Same-Sex Marriage in America, Patricia A. Gozemba and Karen Kahn, Boston, MA: Beacon Press, 2007.

Courting Justice: Gay Men and Lesbians vs the Supreme Court, Joyce Murdoch and Deb Price, editors, New York, NY: Basic Books, 2001.

Defending Same-Sex Marriage (Praeger Perspectives Series) Volume 1, "Separate But Equal No More: A Guide to the Legal Status of Same-Sex Marriage, Civil Unions and Other Partnerships," Mark Strasser, editor, Westport, CT: Praeger Publishers, 2007.

Defending Same-Sex Marriage (Praeger Perspectives Series) Volume 2, "Our Family Values: Same-Sex Marriage and Religion," Traci C. West, editor, Westport, CT: Praeger Publishers, 2007.

Defending Same-Sex Marriage (Praeger Perspectives Series) Volume 3, "The Freedom-to-Marry Movement: Education, Advocacy, Culture and the Media," Martin Dupuis and William A. Thompson, editors, Westport, CT: Praeger Publishers, 2007.

Entry Denied: Controlling Sexuality at the Border, Eithne Luibheid, Minneapolis: University of Minnesota Press, 2005.

Epistemology of the Closet, Eve Kosofsky Sedgwick, Berkeley and Los Angeles, CA: University of California Press, 1990.

Equality Practice: Civil Unions and the Future of Gay Rights, William N. Eskridge, Jr., New York, NY: Routledge, 2002.

Everyday Activism: A Handbook for Lesbian, Gay, and Bisexual People and Their Allies, Michael R. Stevenson and Jeanine C. Cogan, New York, NY: Routledge Press, 2003.

Family, Unvalued: Discrimination, Denial, and the Fate of Binational Same-Sex Couples Under U.S. Law, New York, NY: Human Rights Watch/Immigration Equality, 2006. (Note: Book is also available as a free download at *www.immigrationequality.org/uploadedfilesFamilyUnvalued.pdf*).

Fear Of A Queer Planet: Queer Politics and Social Theory (Studies in Classical Philology), Michael Warner, Minneapolis: University of Minnesota Press, 1993.

50 Ways to Support Lesbian and Gay Equality: The Complete Guide to Supporting Family, Friends, Neighbors or Yourself, Meredith Maran, editor, Angela Watrous, contributor, Makawao, Maui, HI: Inner Ocean Publishing, Inc., 2005.

Forced Apart: Families Separated and Immigrants Harmed by United States Deportation Policy, Human Rights Watch, July, 2007, *http://www.hrw.org/reports/2007/us0707/* (download pdf).

From Identity to Politics: The Lesbian and Gay Movements in the United States, Craig A. Rimmerman, Philadelphia, PA: Temple University Press, 2002.

Gay/Lesbian/Bisexual/Transgender Public Policy Issues: A Citizen's and Administrator's Guide to the New Cultural Struggle, Wallace Swan, ed, New York, NY: Harrington Park Press, 1997.

Gay Marriage: for Better or for Worse? What We've Learned from the Evidence, William N. Eskridge, Jr. and Darren R. Spedale, New York, NY: Oxford University Press, 2006

Gay Marriage: Why It Is Good for Gays, Good for Straights, and Good for America, Jonathan Rauch, New York, NY: Henry Holt & Co., LLC, 2004.

Gay Rights, Rachel Kranz and Tim Cusick, New York, NY: Facts on File, 2005.

Gays and Lesbians, Kate Burns, editor, San Diego, CA: Greenhaven Press, 2005.

Gays and Lesbians in the Democratic Process: Public Policy, Public Opinion, and Political Representation, Ellen D. B. Riggle and Barry L. Tadlock, editors, New York, NY: Columbia University Press, 1999.

Gender and U.S. Immigration: Contemporary Trends, Pierrette Hondagneu-Sotelo, editor, Berkeley and Los Angeles, CA: University of California Press, 2003.

Gendered Transitions: Mexican Experiences of Immigration, Pierrette Hondagneu-Sotelo, Berkeley and Los Angeles, CA: University of California Press, 1994.

God's Profits: Faith, Fraud, and the Republican Crusade for Values Voters, Sarah Posner, Sausalito, CA: PoliPoint Press, LLC, 2008.

Homo Domesticus: Notes From a Same-Sex Marriage, David Valdes Greenwood, Cambridge, MA: Da Capo Lifelong, 2008.

How the Religious Right Shaped Lesbian and Gay Activism, Tina Fetner, Vol. 31, Social Movements, Protest, and Contention Series, Minneapolis: University of Minnesota Press, 2008.

I Came Out for This? Lisa Gitlin, Ann Arbor, MI: Bywater Books, 201.0

Identity and the Case for Gay Rights: Race, Gender, Religion as Analogies, David A. J. Richards, Chicago, IL: University of Chicago Press, 1999.

Illegal People: How Globalization Creates Migration and Criminalizes Immigrants, David Bacon, Boston, MA: Beacon Press, 2008.

Impossible Subjects: Illegal Aliens and the Making of Modern America (Politics and Society in Twentieth Century America), Mae M. Ngai, Princeton, NJ, and Woodstock, Oxfordshire, UK: Princeton University Press, 2004.

In a New Land: A Comparative View of Immigration, Nancy Foner, New York, NY, and London, England: New York University Press, 2005.

Jesus, the Bible, and Homosexuality, Revised and Expanded Edition: Explode the Myths, Heal the Church, Jack Rogers, Louisville, KY: Westminster John Knox Press; revised expanded edition, 2009.

King and King, Linda de Haan and Stern Nijland, Berkeley, CA: Tricycle Press/Ten Speed Press, 2000

King and King and Family, Linda de Haan and Stern Nijland, Berkeley, CA: Tricycle Press/Ten Speed Press, 2004.

Leading the Way: Young Women's Activism for Social Change, Mary K. Trigg, editor, Mary S. Hartman, foreword, New Brunswick, NJ: Rutgers University, 2010.

Legally Wed: Same-Sex Marriage and the Constitution, Mark Strasser, Ithica, NY: Cornell University Press, 1997.

Love the Sin: Sexual Regulation and the Limits of Religious Tolerance, Janet R. Jakobsen and Ann Pellegrini, New York, NY: New York University Press, 2003.

Love Warriors: The Rise of the Marriage Equality Movement and Why It Will Prevail, Davina Kotulski, Ph.D., Seattle, WA: CreateSpace, 2010.

Making Gay History: The Half-Century Fight for Lesbian and Gay Equal Rights, Eric Marcus, New York, NY: Perennial, 2002.

Making It Legal: A Guide to Same-Sex Marriage, Domestic Partnership and Civil Unions, Frederick C. Hertz with Emily Doskow, , Berkeley, CA: Nolo Press, 2009.

Marriage and Same-Sex Unions: A Debate, Lynn D. Wardle, Mark Strasser, William C. Duncan and David Orgon Coolidge, editors, Westport, CT: Praeger Publishers, 2003

Modern American Queer History, Allida M. Black, editor, Philadelphia, PA: Temple University Press, 2001.

Obama and the Gays: A Political Marriage, Traci Baim, Prairie Avenue Productions, available as a print-on-demand and ebook from amazon.com, October 1, 2010, *www.obamaandthegays.com*

On Same-Sex Marriage, Civil Unions, and the Rule of Law: Constitutional Interpretation at the Crossroads, Mark Strasser, Westport, CT: Praeger Publications, 2002.

Perfect Enemies: The Battle Between the Religious Right and the Gay Movement, Chris Bull and John Gallagher, editors, Lanham, MD: Madison Books, 2001.

Queer Family Values: Debunking the Myth of the Nuclear Family, Valerie Lehr, Philadelphia, PA: Temple University Press, 1999.

Queer/Migration (Journal of Lesbian and Gay Studies), Eithne Luibheid, editor, www.glq. dukejournals.org/cgi/reprint/14/2-3/169.pdf.

Queer Migrations: Sexuality, U.S. Citizenship, and Border Crossings, Eithne Luibheid and Lionel Cantu, Jr., editors, Minneapolis: University of Minnesota Press, 2005.

Reforming the Immigration System: Proposals to Promote Independence, Fairness, Efficiency, and Professionalism in the Adjudication of Removal Cases (Executive Summary), Chicago, IL: Arnold and Porter, LLP, American Bar Association Commission on Immigration, 2010

Reforming the Immigration System: Proposals to Promote Independence, Fairness, Efficiency, and Professionalism in the Adjudication of Removal Cases (Full Report), Chicago, IL: Arnold and Porter, LLP, American Bar Association Commission on Immigration, 2010.

Same Sex, Different States: When Same-Sex Marriages Cross State Lines, Professor Andrew Koppelman, Ann Arbor, MI: Sheridan Books, 2006.

Same-Sex Marriage, Tricia Andryszewski, Minneapolis, MN: Twenty-First Century Books, 2008.

Same-Sex Marriage? A Christian Ethical Analysis, Marvin M. Ellison, Cleveland, OH: Pilgrim Press, 2004.

Same-Sex Marriage in the Americas: Policy Innovation for Same-Sex Relationships, Jason Pierceson, Adriana Piatti-Crocker and Shawn Schulenberg, editors, Lanham, MD: Lexington Books, 2010.

Same-Sex Marriage: Pro and Con, Andrew Sullivan, editor, New York, NY: Vintage Books, Random House, Inc., 1997.

Same-Sex Marriage: The Cultural Politics of Love and Law, Kathleen E. Hull, Cambridge, UK, and New York, NY: University Press, 2006.

Same-Sex Marriage: The Legal and Psychological Evolution in America, Donald J. Cantor, Elizabeth Cantor, James C. Black and Campbell D. Barrett, Middletown, CT: Wesleyan University Press, 2006.

Same-Sex Marriage: The Moral and Legal Debate, Robert M. Baird and Stuart E. Rosenbaum, editors, Amherst, NY: Prometheus Books, 1997.

Sexual Politics: The Gay Person in America Today, Shannon Gilreath, Akron, OH: University of Akron Press 2006.

Stonewall: the Riots that Sparked the Gay Revolution, David Carter, New York, NY: St. Martin's Griffin, 2004.

Stories of Gay and Lesbian Immigration: Together Forever? (Haworth Gay and Lesbian Studies), John Hart, Binghamton, NY: Harrington Press, an imprint of The Haworth Press, Inc., 2002.

Straight Parents, Gay Children: Keeping Families Together, Robert Bernstein, Robert MacNeil, and Betty DeGeneres, New York, NY: Thunder's Mouth Press, 2003.

Straight to Jesus: Sexual and Christian Conversions in the Ex-Gay Movement, Tanya Erzen, Berkeley and Los Angeles, CA: University of California Press, 2006.

Straightforward: How to Mobilize Heterosexual Support for Gay Rights, Ian Ayres and Jennifer Gerarda Brown, Princeton, NJ: Princeton University Press, 2005.

Stranger Among Friends, David Mixner, New York, NY: Bantam, 1997.

Strangers to the Law: Gay People on Trial, Lisa Melinda Keen and Suzanne Beth Goldberg, Ann Arbor, MI: University of Michigan Press, 2000.

The Challenge of Same-Sex Marriage: Federalist Principles and Constitutional Protections, Mark Strasser, Westport, CT: Praeger Publishers, 1999.

The Commitment, Dan Savage, Dutton, New York, NY: The Penguin Group, 2005.

The Idealist.org Handbook to Building a Better World, Action Without Borders, New York, NY: Perigee Book Penguin Group, 2009.

The International Homosexual Conspiracy, Larry-Bob Roberts, San Francisco, CA: Manic D Press, Inc., 2010.

The Latino Threat: Constructing Immigrants, Citizens and the Nation, Leo R. Chavez, Stanford, CA: Stanford University Press, 2008.

The Lesbian and Gay Studies Reader, Henry Abelove, Michele Aina Barale and David M. Halperin, editors, Abingdon, Oxford, UK, and New York, NY: Routledge, 1993.

The Limits to Union: Same-Sex Marriage and the Politics of Civil Rights, Jonathan Goldberg-Hiller, Ann Arbor, MI: University of Michigan Press, 2002.

The Politics of Gay Rights, Craig A. Rimmerman, Kenneth D. Wald and Clyde Wilcox, editors, Chicago, IL: University of Chicago Press, 2000.

The Private Roots of Public Action: Gender, Equality, and Political Participation, Nancy Burns, Kay Lehman Schlozman and Sidney Verba, editors, Cambridge, MA: Harvard University Press, 2001.

The Transnational Villagers, Peggy Levitt, Berkeley and Los Angeles, CA, and London, UK: University of California Press, 2001.

The Trouble with Normal: Sex, Politics, and the Ethics of Queer Life, Michael Warner, Cambridge, MA: Harvard University Press, 1999.

The Williams Project on Sexual Orientation Law and Public Policy, UCLA School of Law: "Bi-National Same-Sex Unmarried Partners in Census 2000: A Demographic portrait," pdf download at: *www.law.ucla.edu/williamsinstitute//publications/Binational_Report.pdf.*

"'They Take Our Jobs!' and 20 Other Myths about Immigration," Aviva Chomsky, Boston, MA: Beacon Press, 2007.

Value War: Public Opinion and the Politics of Gay Rights, Paul R. Brewer, Lanham, MD: Rowman and Littlefield, Publishers, Inc., 2008.

Virtual Equality: The Mainstreaming of Gay and Lesbian Liberation, Urvashi Vaid, New York, NY: Knopf Doubleday Publishing, 1996.

Voice and Equality: Civic Voluntarism in American Politics, Sidney Verba, Kay Lehman Schlozman and Henry E. Brady, editors, Cambridge, MA: Harvard University Press, 1995.

When Gay People Get Married: What Happens When Societies Legalize Same-Sex Marriage, M.V. Lee Badgett, New York, NY: New York University Press, 2009.

Why Marriage Matters: America, Equality and Gay People's Right to Marry, Evan Wolfson, New York, NY: Simon and Schuster, 2004.

Why You Should Give a Damn About Gay Marriage, Davina Kotulski, Ph.D., Los Angeles, CA: Advocate Books, 2004.

Children's Books (Not Just For Kids)

And Tango Makes Three, Justin Richardson and Peter Parnell, New York, NY: Simon and Schuster Children's Publishing, 2005

Daddy, Papa and Me, Leslea Newman, Berkeley, CA: Tricycle Press, Berkeley, 2009

Heather Has Two Mommies, Leslea Newman, Los Angeles, CA: Alyson Publications, 2000.

King and King, Linda de Haan and Stern Nijland, Berkeley, CA: Tricycle Press/Ten Speed Press, 2000.

King and King and Family, Linda de Haan and Stern Nijland, Berkeley, CA: Tricycle Press/Ten Speed Press, 2004.

Mommy and Mama, Leslea Newman, Berkeley, CA: Tricycle Press, 2009

My Princess Boy (A Mom's Story About a Young Boy Who Loves to Dress Up), Cheryl Kilodavis, Seattle, WA: KD Talent LLC, 2009.

Oliver Button is a Sissy, Tomie dePaola, San Diego, CA and New York, NY: Voyager Books/Harcourt, Brace & Company, 1979

The Family Book, Todd Parr, New York, NY: Little, Brown Books for Young Readers, 2003

The Sissy Duckling, Harvey Fierstein, New York, NY: Simon & Schuster Books for Young Readers, 2002

Uncle Bobby's Wedding, Sarah S. Brannen, New York, NY: G.P. Putnam's Sons/Penguin's Young Readers Group, 2008

William's Doll, Charlotte Zolotow, New York, NY: HarperCollins Publishers, 1972.

Book Publishers/Book Reviews/Book Sites

A&M Books: *http://www.sarahaldridge.com*
Absolute Press: *www.absolutepress.demon.co.uk*
Alyson.com: *www.alyson.com*
Amazing Dreams :*www.amazingdreamspublishing.com/*
ArtemisPress: *http://www.artemispress.com*
AttaGirl Press: *www.attgirlpress.com*
Aunt Lute Books: *www.auntlute.com*

Bella Books: *www.bellabooks.com*
Blue Feather Books: *www.bluefeatherbooks.com*
Bold Strokes Books: *www.boldstrokesbooks.com*
Bywater Books: *www.bywaterbooks.com*

Cleis Press: *www.cleispress.com*
Colbere Publishing: *www.colberepublishing.co.uk*
Crossing Press: *crossingpress.org*

Diverse Planet International, Inc.: *www.diverseplanet.com*

Elysium Press: *www.elysiumpress.com*
Findhorn Press: *www.findhornpress.com*
Firebrand Books: *www.firebrandbooks.com*

Gay Sunshine Press: *www.gaysunshine.com*
GLB Publishers: *www.glbpubs.com*
Goodreads: *www.goodreads.com/*

Intaglio Publications: *www.intagliopub.com*

Kirkus Book Reviews: *www.kirkusreviews.com*
Kore Press: *www.korepress.org*

Lambda Literary Foundation: *www.lambdaliterary.org*

Naiad Press: *www.naiadpress.com*
New Victoria : *www.newvictoria.com*

Onlywomen Press: *www.onlywomenpress.com*

Regal Crest Enterprises, LLC: *www.regalcrest.biz*

P.D. Publishing, Inc.: *www.pdpublishing.com*

Spinsters Ink: *www.spinstersink.com*
STARbooks Press: *www.starbookspress.com*

Suspect Thoughts: *www.suspectthoughts.com*
The Gay Publishing Company: *www.thegaypublishingcompany.com*
Virago Press: *www.virago.co.uk*
Way Out: *www.way-outpublishing.com*

DVDs

I would love it if you could support an LGBT company, Wolfe Video, by buying titles from them at www.wolfevideo.com. It doesn't hurt to tell them you read about them in *Torn Apart*. I met Kathy Wolfe way back in the 1980s.

If you can't afford to buy them, you can check with your library, your LGBT center or other organizations to see if you can borrow the DVD you want to see. You can also check availability of these titles to buy or rent or stream with the regular mainstream online video sites.

Breakfast with Scot: *www.wolfevideo.com*
Coming Out, Coming Home: *Asian families talk about accepting their GLBTQ children order for $15 (includes shipping in U.S.) from info@apifamilypride.org, www.apifamilpride.org*
Corpus Christi: Playing with Redemption *www.corpuschristi-themovie.com/*
Crossing Arizona: *www.crossingaz.com*
Dying to Live: A Migrant's Journey: *http://dyingtolive.nd.edu*
Edie & Thea: *www.queerfilm.de*
8: The Mormon Proposition: *www.wolfevideo.com*
Entre Nous: *www.entrenousfilm.com*
Excluded: *excludedthemovie.com/*
Farmingville: *www.farmingvillethemovie.com*
Floored by Love: *www.wolfevideo.com*
Follow My Voice: *www.wolfevideo.com*
God and Gays: Bridging the Gap: *www.godandgaysthemovie.com/*
God Grew Tired of Us: *www.godgrewtiredofus.com*
Half-Life: *www.wolfevideo.com*
Hannah Free: *www.wolfevideo.com*
How to Get a United States Student and Tourist Visas: *www.immigrationdirect.com/ visas/student/Student-Tourist-Visas-dvd.jsp*
"I do. Who can't?": *http://idowhocant.com/*
Made in L.A.: *www.madeinla.com*
9500 Liberty: *www.9500liberty.com*
Out in the Silence: *www.wpsu.org/outinthesilence*
Out of the Past: The Struggle for Gay and Lesbian Rights in America: *http://www.glsen.org/cgi-bin/iowa/all/booklink/record/1507.html*
Papers: *www.papersthemovie.com*
Pedro: *www.wolfevideo.com*

Prom Queen: *www.wolfevideo.com*
Pursuit of Equality: The Unfinished Work of American Freedom: *www.pursuitof equality.com/filmakers.html*
Saving Marriage: *www.regentreleasing.com*
Shelter: *www.wolfevideo.com*
Sin Nombre (Without a Name): *www.filminfocus.com/focusfeatures/ film/sin_nombre*
The ACLU Freedom Files: *http://aclu.tv/*
The Anatomy of Hate: A Dialogue for Hope: *http://theanatomyofhate.com/dvd*
The Campaign: *http://thecampaigndocumentary.com/*
The Visitor: *www.thevisitorfilm.com*
Through Thick and Thin: *http://www.7thart.com/films/Through-Thick-and-Thin*
Tying the Knot: *www.1049films.com/*
Which Way Home: *www.whichwayhome.net*

Facebook Pages

A Call to Action: Asian Americans Impacting Immigration Reform: *http://www.facebook.com/AsianAmericanImmigration?v=wall* Sign our online petition at: *http://www.advancingequality.org/familypetition*
A Day in Hand: *http://www.facebook.com/l/205729Y49gfAmfvZoZ1GwZykYbw; www.adayinhand.com*
Americans United for Separation of Church and State: *http://www.facebook.com/betsy.carr.arroyo?v=wall&story_fbid=103859816345529#!/americansunited*
Butch Voices: *http://www.facebook.com/profile.php?id=1510232652&ref=pymk*
Center for LGBTQ Evidence-Based Applied Research (CLEAR): *http://www.facebook.com/?ref=home#!/CLEAR.TEAM*
Christians for Comprehensive Immigration Reform (CCIR): *http://www.facebook.com/faithandimmigration?v=wall*
Demand Equality (Jessica Naomi): *http://www.facebook.com/DemandLGBTEquality1868*
DOMA Stories: Federal Marriage Discrimination Hurts Families: *http://www.facebook.com/?ref=home#!DOMAStories?ref=ts:*
DreamACTivist.org: *http://www.facebook.com/dreamactivist.org*
Equality America: *www.facebook.com/pages/Equality-America/114055221948808*
GAY EXILES: *http://www.facebook.com/permalink.php?story_fbid=462980092736&id=568827736#!/pages/GAY-EXILES/166606481743*
Have a HART Campaign, Gay & Lesbian Rights to Equality: *http://www.facebook.com/pages/Have-a-HART-Campaign-Gay-Lesbian-Rights-to-Equality/139941882690051?v=wall&story_fbid=165019756848930&po=1&ref=notif&notif_t=feed_comment*
HONOR PAC: *http://www.facebook.com/HONORPAC?v=wall*
I Do. Who Can't?: *http://www.facebook.com/pages/I-do-Who-cant/146367765390621?v=wall*
I Support Equal Immigration Rights for Same Sex Binational Couples!: *http://www.facebook.com/?ref=home#!/group.php?gid=350533207638*

Keep Ed & Tim Together: Fight Immigration Injustice: *http://www.facebook.com/pages/*
Keep-Ed-Tim-Together-Fight-Immigration-Injustice/118576734849352?ref=ts:

Lambda Literary Foundation:
http://www.facebook.com/home.php?sk=lf#!/LambdaLiterary
LGBT Asylum News: *http://www.facebook.com/pages/LGBT-Asylum-News/*
336394400652
Lifeworks Mentoring: *http://www.facebook.com/lifeworksmentoring*
Mine : *http://www.facebook.com/video/video.php?v=1143260075848*

Outbeat.Now!: *http://www.facebook.com/pages/Outbeat-Youth/125116027845?v=wall#!/*
outbeatnow
Outbeat Youth: *http://www.facebook.com/pages/Outbeat-Youth/125116027845?v=wall*
http://www.facebook.com/pages/Outbeat-Youth/125116027845?ref=ss:
Out4Immigration: *http://www.facebook.com/Out4Immigration*
Out Spoken: *http://www.facebook.com/permalink.php?story_fbid=108044789266270&i*
d=568827736&ref=notif&notif_t=like#!/profile.php?id=100000512087504
Out to Protect Scholarship Program: *http://www.facebook.com/pages/Out-To-Protect-*
Scholarship-Program/187795699129?ref=ts&v=wall

Positive Images: *http://www.facebook.com/pages/Positive-Images/113431267460?v=wall*
"President Obama: It Gets Better": *http://www.facebook.com/permalink.php?story_fbid=*
46298009236&id=568827736#!/

Queer Alliance and Resource Center: *http://www.facebook.com/pages/Berkeley-CA/*
Queer-Alliance-and-Resource-Center/10592192274?v=wall

SameSexSunday: *http://www.facebook.com/?ref=home#!/pages/SameSexSunday/2397350*
75877?ref=ts:
Save Our Marriage - Stop the Deportation of Henry Velandia: *http://www.facebook.*
com/SaveOurMarriage?v=wall, http://www.facebook.com/permalink.php?story_fbid=1
61612290536497&id=568827736#!/SaveOurMarriage
Silicon Valley Alliance for Immigration Reform (SVAIR): *http://www.facebook.com/*
pages/Silicon-Valley-Alliance-for-Immigration-Reform-SVAIR/149164630851

Talk About Equality: *http://www.facebook.com/group.php?gid=47069401538*
10,000 Committed Gay and Lesbian Couples Joined Together : *www.facebook.com/*
group.php?gid=87441352998&v=info
The American Equality Bill (AEB): *http://www.facebook.com/pages/The-American-*
Equality-Bill/152463468103529?ref=ts&v=wall
The American Equality Bill ONE Bill for Equal LGBT Civil Rights Join: *http://www.*
facebook.com/group.php?gid=278882199073&v=info&ref=ts
The Trevor Project: *www.facebook.com/TheTrevorProject*

We Support Uniting American Families Act
http://www.facebook.com/pages/We-Support-Uniting-American-Families-
Act/107000089351601?v=wall

Groups on Facebook

Immigration Equality: *http://www.facebook.com/photo.php?fbid=485501278409&set =a.82372823409.102472.643873409#!/ImmigrationEquality*
Love Exiles Foundation: *http://www.facebook.com/photo.php?fbid=485501278409&set =a.82372823409.102472.643873409#!/group.php?gid=23787240683*
Out4Immigration: *http://www.facebook.com/Out4Immigration*

Online Videos

"A New Same-Sex Fight": *http://www.out4immigration.org/immigration/content_detail. asp?s=immeqla&id=1380&ctid=114*
"An Anti-Bullying Message from the NOH8 Campaign": *http://www.youtube.com/ watch?v=MhFZ7qjrw5U&feature=player_embedded*
"AllMyLove.Org Gives a Damn": *http://www.youtube.com/watch?v=ziQhU5oHE5A&fe ature=player_embedded*
"Balitang America: Shirley Tan to Stay": *http://www.youtube.com/watch?v= JMljnfS4VJM*
"Binational Couples at The Wedding March 09-26-2010": *http://www.youtube.com/ watch?v=VVTOLtd4aBE*
"Binational LGBT Couples Join New York's Wedding March": *http://www.youtube. com/watch?v=VVTOLtd4aBE&feature=player_embedded*
"Carl and Darin, All Any Parent Should Want is For Their Child to Be Happy (Carl's Mom)," 10,000 Couples, October 2010: *http://10thousandcouples.com/page/ same-gender-wedding-competition-honors-civil-rights-and-love*
"Citizen Non-Citizen": *http://www.youtube.com/watch?v=dcD5eHsgHLY*
"Civil Rights Fast – Day 10": *https://mail.google.com/mail/?shva=1#inbox/12c466bcd6 ec8580*
"Cynthia Nixon to NOM Pres.: 'We Have No Desire to Change Marriage'": *http://www.towleroad.com/2010/10/cynthia-nixon.html*
"Dunno Y": *http://www.huffingtonpost.com/2010/11/12/dunno-y-bollywood-gay- rom_n_782705.html*
"Equality4All": *http://www.youtube.com/user/Equality4All*
"Ex Gay Couple": *http://www.youtube.com/watch?v=HkB8isr3bZQ&feature=player_ embedded*
"FCKH8.com Straight Talk About Gay Marriage": *http://vimeo.com/15550574*
"Fight for Love": *www.youtube.com*
"Friendfactor": *cfdl1.dev.videogenie.com*
"Glad to Be Gay vs Before Stonewall": *http://www.youtube.com/watch?v=v-idDXYKd_ M&N=1*
"Henry & Luz at 'Despierta' Gathering for Latino Youth and Parents": *http://www. youtube.com/watch?v=L4Q4DodsPUA*
"Hillary Clinton: Tomorrow Will Be Better": *http://www.youtube.com/watch?v= zXBpW8GCDtY&sns=fb*

"Holly and Alyson: Freedom Should Never Be Conditional," 10,000 Couples, October 2010: *http://10thousandcouples.com/page/same-gender-wedding-competition-honors-civil-rights-and-love*
"Honda Loves Eat, Pray, Love," POLITICO, October 1, 2010, Patrick Gavin: *http://www.politico.com/click/stories/1010/honda_loves_eat_pray_love.html*
"Human Rights Campaign: Stop the Extremists!": *http://www.hrcactioncenter.org/site/PageNavigator/Delivering_letters_to_Boyd_Packer_video*
"Joel Burns and His Husband Discuss Bullying Speech," The Last Word with Lawrence O'Donnell, msnbc.com, The Advocate, October 21, 2010: *http://www.advocate.com/News/Daily_News/2010/10/21/Joel_Burns_and_Husband_Discuss_Bullying_Speech/*
"Joel Burns: It Was an Act of Necessity": *https://salsa.wiredforchange.com/o/5208/t/6988/shop/custom.jsp?donate_page_KEY=4455*
"Kareem and DeWayne, This Confirms the Blessings in Our Lives," 10,000 Couples, October 2010: *http://10thousandcouples.com/page/same-gender-wedding-competition-honors-civil-rights-and-love*
"Law Dividing Love": *http://www.youtube.com/watch?v=4xZRYlgpPNY&feature=player_embedded*
"Let's Make It Better for LGBT Youth," ACLU of Northern California, October 27, 2010: *http://www.aclunc.org/issues/lgbt/let%27s_make_it_better_for_lgbt_youth.shtml*
"Love: A Mission Statement": *http://www.spreadlovelikefire.com*
"Love Exiled": *http://www.youtube.com/watch?v=dvYqpyM4-Ew*
"Melissa and Ana, Being Gay is OK," 10,000 Couples, October 2010: *http://10thousandcouples.com/page/same-gender-wedding-competition-honors-civil-rights-and-love*
"Message from GetEQUAL Youth to President Obama and Congress,": *www.youtube.com, http://www.youtube.com/watch?v=Q67qEiRsHbc&feature=player_embedded*
"Mom in China Advocates for Gay Son": *http://www.youtube.com/watch?v=AIUmyO6Ekxo*
"Nick and Eddie Give a Damn": *http://www.youtube.com/watch?v=NiikStTgg1U&feature=player_embedded*
"New Religious Right Horror Flick": *http://www.newsweek.com/video/2010/08/12/this-film-is-not-yet-rated-activist-judges.html*
"On These Shoulders We Stand": *http://www.youtube.com/watch?v=y-vAE2ETi_A*
"Openly Gay Student Defends Teacher at School Board Meeting": *http://tv.gawker.com/5689407/openly-gay-student-defends-teacher-at-school-board-meeting*
"Our Last Night Together... The Reality Check": *http://www.youtube.com/watch?v=SjsS4Xpzab0*
"President Obama: It Gets Better": *http://www.youtube.com/watch?v=geyAFbSDPVk*
"Prop. 8 Trial Begins": *http://www.msnbc.msn.com/id/34801259/*
"Ricardo & Steve": *http://www.youtube.com/watch?v=3uXGEHJVgAU*
"Robert and Richard, We Want to Serve as an Example for Committed Relationships," 10,000 Couples, October 2010: *http://10thousandcouples.com/page/same-gender-wedding-competition-honors-civil-rights-and-love*
Rosie Perez's Video for LGBT Equality is a Hoot!": *http://www.shewired.com/Article.cfm?ID=25834*
"Rudolf Brazda, Last of the Pink Triangles, Tells His Story": The Advocate, October 20, 2010: *http://www.youtube.com/watch?v=x-1uFsOXWhQ*

"Same-Sex Couples Fight for Immigration Rights," CNN: *http://www.cnn.com/2009/POLITICS/06/03/same.sex.immigration/index.html*
"Same Sex Immigration Rights (UAFA), Congress and Lady Gaga,": *http://www.youtube.com/watch?v=YvWNWzxUlG8&feature=player_embedded*
"Things People Ask My Friends Regarding My Gayness,": *http://www.youtube.com/watch?v=PUwHj-fTOd0&NR=1*
"Through Thick and Thin" trailer: *http://www.youtube.com/watch?v=UYI-Lj8ODdA&NR=1*
"Tonya and Amy, March into the World and Do What's Right," 10,000 Couples, October 2010: *http://10thousandcouples.com/page/same-gender-wedding-competition-honors-civil-rights-and-love*
"Torn Apart: One Family, Two Countries," San Jose Mercury News, October 12, 2010, Dai Sugano: *http://www.mercurynews.com/torn-apart*
"UAFA": *http://www.youtube.com/watch?v=gRPgBCnLLRk&feature=related*
"UAFA: Entry Denied": *http://www.youtube.com/watch?v=dlnP1yYvdvU&feature=related*
"UAFA Senate Hearings (6/3/2009): Christopher Nugent (ABA) Testimony": *http://www.youtube.com/watch?v=yD7yOgbaYzo&feature=related*
"UAFA Senate Hearings (6/3/2009): Gordon Stewart Testimony": *http://www.youtube.com/watch?v=GmiVawXrozc*
"UAFA Senate Hearings (6/3/2009): Jessica Vaughn (CIS) Center for Immigration Studies) Testimony": *http://www.youtube.com/watch?v=JBNdy1psA_E&feature=related*
"UAFA Senate Hearings (6/3/2009): Julian Bond (NAACP) Testimony": *http://www.youtube.com/watch?v=70wZwx247MQ*
"UAFA Senate Hearings (6/3/2009): Senator Arlen Specter": *http://www.youtube.com/watch?v=TIVH0HH9ay8&feature=related*
"UAFA Senate Hearings (6/3/2009): Senator Charles Schumer": *http://www.youtube.com/watch?v=xQBmcgIU_1Q&feature=related*
"UAFA Senate Hearings (6/3/2009): Senator Jeff Sessions": *http://www.youtube.com/watch?v=i5YJCDAVe2I&feature=youtube_gdata*
"UAFA Senate Hearings (6/3/2009): Senator Patrick Leahy": *http://www.youtube.com/watch?v=ct7Vr62-62U*
"UAFA Senate Hearings (6/3/2009): Shirley Tan Testimony": *http://www.youtube.com/watch?v=9cTojNqjnP4*
"WE GIVE A DAMN, DO YOU?": *http://www.youtube.com/watch?v=RnaJMgk6-fE&feature=player_embedded*
"What Will You Lose?": *http://www.youtube.com/watch?v=1qIbpGS5Ms8*
"When Did You Choose to be Straight?": *http://www.youtube.com/watch?v=QJtjqLUHYoY*

Groups on YouTube.com

Immigration Equality : *http://www.youtube.com/immigrationequality*
Love Exiles Foundation : *(in process)*
Out4Immigration : *http://www.youtube.com/out4immigration*

Podcasts

GayTalk Radio: *www.gaytalkradio.org*
Immigration Podcasts: *www.archive.org/details/DillonPro-immigrationPodcast,*
www.immigrateusa.us/content/view/63/69/immigration.avvo.com/immigration-
podcasts, www.immigrationgucl.com/resources/immigration-podcasts/migrationpolicy.
podbean.com/, www.podfeed.net/tags/immigration, www.usimmlawyer.com/us-
immigration-podcasts
Same Sex Sunday: *samesexsunday.podbean.com/*
The Six Pack: *sixpackage.com*
Radio Broadcasts/Stations: *"Gays' Global Search for Acceptance," National Public*
Radio, Talk of the Nation, August 4, 2010, http://www.npr.org/templates/story/story/.
php?storyid=128981230
Out in America Radio: *www.outinamerica.com/*
"Same-Sex Marriage Inches Toward Higher Court," National Public Radio, July 16,
2010, Tovia Smith: *http://www.npr.org/templates/story/story.php?storyId=128572219*
Sirius XM Satellite Radio Channel OutQ, irius 109 and XM 98, free online trial at:
http://www.sirius.com/siriusinternetradio
Song That Radio: *www.songthat.com/WEB.SameSexImmigrantsFIXEDmp3*

Twitter

Immigration Equality: *www.twitter.com/IEquality*
Out4Immigration: *www.twitter.com/out4immigration*

Check the other groups listed in the Resource Groups and Websites in Chapter 35 for their websites and see if you can connect on Twitter for updates and action alerts.

CHAPTER THIRTY-SEVEN

PERTINENT DEFINITIONS AND INFORMATION

Census Data

At the time I was finishing this book, 2010 Census data was not released. The forms were being processed at the national processing centers, according to the U.S. Census website. For updates on the number of same-sex binational couples and other population information from the 2000 Census cited in *Torn Apart*, go to *www.census.gov/*

Definition of Marriage in America

In 1996, marriage in America was defined as one man and one woman. That was the bill passed by Congress with a vote of 85-14 in the Senate and 342-67 in the House of Representatives. The Defense of Marriage Act (DOMA) was signed into law on September 21, 1996 by then-President Bill Clinton.

But same-sex couples could be married in a few states and the District of Columbia, although these marriages were not federally recognized for the purposes of sponsoring same-sex partners for immigration. According to the online encyclopedia *Wikipedia*:

> At the time of passage, it was expected that Hawaii (and possibly other states) would soon legalize same-sex marriage, whether by legislation or judicial interpretation of either the state or federal constitution. Opponents of such recognition feared, and many proponents hoped, that the other states would then be required to recognize such marriages under the Full Faith and Credit Clause of the United States Constitution. Section 3 of the law, the part that defines marriage for federal purposes as the union of a man and a woman, was ruled unconstitutional by a federal district court judge in July 2010.

That was in California, but the status was put on hold because of a stay on the decision that had not been lifted as of the time I finished this manuscript.

In August 2010, a federal district judge in California ruled that the Proposition 8 ban on same-sex marriages (passed in 2008) violated the equal protection provisions of the U.S. Constitution. The decision has been appealed and enforcement (allowing same-sex marriages to be performed) has been delayed until it can be heard by the 9th Circuit Court of Appeals. An expedited hearing was scheduled for December 2010 and the decision is likely to be appealed to the U.S. Supreme Court, per The National Conference of State Legislatures.

Find out more about marriage options for same-sex couples at: *http://www.ncsl.org/ IssuesResearch/HumanServices/SameSexMarriage/tabid/16430/Default.aspx*

Definition of Permanent Partner

This information comes from the Immigration Equality website:

> Under the Uniting American Families Act (UAFA), to qualify as a permanent partner, a person must be able to show: (a) a relationship with another adult in which both parties intend a life-long commitment; (b) financial interdependence; (c) exclusivity; (d) inability to marry in a manner that is "cognizable" under the INA; and (e) absence of close blood relationship.
>
> A permanent partnership is not equivalent to marriage. The UAFA does not seek to add same sex couples to the category of spouse in the Immigration and Naturalization Act (INA). Instead, it creates a new category of relationship, permanent partnership, which is recognized under the INA. Although an application for permanent partner status under the INA would be subjected to the same intense scrutiny as a marriage-based application, a successful application would confer no benefits other than immigration status for the foreign national. Permanent partnership is therefore analogous to local domestic partnerships that only confer limited, enumerated rights to the couple, such as the ability to include a domestic partner on a health insurance policy.

Deportation from America in the 21st Century

The number of U.S. deportations has grown steadily since 2002. Data from the U.S. Department of Homeland Security shows these annual totals: 2002, 165,168; 2003: 211,098; 2004: 240,665; 2005: 246,431; 2006: 280,974; 2007: 319,382; 2008: 358,886; 2009: 393,289.

An article by Jeremy Pelofsky from Reuters noted that a record 393,000 illegal immigrants in the 2009/2010 fiscal year had been been deported, half of whom had committed a crime, according to Department of Homeland Security officials.

While we don't know how many were gay men or lesbians who tried to be with their American partners, the sheer number of people booted out of America astounds me. Deportation is the worst fate anyone can suffer in their immigration struggle and this is part of the mix of what same-sex binational couples face.

You can read more about this data and the overall topic at:
Deportation Tears Apart Families, Some Say, freep.com, Detroit Free Press, *http://m.freep.com/detail.jsp?key=729646&rc=lo&full=1*
You can find out more about deportation at:
www.usimmigrationsupport.org/ or *deportation.html* or
http://immigration.findlaw.com/immigration/immigration-deportation/

Immigration Reform/ Comprehensive Immigration Reform

According to Wikipedia, "immigration reform" is the common term used in political discussions regarding changes to the current immigration policy of a country. In its strict definition, "reform" means to change into an improved form or condition, by amending or removing faults or abuses. In the political sense, immigration reform discussions can be general enough to include promoted, expanded, or open immigration as well as the aspect of reducing or eliminating immigration altogether.

Some want immigration reform to mean fewer immigrants to America. Others want immigration reform to fix what they consider a broken system and offer amnesty to illegal aliens in the United States so that they can apply for green cards and citizenship, allow the children of illegal aliens to go to college and/or serve in the U.S. Armed Forces, to resolve backlogs and quotas that restrict family unification and employment opportunities, and to allow lesbians and gay men to be able to sponsor their permanent partners for immigration.

The term comprehensive immigration reform in general means an effort to fix all (as the author sees it) immigration problems and expand access. To me and Karin and other same-sex binational couples and our allies, no immigration reform and no comprehensive immigration reform is complete and correct if it does not allow American gay men and lesbians, or members of the LGBT community in general, to sponsor our foreign-born partners for immigration to be with us in America. As we have noted in this book, bills that address that issue so far include Uniting American Families Act (UAFA), Reuniting Families Act (RFA) and Comprehensive Immigration Reform of 2010 (CIR 2010).

PERTINENT DEFINITIONS AND INFORMATION

For more about immigration reform go to: *www.topix.com/news/immigration* or *www.usaimmigrationreform.org/* or *www.comprehensive-immigration-reform.com*

For more about comprehensive immigration reform see the various groups working on this issue in the Resource Groups and Sites chapter.

U. S. Immigration Law

This information comes directly from the United States Immigration and Citizenship Services website:

Immigration and Nationality Act

The Immigration and Nationality Act, or INA, was created in 1952. Before the INA, a variety of statutes governed immigration law but were not organized in one location. The McCarran-Walter bill of 1952, Public Law No. 82-414, collected and codified many existing provisions and reorganized the structure of immigration law. The Act has been amended many times over the years, but is still the basic body of immigration law.

The INA is divided into titles, chapters, and sections. Although it stands alone as a body of law, the Act is also contained in the United States Code (U.S.C.). The code is a collection of all the laws of the United States. It is arranged in fifty subject titles by general alphabetic order. Title 8 of the U.S. Code is but one of the fifty titles and deals with "Aliens and Nationality." When browsing the INA or other statutes, you will often see reference to the U.S. Code citation. For example, Section 208 of the INA deals with asylum, and is also contained in 8 U.S.C. 1158. Although it is correct to refer to a specific section by either its INA citation or its U.S. code, the INA citation is more commonly used.

Basically, there are three categories of ways to immigrate to the United States (get a green card), family member, work or personal misfortune. If you go to the USCIS website, you can get the explanations of the categories. Here's some text, but for complete information go to *www.uscis.gov.*

Green Card Through Family

Many people become permanent residents (get a green card) through family members. The United States promotes family unity and allows U.S. citizens and permanent residents to petition for certain relatives to come and live permanently in the United States. You may be eligible to get a green card through a family member who is a U.S. citizen or permanent resident, or through the special categories described. There are two distinct paths through which you can get your green card. Many family members who are already in the United States may qualify for adjustment of status to permanent residence in the United States, which means they are able to complete their immigrant processing without having to return to their home country. Those relatives outside the United States or those who are not eligible to adjust status in the United States may be eligible for consular processing through a U.S. embassy or consulate abroad that has jurisdiction over their foreign place of residence.

If Your Family Member is a U.S. Citizen

You may be able to get a green card as an immediate relative or as a family member in a preference category if your U.S. citizen relative files a Form I-130, Petition for Alien Relative, for you.

Immediate Relative of a U.S. Citizen

You are an immediate relative of a U.S. citizen if you are:
- The child (unmarried and under 21 years old) of a U.S. citizen
- The spouse (husband or wife) of a U.S. citizen
- The parent of a U.S. citizen (if the U.S. citizen is 21 years or older)

Family Member of a U.S. Citizen in a Preference Category

You are a family member of a U.S. citizen in a preference category if you are:
- An unmarried son or daughter (21 years or older) of a U.S. citizen
- A married son or daughter (any age) of a U.S. citizen
- A sibling (brother or sister) of a U.S. citizen

If Your Family Member is a Permanent Resident

You may be able to get a green card as a family member in a preference category if your family member filed a Form I-130 on your behalf.

Family member of a permanent resident in a preference category

You are a family member of a permanent resident in a preference category if you are:
- The spouse of a permanent resident
- The child (unmarried and under 21 years old) of a permanent resident
- The unmarried son or daughter (21 years or older) of a permanent resident

Green Card Through Special Categories of Family

You may also be eligible to get a green card if you:
- Are a battered child or spouse of a U.S. citizen
- Entered the United States with a K visa as the fiancé(e) or spouse of a U.S. citizen or an accompanying child
- Obtained V nonimmigrant status
- Are a widow(er) of a U.S. citizen
- Are born to a foreign diplomat in the United States

Green Card Through a Job

Many people become permanent residents through a job or offer of employment. Some categories require a certification from the U.S. Department of Labor to show that there are not enough U.S. workers who are able, willing, qualified, and available in the geographic area where the immigrant is to be employed and that no American workers are displaced by foreign workers. In other cases, highly skilled workers, those with extraordinary ability in certain professions, and investors/entrepreneurs are given priority to immigrate through several immigrant categories. In all cases, the process involves several steps.

The main ways to immigrate based on a job offer or employment are listed below.

Green Card Through a Job Offer

You may be eligible to become a permanent resident based on an offer of permanent employment in the United States. Most categories require an employer to get a labor certification and then file a Form I-140, Immigrant Petition for Alien Worker, for you.

Green Card Through Investment

Green cards may be available to investors/entrepreneurs who are making an investment in an enterprise that creates new U.S. jobs.

Green Card Through Self-Petition

Some immigrant categories allow you to file for yourself ("self-petition"). This option is available for either "Aliens of Extraordinary Ability" or certain individuals granted a National Interest Waiver.

Green Card Through Special Categories of Jobs

There are a number of specialized jobs that may allow you to get a green card based on a past or current job. All of these require a Form I-360, Petition for Amerasian, Widow(er), or Special Immigrant, and are described in Section 101(a)(27) of the Immigration and Nationality Act (INA):

- Afghan/Iraqi Translator
- Broadcaster
- International Organization Employee
- Iraqi Who Assisted the U.S. Government
- NATO-6 Nonimmigrant
- Panama Canal Employee
- Physician National Interest Waiver
- Religious Worker

In some cases, you may be able to file the immigrant petition (either a Form I-140 or I-360, depending on your category) at the same time that you file Form I-485, known as "concurrent filing."

If you are not eligible to adjust your status inside the United States to a permanent resident, the immigrant petition will be sent to the U.S. consulate abroad to complete the visa process. In order to apply for a green card, there must be a visa immediately available to you.

Green Card Through Refugee or Asylee Status

If you were admitted to the United States as a refugee or as a qualifying family member of an asylee, you are eligible to apply for permanent residence (a green card) 1 year after your entry into the United States.

If you were granted asylum in the United States, you are eligible to apply for permanent residence 1 year after the grant of your asylum status.

As a refugee, you are required by law to apply for permanent resident status 1 year after being admitted to the United States in refugee status. As an asylee, you are not required to apply for permanent resident status after being granted asylum for 1 year, although it may be in your best interest to do so.

Other sections/links gave information for many other ways to get a green card, including:

- Amerasian Child of a U.S. Citizen
- American Indian Born in Canada
- Armed Forces Member

- Cuban Native or Citizen
- Diversity Immigration Visa Program
- Haitian Refugee
- Indochinese Parole Adjustment Act
- Informant (S Nonimmigrant)
- Lautenberg Parolee
- Legal Immigration Family Equity (LIFE) Act
- Person Born to a Foreign Diplomat in the United States
- Registry
- Section 13 (Diplomats)
- Special Immigrant Juvenile
- Victim of a Crime (U Nonimmigrant)
- Victim of Trafficking (T Nonimmigrant)

Find out more at: *www.uscis.gov/*

Visa Information (B1/B2)
According to the glossary in *Family Unvalued*, the B1/B2 visa includes these parameters:

- **B-1 visa**: a visitor's visa for business. These visas are available for up to six months for persons entering the United States to conduct business affairs such as: consulting with clients, meeting with business associates or attending professional, scientific or religious conventions. B-1 visitors are allowed to receive money for expenses in the U.S., but they cannot be paid a salary by an employer in this country.

- **B-2 visa**: a visitor's visa for pleasure. These visas are available for a stay of up to six months for persons entering the United States for reasons of leisure or pleasure such as: tourism, amusement, visiting friends or relatives, rest, medical treatment, or activities of a social or service nature. The B-2 visa can also be used by a non-spousal partner (including a same-sex partner) of the holder of certain other visas to visit them in the United States.

The Immigration Direct website (*www.immigrationdirect.com*) explains the B1/B2 visa categories thus:

- **Business:** A B-1 visa is granted to business visitors who wish to enter the

U.S. for a temporary period to engage in legitimate business activities, such as meetings, conferences, negotiating contracts and consultations. B-1 visa holders may not work in the U.S. and may not be paid from a U.S. source. Individuals who seek to work in the U.S., should apply for a work visa, such as an H-1B, TN or L-1 visa.

- **Pleasure:** A B-2 visa is granted to visitors who wish to enter the U.S. for a temporary period to engage in tourist activities or visit families or friends. In addition, in certain situations, a B-2 visa may be issued to individuals who will accompany a spouse or partner who holds another visa status.

Qualifying B-1/B-2 visa holders are even authorized to adjust status to Lawful Permanent Resident (apply for a Green Card) after they have entered the U.S. Because of this, individuals who would otherwise be eligible to enter the U.S. without a visa (pursuant to the Visa Waiver Program) may choose to go through the process of applying for a B-1/B-2 visa instead. (Individuals who enter the U.S. pursuant to the Visa Waiver Program are not authorized to change or extend status in the U.S.)

Working in the United States

If you wish to engage in productive employment in the United States you have several options:

Employer-Sponsored Work
Most people with work visas in the United States begin by finding a company that will sponsor them. The most common work visas are as follows:

- **H-1B classification:** Available to individuals performing services in a specialty occupation, fashion models of distinguished merit and ability, or certain individuals working on projects for the Department of Defense. A specialty occupation is one requiring the theoretical and practical application of highly specialized knowledge. Generally, the position itself must require completion of a Bachelor's Degree in a specialized field, and the individual applying for H-1B classification must have earned a Bachelor's Degree, or equivalent education or work experience in the field. The H-1B classification allows dual intent, which means that H-1B workers are not required to maintain a foreign residence and may seek permanent residence in the United States.

- **L-1 classification:** For employees who are transferring to a U.S. branch, parent, affiliate, or subsidiary of a non-U.S. employer for whom they worked for at least one continuous year over the three-year period prior to transfer. The transferred employees must have special knowledge of the company's product, technologies, or procedures, or be a manager/executive.

- **E-2 classification:** Allows individuals who are nationals of countries with which the United States maintains certain treaties to come to the United States to further a U.S. enterprise that is a result of a substantial investment by individuals or businesses that are nationals of the treaty country. Eligible treaties include treaties of friendship, commerce, and navigation, bilateral investment treaties, or other arrangements such as the North American Free Trade Agreement (NAFTA). E-2 nonimmigrants may develop and direct (or act in a supervisory, executive, or essential employee capacity for) the U.S. enterprise. Whether the actual amount invested is substantial depends on the type of business and the amount normally necessary to establish a viable enterprise.

- **E-1 classification:** Allows individuals who are nationals of countries with which the United States maintains certain treaties to come to the United States to conduct substantial trade that is international in scope, including trade in services or technology. Eligible treaties include treaties of friendship, commerce, and navigation, bilateral investment treaties, or other arrangements, such as the North American Free Trade Agreement (NAFTA). The qualifying trade must be primarily between the United States and the country of the E-1 applicant's nationality, meaning that more than 50 percent of the total volume of international trade conducted by the U.S. entity must be between the United States and the treaty country. If the U.S. entity is a branch office, then the foreign entity must conduct more than 50 percent of its trade with the United States. The E-1 applicant generally must demonstrate that the trade is already in existence at the time of the application for E-1 status.

- **O-1 classification:** Available to a person who has extraordinary ability in the sciences, arts, education, business, or athletics, demonstrated by sustained national or international acclaim. Special rules apply to artists and entertainers in the motion picture or television industries, who must have a demonstrated record of extraordinary achievement. Individuals seeking to qualify for O-1 status must demonstrate their achievements through extensive documentation from objective sources in their occupational field, including expert affidavits, contracts, awards, and other documentation.

- **J-1 classification:** Available to individuals participating in programs designated by the U.S. Department of State to promote educational and cultural exchange between the United States and other countries. Common J-1 visa categories include Trainees, Interns, Professors and Research Scholars, Short Term Scholars, and College or University Students. Other categories are Teachers, Secondary School Students, Graduate Medical Education or Training, International and Government Visitors, Camp Counselors, Summer Work/Travel Students, and Au Pairs. J-1 programs for trainees and interns allow foreign nationals to complete paid or unpaid training programs with private companies or non-profit organizations. In order to qualify as a J-1 trainee, the foreign national must: 1) have a degree or professional certificate from a foreign post-secondary academic institution and at least one year of related work experience in his or her field acquired outside the U.S; or 2) have five years of related work experience outside the U.S. in his or her field. In order to qualify as an intern, the foreign national must: 1) be currently enrolled in and pursuing studies at a degree or certificate granting post-secondary academic institution outside the U.S; or 2) have graduated from an academic institution no more than 12 months prior to his or her internship program start date.

Living Permanently in the United States

There are two principal methods for obtaining permanent residence in the United States—through employment and through family relationships.

Employment-Based Permanent Residence

Employment-based permanent residence applications typically require sponsorship by a U.S. company through the "labor certification process." To obtain a labor certification, the sponsoring U.S. company must prove to the satisfaction of the U.S. Department of Labor (DOL) that, after reasonable recruitment efforts, it has been unable to locate a minimally qualified U.S. worker willing to accept the position. If the company is successful in this endeavor then it may use the Department of Labor certification to obtain permanent residence on behalf of the sponsored employee. The process currently takes between two and five years.

Family-Based Permanent Residence

There are several familial relationships that may serve as the basis for rapid eligibility for U.S. permanent resident status. As you may have guessed, if you marry an opposite-sex U.S. citizen, then your spouse may apply directly for your permanent resident status. Also, if you have a child over the age of 21 who is a U.S. citizen, that child may sponsor you. Finally, if you yourself are unmarried, under 21, and your parent is a U.S. citizen, then your parent may sponsor you for permanent resident status.

There are a number of other familial relationships that may serve as the basis for a permanent residence application, but the waiting times are quite lengthy under these categories. These relationships are: opposite-sex spouses, unmarried minor children, and unmarried sons and daughters (21 or older) of lawful permanent residents; married sons and daughters of U.S. citizens; and brothers and sisters of U.S. citizens, provided the U.S. citizens are 21 or older.

Working in America visa information was kindly provided by Kelly McCown, McCown & Evans LLP. For additional detail see *www.mccownevans.com.*

ACKNOWLEDGMENTS

Judy's Litany of Thanks

TO FINDHORN PRESS: Thank you for making this book a reality. I was fortunate to have a well-established and respected publishing house like Findhorn see the merit in this book project. Thierry and Karin placed their faith in my word and reputation and demonstrated the utmost respect for me throughout. They were brave to take a chance on a new author with an idea for a book not only built around the stories of so many people but supported by even more individuals who, while not in the book, recognize the importance of the cause and are working for its solution. Thank you all—Thierry, Gail, Carol, Sabine, Mieke, Nicky, and Damian. This is a whole new chapter in my life.

Thanks to Andrew Oldershaw, Fifteen Minutes Public Relations, for helping get this book noticed so it can help same-sex binational couples keep their families together.

To my birth mother (who didn't want to meet me after I found her): Thank you for carrying me to term and placing me for adoption. I was lucky!

To my beloved Karin: Thank you for the journey we are on—wherever in the world we are at the time. Thank you for not living in fear. Going to Hollywood together to film a public service announcement for Cyndi Lauper's Give a Damn! campaign put the cherry on top of the cake (unless something else tops that).

To the warriors who work for us through Immigration Equality in New York and Washington, D.C.—Rachel, Victoria, Aaron, Christopher, Julie, Steve, Gannon, Stephen, Eric, Gary, Pamela, Rosalba, Win, Gabe, Constance and anyone who has joined since; for those who do grassroots activism for Out4Immigration from San Francisco and everywhere else—Amos, Mickey and Kathy from the beginning and all those who have helped since; for Martha and Lin McDevitt-Pugh of Love Exiles in The Netherlands and their board members Kirsten Anderson and Janherman Veenker (founding board members) and Bob Bragar and Robbie Checkoway; and Leslie and Marta in California who pioneered this immigration reform work with Love Sees No Borders: Thanks for educating me and supporting me and giving me hope that things would change!

To Elizabeth Gilbert and her publicity-shy husband: Thank you for paving the way for us. More people will know about our struggle because of yours. Your celebrity in the media world, Liz, and your fight for us in the halls of Congress will make things better for those of us still facing separation or exile.

To Juan Carlos, who first made me aware of Elizabeth Gilbert's role in our fight: Thanks for asking Elizabeth Gilbert your question at her book signing and then reporting it on Facebook. I pray your struggle to be together with your partner turns out well. You are helping us all.

To the brave couples who are doing their best to be together when American law tears you apart: I pray your struggle to be together with your partner and family turns out the way you need it to. Those of you who have shared stories in this book have made a tremendous difference to the conversation. I appreciate your bravery more than I can say. Sometimes I cried so much I had to take a break from the work…

To those in all other groups who work on immigration reform, immigrants' rights, civil rights, LGBT equality, and the related and crossover issues involved: I appreciate all you have done to help men and women find the answers they need for their challenges. Thanks for your tireless efforts to keep America and the rest of the world a safer place. A special thanks to those who work to make America a welcoming place for men and women with immigration and sexual orientation discrimination issues. I have listed all groups I could find in the Resource Groups and Websites chapter and more will be added in the blog and website to accompany this book.

To all those senators and members of Congress who have introduced and co-sponsored Uniting American Families Act and Reuniting Families Act and Comprehensive Immigration Reform Act of 2010 and have worked on truly comprehensive immigration reform that did not leave out same-sex binational couples: Thank you for making me proud of America and its potential. You are all heroes!

To the late longtime human rights activists in my community Jim McEntee, Gertrude Welch, Shorty Collins and Darline Krause: Your lives touched me for decades, and your example is one I took to heart. You made a huge impact on me and on Santa Clara County, California. Heaven is a brighter place with you four there.

To Wiggsy Sivertsen and Hon. Ken Yeager and my BAYMEC political action committee friends: Thanks for teaching me over the years how to help the LGBT community and get things done so we can have equality—even if it had to be bit by bit! This old dog has learned a few new tricks, too!

To my local, regional and state elected official friends who helped with letters and resolutions about Uniting American Families Act or helped share my story and asked how you could help: Thanks from the bottom of my heart to those not mentioned in the book yet: Hon. Joe Simitian, Hon. Jim Beall, Hon. Ken Yeager, Hon. Rich Gordon, Hon. Judy Chirco, Hon. Evan Low, Hon. Jamie McLeod, Hon. Gavin Newsom, Hon. John Laird, Hon. Ash Kalra, Hon. Sam Liccardo, Hon. Nancy Pyle, Hon. Kansen Chu, and the Hon. Paul Fong. You rock!

My California state legislature voted overwhelmingly in a bipartisan way for AJR15—a joint Assembly/Senate resolution that makes California the first state to support the passage of federal law Uniting American Families Act and its inclusion in comprehensive immigration reform. California legislators have asked the U.S. Congress to pass, and President Obama to sign, UAFA. I am so proud of my state legislators, including Assembly Member Kevin de Leon (D-45), who introduced the measure. Thanks!

And for this Californian, it is a real thrill to have an openly gay man of color as our Speaker of the Assembly, John A. Perez (D-46). Thank you for your work to make California a safer and more equitable place for LGBT citizens. I look forward to more progress in civil liberties for all Californians.

To my family in America—Joan and John (RIP) and Kate and Mark and the whole Nolen/Shelton/Strom family, as well as Kae and Lloyd and Aunt Fairy and Judy and Aunt Margie; to all my Rickard and Cole and Coleman cousins; and especially to my angel parents Erma and Emmett Rickard (so lucky you welcomed and raised me!): Thanks for being in my life and making it what it is and thanks for accepting me for who I am and what I do.

To my birth father Don Everest and my new mom Jeanette Everest and my expanding American family in Oregon (Everests and Verhelsts and Millers and Soesbes and Handys and Liz and JW, too) and Florida (Mittons and Holladays): Special thanks for accepting me as a lesbian when you first met me. I appreciate that acceptance from my new family in England (Tamsin, Terry, David, Hilary, Adam, Amber, Daniel, Melissa, Samantha, Christina, Veronica, Matthew, Michael, Laurel) and Scotland (Michael, Shirley and Connor) and France (Thierry and Jean-Francois), too.

To lifelong friends who are really family—the Pranters and Brians in Arizona and the Silvas and Brians in California and their families: Thanks for being there for us.

To newer friends in my life who I consider family—Mark Reuter's parents and siblings, I so appreciate your love and support of us and our plight—Bob, Audrey and Mike Reuter, and Jane, Zane, and Mailo Numazu.

And to other newer friends in my life who I consider family—Mike and Cindy Soltis and Brendan and Chasen: Thanks for being there for us.

To special friends who are really family—Bill and Cathy and sons James, David, and Eric, and now April and Jessica, too: The same thanks for acceptance to you all and especially thanks to the overt actions you and your extended family have taken as terrific allies for LGBT folks like me and Karin.

To my brother from another mother, as they say: Thanks to Ed for so many years of good fun and good times and terrific support. When we met in junior high school and attended journalism classes at the same time in college, I never thought our life story through the years would include this part. You always said my life would be a good movie. Stay tuned! Thanks for your sage advice and never-ending encouragement. Thanks, too, for introducing me and Karin to New York City, and for slicing and dicing the first manuscript.

To my special buddy Sai: Thanks for asking me to write a story for your website while I was out of the country in 2009. Thanks for suggesting repeatedly that I should write a book. Now I have! You tell others that I am your mentor, but now the shoe's on the other foot.

To the folks who plowed through the manuscript in various stages—Karin, Ed, Joan, John, Cathy, Sai, Vanessa, Arlene, Clara, Marilyn, Helen, Steve, and Mary Jo: special thanks for bearing with me and helping me fix problems.

To Jennifer Rycenga, thanks for leading me to Matt and Michael and for all your work and support.

To my friend and former BAYMEC board member Robert Greeley, Esq., who bought the first advance copy of this book online: Thanks!

To another BAYMEC board member, Richard Poppen, thanks for meeting with Congressman Michael Honda to share our story of immigration discrimination we face as same-sex binational couples.

Thanks also to Julie Kruse from Immigration Equality for encouraging us to meet with Rep. Honda.

And a very special thanks to Steve Ralls from Immigration Equality for doing so much to make things happen!

To my San José State University colleagues: I miss being with you on campus. Early retirement has been interesting, that's for sure. To my former work group— Waynette (and Allan and Jacinda and Ella) and John (and Terri) and my IT pal Dondi (and Ravisha and Kiran): Thanks for being family and for your love and support through my journey with Karin. Thanks also for replacing the sweatshirt I lost in my French train incident. It was so sweet to see the photo of Cindy modeling the SJSU shirt that came via e-mail while we were in France. Thanks all who chipped in on it!

To those wonderful folks who learned our story and gave us safe and wonderful places to be together when we could not be in America: Thanks. Especially to Peter Allen and family on Salt Spring Island, B.C. Canada, where we enjoyed The Love Shack when we reunited after nine months of separation; and to Tony and Carol Tidswell in Montblanc, France, where we hunkered down for two months as part of our six-month exile from America at Villa Roquette. You are part of this story and made our lives more comfortable and more interesting, too.

To my memoir group friends at the Vintage Group at the Billy DeFrank Center—Arlene, Clara, Jennifer, Bill, Chris (RIP), Dean, Dawn, G.A., Bob, Clay, Karin, Angelique and Pam—as well as the Circle of Friends memoir group—Karin, Cathy, Betty, Helen, and Judi: This project gained traction from my experience with all of you and the wonderful mentoring from our angel instructor Sue Sarbaugh (RIP).

To the women I have loved and been involved with in the past: You have created a part of me, and it is still in here somewhere. Even though each time I started over was because of one of you—and for a different reason each time—I took something of you into the future, whether I could see it then or not. I am not listing names here, but you know who you are, and I hope you know what you meant to me. I appreciate you!

To Bill, the only guy I ever went out with: I didn't realize it at the time, but you need to know the reason I didn't want to do what you wanted to do (and I am flattered!) was because after a few years from those days I finally got it that I am a lesbian. I was a pretty late bloomer. I'd love to catch up with you sometime.

I would be very remiss not to mention the wonderful healthcare folks in my life these days. They keep me going when stress and worry over our future because of Karin's status brings me down. Thanks so much for your healing powers: Anna, Terri, Dr. Gringeri, Dr. Choi, and Dr. Joshi! I so appreciate your roles in my life and your understanding and support of the challenges Karin and I face. You see it in my muscles and nerves and bones and teeth and blood sugar! Thanks for helping me feel better and for keeping me going.

To the women at Supercuts—Nasrin, Fariba, Tiffany, Nancy, Farideh, and Tao, the women who keep us looking great: You deserve a big thanks, too. We appreciate your haircuts and coloring. You make us look better, and we like it!

Because we spend so much time apart, the folks at the U.S. Post Office have learned our story and support us in our struggle. Thanks to the Cambrian gang: Stuart, Donna, Du-Chuan, Amy, Dillon, and Chia-Ching.

And for the good breakfasts and internet when we need it, the people at our local Le Boulanger are tops: Rosario, Donna, Adrienne, Arnold, Fernando, Roberto, and the newer employees we are just getting to know.

And finally, to Gerri: Thanks for the great counseling Karin and I got when we were first together. I appreciate all of your energy and communication exercises, even if I didn't always like them at the time. Karin and I are still together!

How to Order *Torn Apart: United by Love, Divided by Law* As a Fundraiser for Your Organization

If you wish to order quantities of this title at a discounted price in order to resell at full price and make funds for your organization, please send an e-mail with your organization information: work you do, nonprofit (501c3) or 501c4 or political action committee (PAC) status, as well as your contact person and contact information and the quantity desired to: *tornapart@findhornpress.com*. We will get back to you about your fundraiser.

You can also raise funds for your organization by sharing the information with your group and having them buy directly online from Findhorn Press at *www.findhornpress.com*, using a unique ordering code that we will provide when you contact us with the information requested above.

Besides buying the book you are holding right now, that's two more ways to raise money to help in the immigration challenge situation that same-sex binational couples and immigrants in general face with today's U.S. law. Every book sold shares the information, advocates for a solution, and raises money for those who help in the process. We all appreciate it!

FINDHORN   PRESS

Life Changing Books

For a complete catalogue,
please contact:

Findhorn Press Ltd
117-121 High Street,
Forres IV36 1AB,
Scotland, UK

t +44 (0)1309 690582
f +44 (0)131 777 2711
e info@findhornpress.com

or consult our catalogue online
(with secure order facility) on
www.findhornpress.com

For information on the Findhorn Foundation:
www.findhorn.org